Praise for Living Passages for the Whole Family

"For such a ritually starved people as ourselves, this is a masterpiece. Shea is doing us an immense favor here, not just in offering us honest rituals and prayers for every aspect of our lives, but, in effect, letting us know we can do the same."

Fr. Richard Rohr, O.F.M.
Franciscan Priest
Author of *Adam's Return*,
on male rites of passage

"What an encouraging and empowering book! Shea has shared her family's rich journey raising children from infancy to adulthood in a way that will inspire anyone with children to take the 'next step' in creating meaningful celebrations and ceremonies to mark life's transitions. No longer having children at home, I was inspired by *Living Passages* to create a ceremony to mark a huge transition for a colleague at work. What a gift!"

Rahima Baldwin Dancy
Parenting Educator and Author of
You Are Your Child's First Teacher

Front Cover Art Legend:

The front cover art was designed by Keri Lehr, Birch Design Studios. It was chosen as a symbol to represent honoring rites of passage in the family. The art visually reflects the meaning of Rebecca Danica's song "Circle of Life" (page 207):

> I stand as one, yet not alone,
> Here on this earth I call my home,
> The circle of Life I now embrace
> And all who join this sacred space.

The cover image represents an individual pausing in their life journey to stand in the center of compassion, surrounded by the love and support of the family circle. The four stars at each corner of the image symbolize the four corners of the earth and the heavens beyond. When we embrace the circle of Life, we learn to carry our true home and family within us wherever we journey. The colors in the image represent qualities cultivated through meaningful rites of passage: red for love and will forces, blue for tranquility and peace, green for growth and healing, and yellow for joy and celebration. The blue and green background coming together within the circle reminds us that we humans are made of earth and spirit. A person's life journey is measured not so much by forward movement as it is measured by soulful deepening. When we are able to experience such soulful deepening together in the circle of family, we find inspiration and sustenance for living boldly with compassion.

Also by Shea Darian~

Books

Sanctuaries of Childhood:
Nurturing a Child's Spiritual Life

Seven Times the Sun:
Guiding Your Child Through the Rhythms of the Day

Grandpa's Garden

CDs

Living Passages Song Collection

Seven Times the Sun Song Collection

Celtic Quest/Avalon a cappella

Upcoming Titles

Mourning Light:
Honoring Family Passages of Grief, Death & Change

Mourning Light Song Collection

Living Passages
for the Whole Family

Celebrating Rites of Passage
from Birth to Adulthood

Shea Darian

Gilead Press

Gilead Press   www.gileadpress.net

Library of Congress Cataloging-in-Publication Data
Darian, Shea, 1959-
    Living passages for the whole family: celebrating rites of passage from birth to adulthood

       p. cm.
    Includes bibliographical references and index.
    ISBN 978-0-9675713-2-4
    1. Rites of passage
    2. Rites and ceremonies
    3. Life change events
    4. Life Cycle, Human
    5. Parent and child-Miscellanea.
    6. Family Life-Miscellanea.
    I. Title.   II. Title: Living Passages for the Whole Family

GT2420.D376 2008

  392.1-dc 22   Library of Congress Card Number: 2007905504

Grateful acknowledgment is made for permission to reprint the following copyrighted material. Every effort has been made to trace ownership of all copyrighted material. If any omission has been made, please bring this to the attention of the publisher so that proper acknowledgment may be given in future editions.

Quotation from the movie *Shall we Dance* by Audrey Wells. Copyright © 2004, Miramax. Reprinted by permission of Miramax Studios.

"African Birth Song" retold by Anita Jones. Copyright © by Anita Jones. Reprinted by permission.

"From boundless cosmic regions" verse from *The Incarnating Child* by Joan Salter. Copyright © Joan Salter. Reprinted by permission of Hawthorn Press UK, www.hawthornpress.com.

A Family Adoption Ceremony, Parent Covenant, Celebration for a Child's First Lost Tooth, Poem "From the Tooth Fairy," Ceremony "Blessing the Journey Into Manhood" (adapted by Shea Darian), Songs: "Mensi Com Ni" and "Circle of Life," and author photo (page 336) all by Rebecca Danica. Copyright © by Rebecca Danica. Reprinted by permission.

Poem "Carry Our Flame" (and adapted excerpt) by Jim Bagbey. Copyright © by Jim Bagbey. Reprinted by permission.

Poem "A Welcoming World" by Andrea Goslin from the book, *Welcoming Ways*. Copyright © 2000 by Andrea Alban Gosline & Lisa Burnett Bossi. Reprinted by permission of Ambledance Pictures and Verse, www.ambledance.com. (San Rafael, CA: Cedco Publishing, 2000)

"Love Grows One by One" © 1981 Carol Johnson, Noeldner Music, BMI www.caroljohnsonmusic.com from her recording "Might As Well Make It Love." Reprinted by permission.

"Mother, sweet mother" verse by Sonika Tinker and Dinyah Rein. Copyright © by Sonika Tinker and Dinyah Rein. Reprinted by permission. (*Contributors, please update contact information.*)

"Being Tucked into Bed" verse by Brit Reis. Copyright © by Brit Reis. Reprinted by permission.

Quotation from the book *Letters to My Son*. Copyright © 1994, 1999 by Kent Nerburn. Reprinted with permission of New World Library, Novato, CA. www.newworldlibrary.com.

"Blessing Song" from *Woman Prayer, Woman Song* by Miriam Therese Winter. Copyright © 1987 Medical Mission Sisters. Reprinted by permission.

Poem "The Journey" by Morgan Darian. © 2005 by Morgan Darian. Reprinted by permission.

Portions of this book first appeared in *Mothering* magazine.

To Andrew. . .
how could we make this journey,
except for the strength of the other's arm?
I am indebted to your adventurous
and steadfast love.

Thanks to:

. . . Rebecca Danica – my unwavering source of inspiration and support, and my editing guru. Rebecca's ceremonies, poetry, and music grace these pages with the beauty of her poet's soul; her presence, wisdom, and love grace the contours of my heart.

. . . those who were willing to share stories, poetry, songs, and words of wisdom included in these pages, especially my intimates – Andrew, Morgan, and Willa.

. . . those who were willing to read and comment on the manuscript as it took form: Kim Chotzen, Andrew Darian, Maggie Jezreel, Dana Larson, Leslie Putt, Diane Saunders and, especially, Tammy Corwin-Renner whose enthusiasm and wisdom were like beacons to help guide my way.

. . . Kat Brenner whose extraordinary proofing skills transformed the final draft.

. . . the Waldorf educators who helped to illumine my family's path when my children were young.

. . . and, finally, to all the parents, grandparents, and caregivers who have attended my talks and workshops through the years and added their wisdom to the ongoing conversation.

Table of Contents

I ⚬ Behold the Miracle
Rites of Passage For Birth & Arrival 33

2 &ivin; The Wonder Years
Rites of Passage for the Growing Child 79

3 &ivin; The Awakening
Rites of Passage for the Growing Youth 111

4 ᴥ At the Crossroads

Rites of Passage for Coming of Age 167

5 ✺ Fully Growin'

Rites of Passage for the Young Adult 209

6 ✺ Knowing the Miracle by Heart

Celebrating Birthdays 275

Conclusion ❧ Fostering Faith in the Future 319

Appendix ❧ Resources for the Journey 323

A Note to the Reader

> . . . things can look dark,
> then a break shows in the clouds,
> and all is changed.
>
> ~ E. B. White

In today's fast-paced society, it's easy to forget who we are. It's easy to forget why we are here. In recent decades, our forgetfulness as a culture led us to routinely medicate births and deaths. We hurried our children to become adult-like, yet flippantly defined "adulthood" as the time one reaches "drinking age." We taught women to dread aging after 29 and encouraged men to cover their balding heads. We had so little time or energy to consider an individual's growth from year to year that birthdays became centered on a bounty of material gifts rather than the soulful meaning of the occasion. No wonder there's a burgeoning interest in creating new rites of passage for the 21st century!

A growing number of parents, grandparents, therapists, healers, teachers and religious educators are seeking meaningful ways for families to celebrate rites of passage that allow a young person to experience the fullness of their childhood, youthhood, and young adulthood. Families are reclaiming the home as a vital center of spiritual growth and renewal where family members and friends can create rites of passage that are more relevant and participatory. Religious leaders are asking new questions about the faith community's role in assisting children, youths, and young adults to reflect on, acknowledge, and celebrate significant times of growth and change. Therapists are recognizing the power of rites of passage in healing past wounds, assisting individuals and families through times of transition, and honoring developmental milestones. New sparks of interest have been ignited in the natural birth and hospice movements, allowing those of all ages to experience the passages of birth and death with greater awareness and courage. As members of an evolving culture, we're opening our hearts and minds to receive new visions in which "a break shows in the clouds, and all is changed."

Living Passages for the Whole Family: Celebrating Rites of Passage from Birth to Adulthood is intended for families of all faiths. This book is a treatise on the value of being witnesses for one another, celebrating the unfolding of one another's lives as a sacred gift. Most humbly, it's an account of many of the rites of passage my family has created (or taken part in) to honor such life passages as birth and adoption, weaning, honoring birthdays, celebrating puberty and menses, making commitments of friendship, preparing to date for the first time, earning a driver's license, graduation, and redefining family bonds, among others. Such rites of passage engrave upon our hearts and minds the spiritual significance of our lives and relationships.

The celebrations included in *Living Passages for the Whole Family* are merely examples of what's possible when a family honors the significance of a young person's life passages from birth to adulthood. My family and I offer these pictures to inspire you to create rites of passage that reflect your own family's journey, identity, beliefs, and values. Of course, you're welcome to use these ideas as they are, transform them, or play with them until they inspire unique life passage celebrations of your own.

This book has been a long time coming. I promised it to my readers years ago, yet the muse saw it differently. So now, a handful of years have passed, and I can speak more intimately on such topics as young adults driving, dating, and leaving home for the first time. Life always has a way of bringing the next lesson when it's due. And, for me, the lessons have been plentiful. . .

Verbiage Defined ✧
Helpful Terms & Word Reflections

The words I use
are everyday words
and yet are not the same!

~ Paul Claudel

RITE: an act, custom, or ceremony steeped with soulful meaning.

SOULFUL: pertaining to the eternal essence of a human being and to the life forces that animate a human's feeling, thinking, and action.

LIFE PASSAGE: a period of transition from one stage of life to another that brings significant change in a person's consciousness, status, relationships or ways of being in the world.

RITE OF PASSAGE: a rite enacted to celebrate a person's passage from one stage of life to another.

CELEBRATE: to observe, honor, applaud, or proclaim; one may celebrate with expressions of grief, joy, reverence, revelry, formality, spontaneity, reflection, action – whatever responses an occasion draws forth.

LIVING PASSAGE: observing or celebrating a life passage in such a way that the person (or people) experiencing the passage (or their caregivers) are inspired to consider the soulful meaning of the passage and how the passage may enrich, change, or inform their journey.

BLIND PASSAGE: being unaware of, ignoring, or numbing oneself (through an addiction or other diversion, or for purposes of self-preservation) from fully experiencing a significant life passage or an intended rite of passage.

RECLAIMING A BLIND PASSAGE: identifying a blind passage for which one feels loss, regret, or pain, and creating a ceremony, action, or event to bring healing; remembering and articulating the significance of a blind passage in the context of one's present life and embracing the gifts the passage has to offer.

MULTILAYERED PASSAGE: when a person experiences more than one life passage at the same time, such as starting first grade and getting a new sibling, or simultaneously being weaned and experiencing a geographical move.

COLLECTIVE PASSAGE: a life passage that is observed or celebrated by two or more family or community members who are experiencing the same passage at the same time, such as a group of young people being confirmed or children beginning first grade together.

INTERCONNECTED PASSAGE: when a family or other significant community experiences the same passage at the same time and it represents different life passages for different members of the family or community; for example, when birth for a baby represents the passage of parenthood for the baby's parent/s and a passage into grandparenting for the baby's grandparent/s.

YOUTHHOOD: the stage of life in which a person deepens their conscious view of themselves and their relationships, is able to more clearly distinguish between reality and fantasy, and sees themselves as an individual in their own right; includes the time of life often referred to as "puberty" (when a person's sexual organs develop) and the cycle of life referred to as "adolescence."

ELDERHOOD: the stage of adulthood in which a person embraces the wisdom they have gleaned from many years of life, chooses to live by that wisdom, and makes that wisdom available to those who seek it.

CELEBRATION COMMUNITY: a group of people who observe and celebrate significant life passages with one another, such as a family, church or synagogue community, school, civic or ethnic community, or any group or community of people that gathers for such celebrations; any group of people that gathers to celebrate a particular rite of passage.

Introduction ❧
Reflecting on the Journey

There are only two or three human stories,
and they go on repeating themselves as fiercely
as if they had never happened before.

~ Willa Cather

Assimilating Change

Since ancient times, people have celebrated rites of passage to help make sense of the evolving human journey – to acknowledge the turning of life, bring order to chaos, clarify one's changing identity. Throughout centuries, people have participated in ceremonies to welcome the newly born and send forth those who have died, wean a child from their mother's breast or their parents' bed, declare a newcomer as an accepted member of a community, recognize one's changing status from child to adult to elder, or bless a traveler embarking upon a significant journey.

We humans are creatures of change. Change is an element of our being, like water or air. We are continually and simultaneously being born and dying, experiencing endings and beginnings. To be an eager student of life, one must learn to accept change as the core curriculum.

The trouble with change today is that there is just so darned much of it! Change seems to summon us at every turn as our technological inventions, changing definitions of family, cultural assimilation, and mobility wear away at our desire to meet change with an open heart and mind.

Consider the cultural changes a person experiences today, along with the personal changes one evolves through in a lifetime, and it's easy to understand how a person might become overwhelmed. This is one reason why meaningful rites of passage are crucial to 21st century life; they allow us moments of pause to assimilate change and inwardly reconstruct our perceptions and expectations of ourselves and one another. In such vulnerable moments of transition, rites of passage allow us to be held by something larger than ourselves, something bold enough to speak our joys, strong enough to bear our sorrows, insightful enough to hold us tenderly in moments of crisis, growth, and transformation.

In Anthony de Mello's story collection, *Song of the Bird*, he includes a story about a salt doll. The salt doll didn't know what she was until she came to the ocean – a great body of water that so transfixed her, she desired to know who the ocean was. The ocean lured her in, and it was in coming to know the ocean that the salt doll finally came to know the essence of herself.

So it is with humans. We can forever contemplate the great questions we've asked ourselves through the ages:

- Who am I?
- Why am I here?
- What is my purpose?
- Who are my people?
- Where is my place in the world?
- How can I be useful?

Yet, it's in freely entering into the soulful element of change, and letting go of life as we've known it, that we become vulnerable enough to remember once again who and what we are.

Just before graduation, when I was a high school senior, my principal told me, "Enjoy these years! This is the best time of your life!" I was puzzled, then saddened by his words, thinking of this middle-aged man who felt the best years of his life were behind him. The idea that the richness of my early adulthood might surpass that of the years to come had never entered my mind. Fortunately, I chose to disregard the message.

If we're paying attention, we see that *every* life passage, including our final breath, leads us into a world of new possibilities. Of course, this perspective clashes loudly with the societal messages children, youths, and adults often receive – messages that sometimes persuade us to believe there is an *optimal age* of being. Thus, children tend to be hurried toward adulthood, just as adults often dig in their heels at some critical moment of their journey. We valiantly fight off the realities of aging. We refuse to be thrust to the tragic summit from which we glimpse that ill-conceived land called "over-the-hill." But a life well-lived may not be hurried *or* resisted. A life well-lived is a sacred journey – a journey to be savored.

The more fully we live into each new stage of our lives, with all its challenges and delights, the more fully and wholly human we become. Through each life passage, we're handed a clue – sometimes more than one – that helps us unravel the mysteries of life. Our ability to decipher each clue depends upon our willingness, and that of our caregivers, to learn the soulful language of each new stage of our human experience. What greater gift can we bestow on today's young people than to learn this language with them. As we do, we not only teach our children to meet the transitions of their lives with a sense of awareness and wonder, we receive an advanced course in the art of graceful change.

Nurturing Community

As much as we humans are creatures of change, we are also seekers of community. We yearn for companionship. We crave to dwell among those who lovingly know who we are, where we've been, and what visions we hold for the future.

In the movie *Shall We Dance,* Susan Sarandon's character, Beverly Clark, says it best when she reveals her perspective on why people get married:

> ". . . we need a witness to our lives. There's a billion people on the planet, I mean, what does any *one* life really mean? But in a marriage, you're promising to care about *everything*: the good things, the bad things, the terrible things, mundane things. . . all of it, all the time, every day. You're saying: 'Your life will not go unnoticed, because I will notice it. Your life will not go unwitnessed, because I will be your witness.'"

This is one of the ultimate functions of a true family, one of the highest priorities of a genuine community: *to witness one another's lives.* However, this "loving attention," this collective witnessing doesn't merely happen. With today's frantic pace and busy schedules, a community (whether it's a family, faith community, or any circle of friends or companions) must find *intentional ways to commit ourselves* as witnesses for one another. Making time and space in our lives for meaningful rites of passage is just such an intentional commitment. Rites of passage clear our vision for seeing one another and deepen our gestures of listening to one another's lives. Rites of passage are covenants of encouragement we bestow on each other.

By the time my partner, Andrew, and I were in the throes of parenting two young children, I was an avid believer in the importance of celebrating rites of passage. I had already experienced a handful of meaningful rites throughout my life. In my early years, my mother was the queen of birthday celebrations. When I was five, I was awed by the rite of immersion baptism – a powerful symbol of spiritual rebirth. When I began my menses at 11, I recall my delight when my parents granted me the right to get my ears pierced soon afterward. In early adulthood, I experienced the life-changing rites of ordination, marriage, and naming ceremonies. Still, as I began celebrating rites of passage with my own children, I had no idea what would become, for me, one of the most profound gifts of such rites. The gift is simply this: *meaningful rites of passage teach us crucial aspects of community building. They assist us in bringing to light the soulful and spiritual substance of our intimate relationships.*

As a parent, I greatly cherish the strong social skills both my children display in their peer groups and in intergenerational settings. I have no doubt their ability to retain a strong sense of self-identity, while extending themselves to encourage and care for others, is a skill that's been heightened through participating in rites of passage. Rites of passage teach us to encourage and support one another just as we are encouraged and supported by such rites. Rites of passage teach us the dance of giving and receiving, the dance of autonomy and interdependence.

When we intentionally welcome a baby into the world, we learn the gesture of welcoming newcomers into our midst. When we celebrate bar/bat mitzvah and confirmation ceremonies in which young people become worship leaders and mature members of their faith communities, we're reminded that our memberships and alliances require our dedicated responsiveness and the timbre of our own unique voice. When we gather to honor a young adult's right to drive or drink alcoholic beverages, we have the opportunity to clarify how our decisions and choices affect others. When we participate in a remembrance ceremony for loved ones who have crossed the threshold of death, we're given access to the mystery of life beyond life and the opportunity to commune with these loved ones still.

Meaningful rites of passage bond us to the priorities of our significant communities and link us to our companions, past, present, and future. Rites of passage strengthen our commitments. It shouldn't surprise us that meaningful rites of passage tend to be nonexistent or ineffective where community relationships are ailing. The most potent and life-affirming rites of passage spring up in families, school and faith communities, ethnic and civic groups that make community building a priority.

Rites of Passage in the 21st Century

In ancient times, rites of passage sprang up from cultures that were cohesive and well-defined. Rites of passage were powerful symbols for translating cultural beliefs and values into ceremonies that could be experienced physically and soulfully. However, our 21st century culture is changing at such an accelerated rate that, collectively, we have no idea who we are. We have no idea to what people we belong. As a culture, we represent every race and nation, and most of us are of mixed ethnic origin. We have access to all the great religions of the world and the freedom to live and die by one, reap the truths of them all, or set out to find our own unique spiritual path. We choose to marry or not, and when we do, we create interfaith, interracial, and same-sex marriage partnerships. We live in blended families, single-parent families, dual households. Some of us have more step-relatives than we can count. We are one of the most assimilated, mobile, and technologically-advanced cultures of all time. Is this cultural identity crisis the reason our rites of passage are becoming so pale and meaningless today? Some cultural analysts believe so.

I have another theory. I believe many of our rites of passage have become pale and meaningless because, as a culture, we've been living with the misguided notion that we can separate our soul needs from other aspects of our lives. We attempt to do it all the time: in education, politics, the work force, the family, economics, business, medicine, science, even religion. We act as if the human spirit can be compartmentalized, as if we can amputate our souls from our daily experiences. But attempting to separate our souls from any aspect of life is like trying to function physically without a heart or a brain. It simply doesn't work. Thus, our culture's startling statistics on depression, addiction, mental illness, divorce, and crime. Thus, the heart-wrenching realities of child and teen suicides, eating disorders, stress-related neuroses, and gang-related violence. It's time to reclaim the soul as the animating force of human experience! Only by doing so can we heal the wounds that are weakening the human spirit.

The good news is: the same 21st century culture that presents us with such potent soulful challenges also offers us myriad resources for becoming more soulful participants in life. Today we have at our fingertips a mother lode of information to consider on the human life cycle and stages of development, given to us by such theorists as Erik Erikson, Carol

Gilligan, Rudolf Steiner, James Fowler, and Gail Sheehy, to name a few. We have the accumulated wisdom of a multitude of ethnic and religious perspectives to access, so we might learn from one another's rites, traditions, and spiritual practices. Perhaps most importantly, celebration communities – families and friends, faith communities, school and civic groups, even businesses and medical communities – are increasingly creating, reforming, and resurrecting meaningful rites of passage to nurture the soul, assimilate change, build community, and act as a compass to guide individuals, families, and communities in their ongoing life journeys.

Creating, reforming, and resurrecting meaningful rites of passage is an act of cultural revolution, for rites of passage not only *reflect* our beliefs and values, they also *define* them. This soulful revolution is taken up by every doctor or midwife who asks to bless a child at the moment of their birth, every parent who gives their child a strong name by which to live. It's taken up by every teacher who blesses a child on their birthday and every school principal who helps plan a ceremony to initiate students on their first day of grade school. It's taken up by every judge or lawyer who acknowledges the soulful vulnerability of a divorce or adoption, and every nurse, police officer, fire fighter, or hospice worker who attentively guides family members and friends through a loved one's death. It's taken up by every minister or rabbi who thoughtfully works to reform traditional rites to make them more meaningful and relevant to 21st century life. It's taken up by every scientist who acknowledges intuition and imagination giving life to their scientific endeavors and discoveries. It's taken up by every administrator who creates an intentional gesture of welcome for a new employee and their family, or bestows a parting blessing when a coworker moves on. It's taken up by every politician who finally admits that the separation of church and state is not the same thing as the separation of body and soul. It's taken up by you and me, wherever we are, in whatever we do.

Living Passages for the Whole Family is my small contribution to help resource the soulful renewal of our culture. Creating, reforming, and resurrecting meaningful rites of passage are potent strategies for reclaiming the fullness of our humanity. They are acts of soulful revolution to change the world – one soul, one family, one celebration community at a time.

The Gradual Unfolding ᴂ
From Infancy to Adulthood

Although *Living Passages for the Whole Family* is laid out in an approximate chronological order from infancy to young adulthood, it is not my intention to represent the human life cycle in a linear fashion. Infancy, childhood, youthhood, and young adulthood ebb and flow into one another. In these pages, I do not assume that a young person experiencing a life passage of youthhood or young adulthood has necessarily left behind the cycle of life that came before. We parents know from experience that it is wholly possible for a child to live simultaneously in more than one developmental reality at a time. However, if we are to assist our children in living fully into each new stage of their development, we do well to recognize and celebrate the periods of growth in which youthhood calls boldly to a child and in which young adulthood calls boldly to a youth. We celebrate these moments, not with the intention of hurrying our children along their path to adulthood, but with the intention of witnessing and honoring the gradual unfolding of their lives.

How to Use This Book

...to desire to have many books,
and never to use them, is like a child
that will have a candle burning by his bed
all the while he is sleeping.

~ Henry Peacham

1. **Read *Living Passages for the Whole Family* from cover to cover or focus on the passage at hand.**

Even if you skim through the longer ceremonies, one advantage of reading *Living Passages for the Whole Family* from cover to cover is to be reminded of how one cycle of a young person's life flows into another. By reading the book from start to finish, you may also be inspired to contemplate blind passages you need to reclaim for yourself that require attention or healing (see number eight on page 32), or blind passages to reclaim for a child or the entire family.

On the other hand, you may be in the throes of celebrating a particular transition in a child's life, planning a rite of passage for a family member or friend, or contemplating a life passage ceremony within a larger celebration community. For inspiration, feel free to hone in on the chapter or section of *Living Passages for the Whole Family* that is most helpful to you at the present time.

2. **Some of the ideas and ceremonies in *Living Passages for the Whole Family* can be used as they are; others will need to be adapted and edited, as you see fit.**

Along with many simple celebration ideas, *Living Passages for the Whole Family* includes several passage ceremonies – some are simple and brief, others, more elaborate. Some of the ceremonies are written in a generic form, so you can "fill in the blanks" to personalize a particular ceremony. I've included other ceremonies (or parts of ceremonies) in their original form – written for a particular individual, family, or community – because these original ceremonies help tell the story of how each rite of passage was inspired by the values, beliefs, and biographies of the participants. Although these original rites of passage will take a bit more effort to transform, I've placed many of the changes you'll need to consider in italics to make it easier to adapt and edit. With the spoken portions of each ceremony, consider whether it's more meaningful to read the words, recite short passages from memory, or speak more spontaneously.

3. **Revise the ceremonies and celebration ideas included in *Living Passages* to make them more compatible with your own beliefs and faith tradition.**

   Although *Living Passages for the Whole Family* mentions specific religious rites and traditions, and includes references to a higher power (known by many names) and other spiritual inferences, it's not my intention to give the reader guidance from a particular religious standpoint. Many of the celebrations, in fact, include no overtly spiritual references and can be used by those of any or no religious preference. My hope is that readers of all faith perspectives can find meaning in these pages and freely revise this material to make it more meaningful according to a family's own beliefs and faith tradition. Consider scripture and other writings, songs, poetry, names for the Divine, words of wisdom, symbols, and acts of prayer and celebration that can add meaning for you and your family.

4. **As you consider possible rites of passage, remember not all life passages require an elaborate ceremony.**

   Sometimes a rite of passage can be celebrated simply – a gift given, a thoughtful verbal acknowledgment, a sunrise hike, a special dinner, an ear piercing. . . Life passages can be celebrated in the intimacy of the family, large and small community gatherings, or in private moments shared between two family members. Meaningful rites of passage may be elaborate or brief, well planned out or spontaneous. Indeed, at times, a rite of passage only comes clear *after* it's experienced and is celebrated in the act of storytelling. Battling the elements of a snowstorm, meeting the challenges of a caving expedition, receiving a spontaneous spiritual vision, or waking to remember a significant nighttime dream – such events can come into a person's life at the most consequential moments to bring light to the significance of the passage at hand. Sometimes, life presents to us naturally occurring rites of passage we'd never think to plan, and it's up to us to acknowledge, celebrate, and derive meaning from such experiences.

5. **Remember that there may be vast differences in the chronology of each family member's journey.**

   Although *Living Passages for the Whole Family* is organized in approximate chronological order from birth to adulthood, family members may experience developmental and situational passages at significantly different ages and stages of the human journey. Just as puberty may be experienced by one person at the age of eight and another at eighteen, such life passages as giving birth, graduating from high school, marriage, significant religious rites, college graduation, leaving home, learning to drive, or adopting a child may be experienced at significantly different phases of the human life cycle, imbuing the passage with unique elements, depending upon a person's age and stage of growth. Acknowledging and celebrating a life passage experienced at an unusual juncture in the human journey can be especially empowering for all involved.

6. **As you celebrate particular rites of passage, be aware of interconnected life passages in which family members experience different, but related, life passages at the same time.**

Whenever a family member goes through a significant life passage, whether it's a passage of birth, puberty, graduation from high school or college, moving away from the family home, marriage, or parenthood, among others, the experience is a significant passage for other family and community members, as well. To celebrate a passage meaningfully, it's helpful to consider the passage from various perspectives. While a rite of passage may focus on a particular child, youth, or adult who's experiencing the passage most intimately, there may be simple ways to acknowledge the meaning of the passage for others. Asking a grandparent to take part in a rite of passage to welcome and name a newborn allows the grandparent to celebrate and contemplate their role as elder for the child. Ideally, when a family creates a rite of passage at such times as a young adult leaving home or a child attending school for the first time, all family members have an opportunity to recommit their affection and support to one another in the face of changing relationships.

7. *Living Passages for the Whole Family* **focuses on developmental and age-related passages of the first 21 years.**

Families will obviously experience rites of passage beyond the scope of this book. Consider how such passages as the death of a loved one, divorce, or a geographical move may affect the way a young person experiences a particular age- or stage-related passage. Also, keep an eye open for my upcoming book, *Mourning Light: Honoring Family Passages of Grief, Death and Change*, which is scheduled for release in 2009.

8. For adults reclaiming blind passages from the past, refer to the "Reclaiming a Passage" sections toward the end of each chapter.

As you honor rites of passage in the life of a child, youth, or young adult, you may become aware of life passages that were not celebrated or acknowledged in your own past. The "Reclaiming a Passage" section in each chapter offers ideas for acknowledgment and healing. We adults will be much more effective in assisting young people to honor life passages if we learn to acknowledge such passages in our own lives – sometimes in retrospect.

9. For practical guidance in planning effective rites of passage, see the appendix, "Resources for the Journey."

Planning a rite of passage and leading a rite of passage ceremony don't come naturally to everyone, so the appendix includes sections on "Planning a Rite of Passage" (page 324) and "Planning a Ceremonial Rite" (page 326), which offer ideas for thinking through practical and prayerful ways to make a rite of passage more relevant and meaningful.

10. For those who prefer to learn songs by ear, the *Living Passages Song Collection* CD is available.

The song collection CD was delightfully recorded by Avalon Revisited, a women's a cappella trio comprised of my daughters, Morgan and Willa, and me. It can be ordered through Gilead Press (www.gileadpress.net).

11. Interact with *Living Passages for the Whole Family* as a soulful dialogue.

For whatever reasons you're drawn to *Living Passages for the Whole Family*, please make the reading of these pages an inner dialogue. The content of this book is far from comprehensive. It's my hope that parents, grandparents, teachers, therapists, healers, religious educators, and adults from all walks of life will find inspiration in these pages to help guide their own families and others in their care. It's also my hope that each of you will join the conversation and that together we may discover rites of passage that encourage our children to meet life fully, bravely, and with an abundant measure of joy.

1 ↭ Behold the Miracle

Rites of Passage for Birth & Arrival

The story is told of a group of people
somewhere on the vast continent of Africa
who celebrate their birth not on the day they were born,
not even on the day they were conceived,
but on the day they became a thought in their mother's mind.
On that day, the mother goes out and listens for her child's song.
Upon hearing the song, she sings it.
She goes back home and teaches it to her mate.
Each time they mate, they sing the song.
On the day the child is born, the people
gather in the birthing room and sing the song.
This becomes the newborn's song for their whole life.
When they cry for mama as a baby, she sings the song;
when they fall and skin a knee as a child,
the song is there to comfort.
All through life the person can always find solace in their song.
And when the person comes to the time of death,
again the people gather in the room and sing that song.

~ As told by Anita Jones

Celebrating Birth & Arrival

Some children arrive in our midst even before they become a thought in their mother's mind. We talk of parents giving birth to children. Rather, it is my children who are giving birth to me. Singing for *me* the song of *my* life.

In the beginning, I was not prepared, not ready to be a mother. Andrew and I had decided to wait three or four years. Suddenly, a few weeks after our Bermuda honeymoon (with its deserted beach under a cloudless, starlit night), we found ourselves faced with the reality of pregnancy and parenthood.

I was angry. Angry at our carelessness. Angry at Andrew for betraying my disappointment with that gleam of excitement in his eye. Yet, as we talked and I considered welcoming this child into our family, I was gradually swept up by the wonder of a child in our midst. Andrew and I enlisted the services of a midwife at a birthing center and began to prepare for the arrival of our child.

Then, at 3-1/2 months, on Halloween, I began to bleed. In a panic, I called Andrew and we rushed to the birthing center. All along the way, we glimpsed little children happily trick-or-treating in their Halloween costumes. The paradox seemed a bitter foreshadowing. In 24 hours, our baby was gone, as well as our hopes and visions for the future. It felt like a cruel joke. In the days that followed, I was taken aback by my feelings of excruciating loss and sorrow. Whenever I saw a pregnant woman or parents with young children, I wanted to hide myself and weep.

Yet, over the weeks and months, I gradually began to see how this unexpected pregnancy and miscarriage prepared Andrew and me for parenthood in ways I would not have anticipated. Through the brief presence of this child in our family, we had been anointed with a vision of ourselves as parents. This new vision inspired us to begin to create ideals of who we desired to be as parents to our, as yet, unborn children. We began to change our lifestyle and work plans to make room in our lives for a child to be welcomed with open arms. Six months later, we were thrilled to learn we were pregnant again.

Perhaps nothing can fully prepare us for parenthood. Perhaps nothing can fully prepare us for receiving into our lives the complexity of human life we find in a daughter or son. Yet, preparation itself is a passage, an announcement to ourselves and to all who care to listen, that our lives are changing, deepening, widening to hallow a space to receive the miracle of new life.

Interestingly, when our second child, Willa, was a preschooler, she spouted out one day that she "came before, but had to go back," so her older sister, Morgan, could be born first. I stood open-mouthed as Willa ran off to play. We had never mentioned the miscarriage to either of our children. After I absorbed the meaning of Willa's words, I laughed to myself. This was just like Willa – the mover and shaker, the one who stretches Andrew and me to constantly reassess the limits of our parenting wisdom. Willa "came before" to wake us up. She and her sister were waiting, ready to come to us, and I now believe Willa's initial earthly visit was intended to inspire us to make ready for their arrival.

Perhaps nothing can fully prepare us for parenthood. All the more reason to prepare. All the more reason to embrace the daily opportunities our children present to us even before they are born – opportunities to grow and change, to widen our capacities for love and compassion, to be reminded again and again of the deeper significance of our lives and relationships. These opportunities are, perhaps, the most meaningful preparations of all.

Rites of Passage for Birth & Arrival

A Ceremony of Welcoming

We often hear people speak of "life after death," but how often do we consider a person's spiritual existence *before* the person is conceived? How often do we pray for and speak with loved ones as yet unborn?

Perhaps it was the fact that our first pregnancy ended in miscarriage on Halloween, a day when it was supposed, in the ancient Druid tradition, that the dead come back to mingle with the living. Suddenly, as a childless mother, I became keenly aware of the soulful presence of the child who had so briefly blessed our lives. I became aware of the spiritual presence of my future children. The misty veil between the earthly and spiritual realms is, at times, quite thin; just as we humans are visited by the spiritual presence of those who have gone before us, so we are visited by the spirits of those who will take part in our future destiny.

After our Halloween miscarriage, the holiday took on new meaning for Andrew and me. We began to celebrate it more intentionally as a time to honor our ancestors and loved ones who had passed over. When Morgan was ten months old, Andrew and I decided to create a memorial of sorts for the child we miscarried during our first pregnancy. We realized that we hadn't fully acknowledged the significance of that experience. We wanted to bless and thank the miscarried child for enlightening us with new visions of parenthood. Through this celebration, we also desired to welcome a second child into our family before he or she was ever conceived. We didn't fully realize how intimately connected these two pregnancies would be. We had become aware, however, through our Halloween miscarriage, that just as rebirth is an element of death, so death is sometimes intimately connected with the miracle of new life. Moreover, it is this very relationship between life and death that steeps the human journey with meaning and purpose.

Although the following rite of passage could be celebrated any time of year, for us, celebrating it on Halloween, exactly two years after our miscarriage, held special meaning. So, after greeting over 120 trick-or-treaters at our door, when Morgan was asleep and all was quiet, Andrew and I gathered several candles to share the following ceremony. Revise it to reflect your own beliefs and spiritual perspective.

> **Tools** ⧸ For this rite of passage, you'll need several candles to represent departed loved ones (tea lights are fine), a special candle for the child being welcomed to the family, and matches or a candlelighter. You may also want to include pictures and symbols of loved ones who have passed over and symbols of your future child.

Remembering Our Ancestors

To begin our ceremony, we honored our ancestors, family members, and friends who had crossed the threshold of death. We named them one by one, lit a candle for each, and shared cherished memories and gratitude for their presence in our lives. We also offered a special remembrance for the baby we had miscarried. . .

Remembering the Child We Miscarried

For this portion of our ceremony, Andrew and I spoke directly to the child we miscarried two years before. We told the child how unprepared we were for parenthood until we became pregnant for the first time. We thanked the child for visiting us in this initial pregnancy and waking us up to our desire to be committed, loving parents. We offered prayers and blessings for the child. (Speaking with and praying for the spirit of a miscarried or stillborn child can also be deeply healing immediately following the loss or anytime during the grieving process.)

Welcoming Our Future Child

A parent says:

"Just as we commune with loved ones who have died, we also commune with those born of the future. Tonight, we invite our future child into our family." (Child's candle is lit.)

A parent says:

"Dear child, we welcome you with open arms.
We offer visions of our future together. . ."

Parents share desires, hopes, and images of life with their future child. If others are present, they may also share their visions of the child.

Song: Kum ba yah, My Child (page 73)

> (This song is from Angola. Kum ba yah means "come by here.")

> Kum ba yah, my child, kum ba yah, (3 times)
> Dear child, kum ba yah.
>
> We are waiting, child, kum ba yah. . .
>
> We are praying, child, kum ba yah. . .
>
> We are dancing, child, kum ba yah. . .
>
> We are laughing, child, kum ba yah. . .
>
> We embrace you, child, kum ba yah. . .

Invoking the Blessings of Our Ancestors

A parent says:

"We ask our ancestors to impart blessings upon our child/ren. Whatever goodness, whatever protection, whatever love and encouragement you can impart, we ask you to do so now and always."

Everyone stands, raises one hand heavenward in a gesture of blessing, and speaks together:

> "Companions of the spirit,
>   bless us now as you are blessed.
> Child, yet to come,
>   we await the honored guest;
> Come and make this family new
>   as we prepare a place for you,
> Our arms reaching tenderly
>   to welcome you home."

If the candles are left burning after the ceremony, make sure they're in a safe place and don't leave the candles unattended. Before extinguishing the candles, offer a silent or spoken acknowledgment such as: "Your flame burns forever in our hearts."

A Parenting Journal

Because our culture provides few ways for parents to explore and adopt healthy parenting practices, sometimes it takes great initiative for a new parent to prepare inwardly for this major life change. Keeping a parenting journal can be a great help to process the myriad feelings and issues that arise as you become familiar with this new territory.

After our miscarriage, my new identity as a mother did not die with that tiny baby. The picture of myself as a parent continued to grow inside me. I began to dedicate an entire journal to understanding myself as a mother. In my parenting journal, I reflected on my perceptions of motherhood itself. I wrote about mothers I knew, their struggles and joys, and what I could learn from each of them. I wrote about my relationship with my mother, and her relationship with her mother. I considered the gifts I received from these two significant women in my life, as well as the challenges they passed on to me which were now mine to overcome.

In my journal, I wrote about our society's stereotypes and expectations of mothers and the aspects of these images and expectations with which I struggled. I wrote about how I desired to be a mother to my future children and how my identity as a mother related to my marriage, work, passions, spirituality, daily life, and choices.

I found that writing my parenting journal was like planting seeds in a freshly dug garden plot, then eagerly watching to see which seeds would sprout, which I would need to thin, and which would grow fully to harvest. Of course, my perceptions, beliefs, and perspectives evolved with the realities of future pregnancies, births, and the real life experience of nurturing children. The journal became like an invaluable friend and counselor that could reflect to me who I was and who I was becoming as a parent and a human being. It saw me through the passage when I became a parent for the first time and the whole world changed before my eyes.

Your parenting journal can include whatever topics are most helpful to you as you consider your evolving identity as a parent. When you need a prompt, consider one of the following reflections or questions:

- Envision yourself with your child as a newborn, toddler, preschooler, and on through the years. . . What aspects of parenting do you antici-pate with joy and a sense of excitement? What aspects of parenting cause you fear?

- What do you think is expected of you as a father or mother from
    . . . your child?
    . . . your partner?
    . . . your parents, siblings, or other extended relatives?
    . . . your higher power, spiritual companions or guides?
    . . . the larger communities of which you are a member?
    . . . society at large?

    Which of these expectations feel positive to you?
    Which feel restrictive?

- Write a letter, *for your eyes only*, to any one of the people or com-munities listed above, and tell them how their expectations make you feel, which expectations you plan to actualize as a parent to your child, and which you plan not to fulfill and why.

- Describe your relationship with your own mother or father. What are the gifts your parents bestowed on you through the years? What ob-stacles have they set in your path? How have you communicated your gratitude to them for their nurturing and support? How have you taken responsibility to heal any wounds you suffered or created in your relationships with your parents?

- What qualities of your father's or mother's parenting practices do you wish to embody? How will you choose to parent differently?

- If you have unresolved issues with your parents, as many of us do, reflect on the aspects of your relationships with your parents that need attention. What aspects of your relationships with your parents are in need of healing? Can you address these issues directly with your par-ents or is the most positive course of healing an inner or spiritual pro-cess that can take place without your parents' participation? Would a professional counselor or spiritual director be helpful in clarifying the issues and possible tools for resolution? Think of this process as a way to create a healthier, more nurturing environment for your child.

- Of all the parents you know, which do you respect most? Why?

- Identify the qualities you admire in all of the loving, committed parents you know. Which of these qualities come naturally to you? Which will be a challenge to embody?

- If you have a spouse or parenting partner, how would you describe their attitude and level of commitment to parenting?

- How is your partner's attitude or level of commitment similar or different from your own? How does this make you feel? Is it possible that your approaches can be different, yet complementary?

- How will the birth of a child change your relationship with:

  . . . your partner?
  . . . your other children?
  . . . your work?
  . . . your extended family members and friends?
  . . . the larger communities to which you relate?

  Which of these changes do you eagerly anticipate? Which do you imagine will be a challenge for you?

- What values, priorities, and intentions do you hold close to your heart as you strive to be a loving and committed parent?

- Imagine you and your child several years into the future. Write a first-person journal entry of you and your child then, but write it *in the present*, as if you have already actualized the values, priorities, and intentions in your parenting that you hold dear. Allow this description to be a guiding vision for you in the days to come.

- Write about whatever feelings or issues arise, positive or negative, those filled with joy and anticipation, as well as the issues that cause confusion, rage, doubt, fear, etc. How will you allow negative emotions to guide you toward healing and transformation?

- Learn the song "Child of My Heart" on page 76. Sing it as a lullaby to your child. Journal about the images, insights, and feelings that arise.

Even if you aren't a continual or avid journal writer, occasional journaling can be a great self-counseling process. It can also help to clarify your evolving identity as a parent and a person. Think of it as an ongoing conversation with the parent who dwells within you.

A Father's Pregnancy & Birth

When we were pregnant with Morgan, Andrew found it difficult to feel intimate with her. He envied the physical experience I was having and, in some ways, felt like an outsider. As we journeyed through a full-term pregnancy for the first time, we recognized the double standard for fathers in our society. On one hand, fathers are chastised for not being more involved in their children's lives, especially early on when their children are young. Yet, there are so many ways we, as a society, sabotage the father-child relationship from the beginning. The dads in my father's generation were not even allowed in the delivery room when their children were born.

When Morgan was born at a hospital birthing center in Chicago, the midwives were taken aback by Andrew's attentiveness to my every contraction. They told us that most men sat in the next room, watching television, until the "big moment." This didn't surprise me. It's a long road from being completely excluded from childbirth to being included as a knowledgeable, valuable, and irreplaceable participant. During our search to find just the right caregiver for each of our children's labors and births, we encountered midwives and doctors who regarded Andrew only as a secondary participant. Needless to say, these were not the caregivers we chose.

Andrew's enthusiasm and willingness to participate fully in the birth process inspired him to read several books on pregnancy and birth, take time off work for appointments with doctors and midwives, attend birth and labor classes, and help me prepare my body for the coming birth. I believe this was made easier for Andrew because I found tangible ways to welcome him into the birth process.

In our appointments with caregivers, I made a point of including Andrew in the conversation when a caregiver was focusing only on me. I learned to speak of "us" being pregnant, of "us" giving birth. Six months into our pregnancy with Morgan, I also wrote the following letter for Andrew from our baby's perspective. This letter helped Andrew to consider ways he could foster a deeper intimacy with this new child who was growing in my womb, and growing in his heart and mind.

Dear Daddy,

Mama tells me you're having a hard time knowing how to be close to me right now. Since she's the one carrying me inside, she thinks it's easier for her to know who I'm becoming. She thinks it's easier for her to feel close to me. This may be true, but, Daddy, I knew you before I ever came here. I chose you to be my father. You and mama are the most important, cherished, needed people in my life.

I know you want to know me better. I want to know you better, too. So, I've been thinking of ways we can share special time together on this journey to see one another face-to-face. As you learn to be close to me, you may want to. . .

1. Read me a story or sing me a song, so I can learn to use my ears and come to know your voice.

2. Put your hand or face on me and feel my movements. (I'll try not to kick you too hard.) Rub and gently massage me inside mommy's tummy. This feels wonderful and helps me get to know your touch.

3. Give mom a massage. When mom feels relaxed, I do, too.

4. Dance with mommy. I like to hear the music and feel the movement. It helps my sense of balance, too.

5. Go for a walk with me and mama. It makes us both healthier and helps my sense of touch and balance.

6. Shine a light on me. This helps me use my eyes and see amazing shapes and colors.

7. Read about children and parents. Learn about how other babies and parents have learned to live together. We'll have our own style, but this will help you put some of your fears behind you. If other dads can do this, so can you!

8. Imagine positive images of you and me together – playing, laughing, soothing me when I cry, feeding me, diapering me, or taking a nap together. This will help you trust yourself as my father. I trust you already.

9. You and mom keep laughing and finding delight and humor together. When the two of you feel good, so do I!

After reading this, you'll probably come up with some ideas of your own. I love you, Papa, and I'm excited to meet you face-to-face. Until then, we have a lot of growing, loving, and learning to do with one another.

Write back soon, Your Growing Baby

Blessing Ceremonies for Labor & Birth

Over the past few decades a beautiful tradition for expectant mothers, that some call a "blessingway," has risen up in our culture. These nurturing ceremonies are beginning to replace the traditional "baby shower" of gifts and party games. "Blessingway" ceremonies offer tangible nurturing and support for the pregnant mother, often including such tender gestures as brushing, styling, and adorning the mother's hair, giving her a footbath or massage, and special blessings for the labor and birth. The ceremonies often include music and a celebratory feast.

Some "blessingways" take place in intimate circles, including only a few participants; others are celebrated in a larger community circle. Some honor only the expectant mother, others honor the new father or both parenting partners, and some incorporate blessings for the grandparents or older siblings. I know of one birthing couple who created a blessing ceremony in which they honored the baby's older brother, blessing him with positive visions of his relationship with the new baby, bestowing a special gift, and allowing him to lead the children present at the blessing ceremony through a "birth tunnel." The "birth tunnel" was created by two rows of adults, facing each other, holding long scarves overhead between them. His leadership was a symbol of leading the way for his younger sibling. The birthing couple experienced this act as a highlight of the ceremony and an effective way to prepare their son for the changes a new sibling brings.

"Blessingway" ceremonies for expectant mothers were originally inspired by rituals of the Navaho Native Americans. The Navaho people traditionally celebrate many "blessingways" throughout the Navaho life cycle. Recently, however, in consideration of the Navaho people, there has been an impetus to rename the adopted "blessingway" ceremony "mother blessing." ("Parent blessing" or "father blessing" may be used for inclusive ceremonies or ceremonies to prepare a father.) This renaming is an important recognition that when we create rites of passage inspired by the traditions and rites of others, we must do so without co-opting rituals and celebrations we do not own and may not fully understand.

Parent blessings can assist parents and families to feel supported and held during a vulnerable life transition. Single parents, gay and lesbian parents, and adoptive parents have unique challenges in growing a family and may appreciate the nurture and encouragement of such ceremonies as much as anyone. Be creative and put together a blessing ceremony that speaks to your unique situation.

On the following pages are four blessing ceremonies. The first is a blessing ceremony for parents expecting their first child. The final three blessings may be used separately or as a three-part blessing: to prepare birth participants for labor, include long-distance friends and family in the labor and birth, and name and bless the newborn. Feel free to revise these rites of passage or create a new ceremony more relevant to the situation at hand.

A Blessing for New Parents

When our children were young, our dear friends, Tammy and Dan, became pregnant for the first time. Tammy and I had taken part in large "blessingway" ceremonies given to expectant mothers; however, Dan and Tammy desired to be given a parent blessing together in an intimate circle. So one night, after our children were asleep, Andrew and I gifted the new parents with a ceremony similar to the one that follows.

Tools ❧ Candles are lit around the room. Chairs or sitting pillows are set in a circle for participants. In the center of the circle, on the floor or table, are three "family candles" representing mother, father, and child. A decorative length of cord (two feet long or so) is placed in a circle around each candle. A pitcher of water and a bowl are covered with a cloth. If a footbath or handwashing is given, you'll need two basins filled with warm water, scented oils or bath salts (if you choose), towels, and massage oil or lotion (if a foot or hand massage is given). Make sure the oils or lotions don't contain ingredients to which the honored parents are allergic.

Before a mother blessing, sometimes a more experienced mother or small group of women help the new mother prepare for the ceremony by drawing her a bath, assisting her in dressing, brushing or styling her hair, and/or adorning her. A footbath or handwashing is a simpler way to offer this gesture of supportive preparation to one or both parents.

The Preparation

Foot Bath: Outside the celebration circle, or in another room with quiet music playing, the new parents are invited to soak their feet in warm basins of water. (Scented oil or bath salts can be added.)

Someone says to the new parents:
"The water that nurtures you is a symbol for the water of Creation's womb, the water upon which you were born into existence. This water prepares you for your new birth as parents."

If the honored parents enjoy the footbath in another room, other participants can use this time to prepare for the ceremony, learn songs, and review the flow of the celebration so everyone knows what to expect and how and when they will contribute.

Anointing & Invitation to the Circle

Drying and Anointing the Parent's feet

Someone dries the honored parents' feet with a towel and anoints them with a special oil. If the honored parents are comfortable with the idea, someone can massage their feet with oil or lotion to symbolically prepare them to walk with courage and compassion on their journey as parents. The parents are then invited to the circle of celebration.

Song: A New Parent's Prayer (page 74)

Elders who walk before me,
Bless me with your wisdom,
Friends who walk beside me,
Bless me with your love.
Child yearning to be free,
Child, come and learn with me
How we may grow increasingly
Compassionate and strong.

Lighting the Family Candles

Someone says to the new parents:

"Each candle, here in the center, represents the lives of each of you: father, mother, and child."

Reading or Recitation ⁓ Ecclesiastes 4:9-12

Each of the honored parents is invited to light their respective candle and together they read or recite the following passage:

"Two are better than one,
    because they have a good reward for their toil.
If someone falls, one will lift up the other,
but woe to the one who is alone when they fall
and have not another to lift them up.
Again, if two lie together they are warm,
but how can one be warm alone?"

The honored parents are invited to light the candle of their child from the flames of their own candles. Together, they speak these words from the Ecclesiastes passage:

"Three is even better,
    for a triple-braided cord
    is not easily broken."

Blessing the Parents

Gifts for the Parents

A pitcher is given to the father as a symbol of the male life energy, and a bowl is given to the mother as a symbol of the womb. (Getting a matching set from a pottery shop makes a wonderful gift for the new parents.) As the mother holds the bowl, the father is invited to pour the water from the pitcher into the bowl to symbolize the conception of their child.

The Parents Speak

The new parents are invited to speak about their experience of being a parent – the joys and challenges, and how they desire support and encouragement from those gathered. (The honored parents can prepare something for this portion of the ceremony in advance.)

Reflection: "On Children"
excerpts from *The Prophet* by Kahlil Gibran*

Blessing the Mother & Father

Each participant offers a blessing for the new parents. The blessing may be silent, spoken, or even sung. It can be read or given spontaneously. After each blessing, the blessing-giver wets the tips of their fingers with the water from the bowl, touches both of the parents, and speaks this line from the Ecclesiastes passage:

"Three is even better,
for a triple-braided cord
is not easily broken."

Blessing the Child

Someone says:

"When two people face one another to join their right hands and their left hands, the gesture is called 'handfasting.' It's an ancient gesture, originally used to join two people in marriage. The figure eight created by the gesture is a symbol for eternity and wholeness. As we bless your child, we invite you to join your hands in this way. Let the gesture remind you of the whole relationship that's needed to bring this child into the world together with intention and joy."

The honored parents join hands. One by one, participants offer a single word or phrase of blessing: "love," "health," "a safe journey home," etc.

---

*"On Children" is a well known passage from *The Prophet*, often used to celebrate childbirth and parenting. (See the book listing on page 333, under "Soulful Journeys.") Excerpts may be read, recited, or sung. A prepared reading by a small ensemble can be inspiring, or check out the beautiful musical version of this passage, composed by Ysaye Barnwell of Sweet Honey in the Rock. The sheet music can be purchased through The Musical Source (1-800-2-SOURCE); a recorded version of the song is also available on the Sweet Honey in the Rock CD, *Selections: 1976-1988* (www.sweethoney.com).

Braiding the Family Cord

Someone says:

"The members of your family – mother, father, and child – each bring a cord of life to braid together with the other two, creating a strong, triple-braided cord. As we sing, we invite you to take these cords encircling your family candles, cords that represent your individual lives, and braid them together as a symbol of strength and unity. Braid them together as a sign that you welcome this child into your family." (As the parents braid the cords, participants sing:)

Song: Health, Joy & Love (page 75)
Lyrics to verse one offered by Sonika Tinker & Dinyah Rein

Mother, sweet mother,
birthing life, birthing love,
Blessings we bestow upon you,
Health, joy, and love.

Father, dear father. . .

Child, growing child. . .

Fam'ly, loving fam'ly. . .

Final Blessing

Everyone stands and speaks the blessing together:

"Three is even better,
for a triple-braided cord
is not easily broken."

(After you extinguish the candles, you may want to give them to the honored family as a remembrance of the celebration.)

A Meditation to Prepare for Labor

In the last month of our pregnancy with Willa, I prepared a prayer table in my writing/meditation room. We were planning a homebirth with a friend, Julia, present to care for Morgan. I imagined the prayer table as a place for each of the adult participants to prepare ourselves inwardly for the labor and birth. I wrote a meditation in booklet form and explained it briefly to Andrew and Julia a few weeks before the birth. We planned for each of us to come alone to the table for some quiet moments after labor began. However, unlike her sister, Morgan, whose labor had taken an entire day, Willa surprised us and came into the world in a few brief minutes! I was the only one who had time to enjoy the meditation before the pushing stage began. A better plan might be to give all the birth participants a copy of the meditation a few weeks before the birth. That way, everyone can enjoy the blessing ceremony at their leisure, especially if a hospital birth is planned.

> **Tools** ✖ large ceramic bowl (filled with water), hand towels, a candle, matches, CD player set to play soft instrumental music, and a meditation guide or booklet, described below. Page numbers refer to each page of the meditation booklet, if one is made.

Page 1: A Meditation to Prepare for Labor

> I do not know how you appeared in my womb;
> it was not I who endowed you with breath and life,
> I had not the shaping of your every part.
>
> ~ Mother of Seven Sons (Hebrew Scriptures)

Page 2: An Explanation

We each come to this meditation in anticipation of the birth, now imminent. Take time to allow the Divine to speak to you and nurture you. As you read each page of the meditation booklet, consider each passage or suggestion. Then celebrate these prayerful moments in ways that are comfortable and meaningful for you. Light the candle and turn on the CD player, if you prefer.

Page 3: Words of Meditation by William Wordsworth

> Our birth is but a sleep and a forgetting:
> The soul that rises with us, our life's Star,
> Hath had elsewhere its setting,
> And cometh from afar:
> Not in entire forgetfulness,
> And not in utter nakedness,
> but trailing clouds of glory do we come
> From God, who is our home:
> Heaven lies about us in our infancy!

Page 4: Personal Meditation

As we gather to witness and participate in this birth, we're creating a sacred place to welcome this child into the world, into our lives. Each of us brings our unique presence and our particular skills and knowledge to this important passage. Contemplate the gifts you bring to this birth and visualize sharing these gifts with the others present.

Page 5: The Water of the Womb

The water placed before you is a symbol of the Womb of Creation, the Source of All Life.* As we prepare ourselves to support and nurture this child and one another during labor and birth, let's remember that we are supported by the strength, wisdom, and love of one another, and of the Spirit of Life.*

Page 6: Anointing Yourself for the Birth

Now, in preparation for the labor and birth, anoint yourself with this water – the water of Creation's womb. You may want to wash your face and hands in the water, or anoint particular parts of your body (your eyes to see clearly, your mouth to speak wisely, your ears to hear others' needs, your heart to love well, etc.). Imagine yourself being held and supported in the Womb of Creation. Express your gratitude.

**Page 7: A Blessing for the Baby
from *The Incarnating Child* by Joan Salter**

> From boundless cosmic regions,
> From sounding starry spaces,
> (Child who) sought and found us,
> We welcome (you) to earth.

*Insert the names for the Divine most meaningful to you.

Personal Prayer: Offer a prayer for the baby. Imagine positive visions of the labor and birth, and pray for each participant.

Page 8: A Gift for You

Beside the prayer table, you will find an envelope with your name on it. Open it and read it.

(Each note expressed my thanks for important personal gifts I felt each person was bringing to the labor and birth. The one who prepares this rite of passage may want to ask another participant to write such a note for him or her.)

Page 9: The Cycle of Renewal

Now, in a gesture of giving and preparation, empty out the water and fill the bowl again for the next person who will come to this table. Prepare the prayer table as you found it. Extinguish the candle so it may be lit anew.

A Blessing From Afar

A few months before Willa was born, we moved to California where Andrew was attending college. We were far away from all of our close friends and relatives. Several weeks before our due date, in anticipation of our home birth, Andrew and I asked our family and intimate friends to send a blessing for our new baby. In this way, we had a tangible expression of our extended family's love and support during this exceptional passage in our family's life.

We planned to read each blessing at strategic moments as we needed strength and inspiration for the labor and birth. However, since Willa's labor kicked in and hard labor consisted of only two or three brief pushes, we were unable to read the blessings, all but one. So we saved them for the following ceremony a few weeks after her birth.

Naming Ceremony for the New Baby

> **Tools** ↫ Written blessings sent by friends and relatives, a candle to represent the Creative Source of the Universe, a candle to represent the baby's life flame, matches, and anointing oil to anoint the newborn. If the size of the group allows, participants sit in a circle with the new parents seated next to each other.

Coming Together

Song of Celebration: Blessed Child (page 77)

Blessed child, you came from afar,
As full as the moon and bright as a star,
Shine your light, love,
Shine your light, love,
Shine on, dear child, shine on.

Naming and Blessing the New Baby

Participants take turns reading the written blessings for the baby sent by friends and family members who could not be present for the blessing ceremony.

Blessing Song: The Dew of Your Birth (page 78)

The dew of your birth is of the womb of the morning,
The kiss upon your brow is the anointing Divine,
A holy gift, sweet child of mine.

Naming and Anointing

Father or Grandparent: (holding baby)

"It is written that 'a good name is better than precious ointment.' Before all these witnesses, those present in body and those present in spirit, we name this child *Willa Andi Darian: Willa, meaning 'brave will;' Andi, meaning 'of your father Andrew,' and Darian, meaning 'heart of wisdom, compassion, and grace.'* (Elder anoints the baby with oil.) *Willa Andi Darian* may you grow strong, like your name."

Spoken Blessings

Mother: (picks up the baby's birth candle, but doesn't light it)

"This candle represents the light *Willa* brings into the world.
   In silence, let's consider our hopes and prayers for *Willa*. . ."

After a few moments of silence, the mother lights the candle and speaks aloud her hopes and prayers for the child. She passes the candle around the circle (away from the father so he's the last to receive it). Participants are invited to share their hopes and prayers for the child as they receive the candle. After the father shares his blessing, the mother, father, or a grandparent can thank the participants for their support and encouragement and ask for continued prayers and blessings for the child.

Song: Blessed Child (page 77)

Blessed child, you came from afar,
As full as the moon and bright as a star,
Shine your light, love,
Shine your light, love,
Shine on, dear child, shine on.

Final Blessing from *The Incarnating Child* by Joan Salter

Everyone says:

"From boundless cosmic regions,
From sounding starry spaces,
(Child who) sought and found us,
We welcome (you) to earth."

> If the candle is left burning after the ceremony, make sure it's in a safe place and don't leave the candle unattended. Before extinguishing the candle, offer a silent or spoken blessing, such as: "Shine on, dear child, shine on."

Infant Dedication & Baptism

Once, a woman who was a grandmother asked me if I believed an unbaptized infant who died would still experience eternal life with the Divine. As we talked, she revealed to me that a friend's baby had recently died shortly after birth, and the young mother was concerned about the baby's future in the spiritual world. I was taken aback by the woman's question, puzzled that such a wise and seemingly enlightened elder could believe in a higher power who would simply discard the souls of unbaptized children.

I shared with this elder my own view of infant baptism, which includes the moment during labor when the waters of the womb "break" and wash over the infant. In my imaginings, this is the moment the Divine Spirit laughs with joy to welcome each living infant into their new world on earth, or weeps with compassion when a baby's life is redirected back into the spiritual world, leaving their earthly family in a state of grief and confusion. Either way, it is baptism. Each baby's soul is intricately connected with the Divine, as the great poet Wordsworth affirms:

> "...trailing clouds of glory do we come
> From God, who is our home:
> Heaven lies about us in our infancy!"

Unbaptized infants receive no less Divine care than those we rush off to the baptismal font or dedicate to the Divine according to our chosen religious or spiritual path. Yet, those who have the opportunity to witness an infant baptism, dedication, name-giving, or covenant ceremony know such rites of passage grab hold of a vulnerable place in our souls. In that place, we are reminded of how utterly precious life is. We are reminded of the sacred ground of our being, so poignantly reflected in the tiny, extraordinary creation of a newborn baby.

Whenever I have the privilege of baptizing an infant at a church service or home ceremony, or attend an infant dedication or naming as a witness among the throngs of a celebration community gathered, I don't experience such ceremonies being undertaken as an insurance policy to guarantee eternal life for the infant. Rather, I experience such rites of passage as a medium for expressing inexpressible gratitude, making a commitment to nurture a child's soul, and acknowledging that it truly *does* require a village to raise a child.

When we come together to celebrate a new birth, we're calling forth the child's community – companions on earth and companions of the spirit – to bless, hold, guide, and identify the child as the Divine's own. Through such rites of passage, we're reminding ourselves, as parents, grandparents, godparents, aunts, uncles, siblings, cousins, and friends, that we are being entrusted to nurture, love, and support the newborn *without claiming ownership* because each child born comes to us from Divine hands.

The following dedication ceremony is one Andrew and I created for our daughter Morgan when she was nine months old. We hadn't celebrated a naming or blessing ceremony when Morgan was born and became aware of the omission months later. A dedication seemed to us a meaningful way to affirm Morgan's life and presence as a sacred gift.

A Celebration of New Life

Tools ᔆ Set chairs for the participants around a table. On the table, place an altar cloth, blessing bowl, and a pitcher of water. Set a CD player nearby to play a recording of ocean sounds later in the ceremony. In the invitation to the celebration, ask participants (who choose to do so) to contemplate how the child's birth has been a rebirth for them in some way, and invite them to bring a symbolic gift that reflects this sense of rebirth (as described on page 57). Also, ask each participant to prepare a brief written or spoken blessing for the honored child to impart during the ceremony. If the gathering is too large for everyone to bless the child, the child's parents, grandparents, and/or godparents may bless the child on behalf of the entire celebration community.

The Gathering

An Invitation to Celebrate

To begin, someone offers words of welcome and explains briefly the purpose of the dedication ceremony.

Meditation in Song: The Dew of Your Birth (page 78)

The dew of your birth is of the womb of the morning,
The kiss upon your brow is the anointing Divine,
A holy gift, sweet child of mine.

Naming the Gifts Bestowed

The Child's Biography

A parent or grandparent shares a brief biography of the child's life from conception to the present, highlighting events of the pregnancy, naming, birth, and other important remembrances.

Gifts Bestowed By the Child's Presence

Honor a few moments of silence, in which participants contemplate how the child's birth has been a rebirth for them in some way. Perhaps the child's presence brings insight into one's role as a parent, grandparent, godparent, sibling, aunt, or uncle, or the child's birth and presence has blessed one's life with an abundant measure of love, hope, joy for life, sense of mystery, tenderness, sense of purpose, need for organization, commitment to relationship, etc.

At this time in the ceremony, participants are invited to share their reflections. After each participant shares, they offer their symbolic gift for the child.

Anointing the Child With the Water of Life

Meditation in Song

Play a recording of ocean sounds; there are numerous recordings available (with or without instrumental music added).

The Water of Life

After quietly meditating to the ocean sounds for a few moments, some-one pours the water from the pitcher into the blessing bowl. As the ocean sounds continue, someone can speak about water as the suste-nance of all life and a symbol of birth and rebirth.

The Blessings

Standing around the table, one at a time, each blessing giver dips their fingers into the bowl of water, touches the child being dedi-cated and speaks their blessing aloud. Individual blessings can be read or spoken spontaneously. (After the blessings, fade the ocean sounds.)

A Covenant of Support

Everyone says (in unison):

> "(*Full name of child*),
> we love you. We support you.
> We encourage you as you live and grow.
> We rejoice with you in Life."

Going Forth

Song: The Dew of Your Birth (page 78)

> The dew of your birth is of the womb of the morning,
> The kiss upon your brow is the anointing Divine,
> A holy gift, sweet child of mine.

Adopting a Child

Like most children at some juncture of their journey, I remember vividly coming to the conclusion that I *must* have been adopted. For many children, the "adoption theory" comes into play around age nine. For me, it happened before I ever got to kindergarten. There was no fooling this fledgling. After all, it didn't take a third grade graduate to see that I was blonde while all my siblings had dark hair. Then, of course, there was my world view, which, from the time I was three, appeared to be so *utterly different* from the picture of the world my parents and siblings held. And, most importantly, at times, my older brothers and sister ganged up on me, teasing me incessantly, sometimes even coaxing a group of their friends to join in (for extra potency) – surely *that* was proof that I didn't belong.

So one day, at the ripe, old age of four, I decided I'd had enough. I packed my Barbie suitcase with my favorite "Thumbelina" doll, a pair of pajamas, and (my mother, if she really *was* my mother, would be so proud) a clean pair of underwear. Just as I zipped up the suitcase, my father stepped into my bedroom to ask what I was doing. With a trembling lower lip, I straightened my back and willed forth all the courage I could muster to say, "I'm running away." Silence. I shuffled my feet and looked at the floor. "All right," my father finally replied, "if you think that's what you need to do, you better go ahead and do it." I couldn't believe it! My father was actually going to *let* me run away!

Without so much as a glance at him, I marched past my father (if he really *was* my father) and huffed down the hallway to the front door; but just before I reached for the doorknob, I heard his gentle voice behind me, "Aren't you going to give me a kiss goodbye?" I turned around and begrudgingly allowed him one last kiss and hug. Then I was out the door, marching down our long driveway to freedom. At the sidewalk, I turned back for a final look. There, standing in the massive arched doorway of our home, was my father. From that distant perspective, he looked so small, so vulnerable. Suddenly, I knew: my father needed me! After all, if I were gone, who would hug him as I could? Who would listen to his stories the way I did? Who was small enough to sit and cuddle in his big, old easy chair, except for me? I shot off like a flash, running back across our front yard. I dropped my Barbie suitcase and leapt into my father's arms. No doubt this man was family to me. No doubt this was my home.

There's an intriguing paradox we human beings experience that causes quite a bit of inner ruckus while we're here on earth. The paradox is this: each of us is singularly alone in the world; at the same time, our true family abides all around us if we keep our inner eye peeled for them.

Sometimes a person is fortunate enough to discover true family in a birth parent or sibling, as I have, despite my early childish imaginings to the contrary. Yet sometimes we must look beyond blood ties to discover we're not as disconnected from others as we imagine.

My sister, Rebecca, and brother-in-law, Jim, at the ages of 45 and 41, decided to adopt two daughters (and, eventually, settled for three) through their state foster adoption program. They gave certain guidelines to their social worker as she strove to identify children in the foster program who might be available for adoption. Sometimes, the social worker suggested children who didn't meet Jim and Rebecca's criteria, and one day when she suggested such a child, and Rebecca declined, the social worker insisted that Rebecca and Jim at least *visit* the child she had available for them. Reluctantly, they agreed, knowing they could simply stop by her foster home and be on their way in a matter of minutes to enjoy their evening dinner and theater plans. However, when Jim and Rebecca stepped inside that foster home, they weren't prepared for what took place. They looked into the eyes of their then future daughter and *immediately* knew she was family.

Such is not always the case for an adoptive parent, or any parent for that matter. Sometimes our deep family bonds reveal themselves slowly, over time. Unfortunately, for some, these bonds are never quite secured. We're at our most vulnerable in our immediate family relationships, and in few other relationships do we have so much at stake. This is one of the reasons it's crucial, in adopting a child into the family, that a rite of passage is created to welcome the new family member and clarify the meaning of parenthood and family. Consider the rites of passage for adoptive families on the following pages. . .

A Labor of Love

During their wait for their adopted daughter, my friend Dana and her husband Paul created a family album depicting the significance and meaning of their family relationships. It included photos, artwork and words carefully selected to reflect the faith, affection, celebrations, and silliness they manifested as a family through the years. The pages of the album also reflected the great anticipation and preparation the family was experiencing while they awaited the new arrival. The creation of the album helped Paul and Dana clarify their values and priorities as they prepared to widen their family circle. It continues to be a testament of the soulful welcoming awaiting the child's birth and homecoming – a treasure for any child to savor!

Other artistic creations for an adopted child might include a quilt that depicts images and symbols of the qualities and priorities of a family's life together. A family symbol or family crest displayed on a blanket, cradle, toy chest, or work of art might also make a memorable arrival gift for the child. In the Japanese tradition, a family crest is a simple rendering of singular design: for example, the symbol of an orange tree encircled by a ring, or two feathers crossing each other. Consider a symbol that's meaningful for your family; then design, draw, paint, or model it cooperatively. Use your family crest on letterhead or paint it on a large stone for the garden. Use it wherever it will best serve you as a reminder of the deeper meaning of your family life and relationships.

A Blessing for the Birth Mother

My friends Dana and Paul had the good fortune of welcoming their adopted daughter, Anna, into their arms the day she was born. Before they whisked Anna home from the military hospital where her birth mother had labored and delivered the infant, Paul and Dana had the wisdom to ask the hospital chaplain to help them create a rite of passage for blessing the birth mother as she released her child to them. The chaplain helped to choose scripture, prayers, and songs, and the three parents found solace in putting into an experiential ceremony the weighty significance of the life passage at hand for each of them.

Of course, it isn't always possible for adoptive parents to welcome their child on the day of their birth or to meet the birth mother under such conditions. However, such a rite of passage can be celebrated anywhere and anytime adoptive parents desire to create a blessing for the woman or birth couple who brought their child into the world, whether the birth mother or father is present or not. In this way, adoptive parents can more fully acknowledge the monumental life passage taking place for the adopted child, the parents, and the child's siblings, as the mantle of parental nurture is passed from birth mother (or birth couple) to adoptive parent/s.

Birth mothers might consider a ceremony of their own, acknowledging the weightiness of their decision to place their child for adoption. Such a ceremony can serve to clarify the intention of such a decision, acknowledge positive and/or difficult feelings, and provide an opportunity to bless and pray for the birth child. Some birth mothers gather on the Sunday before Mother's Day to honor their role in bringing a child into the world. Other birth mothers prefer to be acknowledged on Mother's Day. Any Mother's Day celebration that acknowledges birth mothers can assist in healing the pain and transforming the invisibility women sometimes feel after placing a child with another family.

A Day in Court

Court proceedings, including adoption legalities, are often experienced as sterile at best. Even in the most positive situations, they can be anxiety-producing. Not so with my nieces' legal adoptions. Oh, their parents were as nervous and excited as any new parents might be, but they were also able to experience some of the legal aspects of adoption as highlights of the adoption process. Weeks prior to Jim and Rebecca hosting a touching adoption celebration in their home with a house full of friends and family, my nieces experienced a celebration of a different kind – in court, of all places!

The lawyer representing my sister and brother-in-law had the wisdom and foresight to suggest to Rebecca and Jim that they invite a handful of close friends to the court proceedings. The lawyer encouraged the new parents to ask each friend (who was willing) to prepare to speak for a few brief moments about the gifts and qualities Jim and Rebecca bring to their parenting. In both court appearances (one for their eldest daughter, and another a few years later for their two youngest children), there were few dry eyes as friends shared images of the love and artistry with which Rebecca and Jim are choosing to parent. The friends also spoke of their own support and devotion to Rebecca's and Jim's children who are joyfully blessing their lives. The new parents were given an opportunity to share brief reflections about their adoption journey, and to thank each participant present (including the lawyer and judge) for their part in supporting their growing family.

Both judges overseeing these adoptions were visibly thrilled to experience such a deep sense of celebration in their court rooms. Pictures were taken – yes, even with the judge – and the friends present joined the family for a special meal after the adoption was official. Oh, that every courtroom could be filled with such unabashed expressions of delight in welcoming children home to their adoptive families!

A Family Adoption Celebration

Rebecca and Jim chose to create an adoption ceremony for their eldest daughter, Fielding, who was two years old at the time. They hosted another a few years later for Fielding's two sisters, who share a birth mother: Zady, who was three years old at the time, and Savanah, who was 18 months. Family members came from all corners of the U.S. to celebrate these events, and a community of friends were thrilled to be invited to take part in this rite of passage for Jim's and Rebecca's growing family.

Each adoption celebration began with a written invitation sent to family and intimate friends, which included a brief explanation and particulars of the event. The invitation included a request, for all who desired to participate, to bring a silver charm for a charm bracelet that would be given to the child at a future date. Those invited were also asked to bring a written blessing and explanation of the particular charm symbol chosen for the child. (For a boy, the charms could be sewn on a special quilt to be stored away and given on a future birthday, or the charms could adorn a specially made craft such as a dreamcatcher or suncatcher.)

The adoption ceremony on the following pages is a weaving together of my nieces' two adoption events. This ceremony can also be used to welcome a birth child.

Tools ➢ For this ceremony, participants brought a silver charm and written blessing as mentioned above. A small decorative tree, used for displaying the charms as they were given, was set on the coffee table. Candles to honor the family ancestors and four candles to light throughout the ceremony were set up high (away from curious little hands) on the fireplace ledge or piano. Also, a handful of participants were each given a small bottle of bubbles to blow over the honored child/ren after each charm and blessing was given. (The small bottles sometimes used at weddings work well.) A younger child included in this task may need an adult companion to hold the bubbles and assist. A bell or chime is needed to begin the ceremony.

Adoption Ceremony

Call to Gather

The honored child rings a bell or chime to begin. If the honored child is too young, an older sibling, cousin or friend can be asked to begin the ceremony. When all is quiet, someone recites the following poem. . .

Poem of Welcoming: "Laughing Song" by William Blake
(revised words in italics)

Now the green woods laugh with the voice of joy,
and the dimpling stream runs laughing by,
Now the air does laugh with our merry wit,
And the green hill laughs with the noise of it.

Now the meadows laugh with lively green,
And the grasshopper laughs in the merry scene. . .
Now the painted birds laugh in the shade,
Where our table with cherries and nuts is spread.

Come live and be merry *with me, let us play,*
To celebrate Fielding's* Homecoming Day!

Honoring and Inviting Family Ancestors

Parent says:

"At this sacred time in our family's life, in the sacred place of our home, we invite our ancestors – those who have gone before us – to be with us here, to bless our family with your presence today and everyday."

Each significant family ancestor who has passed is named and a candle lit in their honor.

*Insert the name of the child being welcomed.

Someone recites: "Carry Our Flame" by Jim Bagbey

> Where will you carry our flame, dear child?
> On wild adventures o'er many a mile,
> taking day in the deep of life's darkest nights,
> to make cold despair, frozen fear take its flight?
>
> Go! Blaze a path, my love, and learn as you grow –
> its song, its joy, its strength, its glow.
> Look! See your reflection and name as it shines
> beside those before you, who once held this light.
>
> Forefathers, foremothers, dear ones who have passed,
> each carried this flame to lighten life's path.
> Some thinking of you, not knowing your name;
> With me, with love, we hand you this flame.
>
> Perseverance and patience, hardship and trial
> are all in this flame that we hand you, my child.
> Find faith, hope and love with strong gentleness;
> Will you find all we give in the warmth of this gift?
>
> One day, when life's full of the light that you live
> and your child reaches forth for this flame that you give;
> When you hand them this fire, when you ask with a smile,
> "Where will you carry our flame, dear child?"
>
> Remember, remember my love.
> Remember, remember our love.
>
> Where will you carry our flame, dear child?

Lighting a candle, someone says:*

"I light this candle in honor of *Fielding*, a Child of God, the Joy of the Spirit embodied."

* In Fielding's ceremony, her older brother, Rion, who was in his early twenties at the time, lit each candle and spoke the written blessings throughout the ceremony. If you wish, you might invite different friends or relatives to light each candle and speak the blessing.

Welcoming from the Parents:

(spoken by parents in unison, cooperatively, or spontaneously)

"We welcome God, Spirit of Life, Source of all Love* to be present and to bless our holy gathering. We welcome *Fielding* and thank *her* for choosing us to be *her* forever parents. We welcome you, our family, and thank you for being here today to celebrate the adoption of *Fielding* and our journey together as a family. We invite *Fielding's* birth parents to be with us today in Spirit and honor them for their part in *her* sacred journey."

Lighting a candle, someone says:

"I light this candle in honor of Family."

Song: On the Day You Were Born (page 316)

On the day you were born, the angels rejoiced,
And a song burst forth from the heavens above,
On the day you were born, the angels rejoiced,
And the earth was shower'd with love.

Grandparent's Blessing:

Grandparents and other significant elders come to stand before the adoptive parents. The elders may choose to lay a hand on each of the parents and bless them silently, or speak their blessings aloud. After the individual blessings are bestowed, the grandparents/elders say together:

"(Today your) life's full of the light that you live
and your child reaches forth for this flame that you give;
(As) you hand (*her*) this fire, (as) you ask with a smile,
'Where will you carry our flame, dear child?'
Remember, remember my love.
Remember, remember our love."

Parent Covenant
written by Rebecca Danica and Jim Robke

The parents speak.

"*Fielding*, we stand in awe of your holiness, of your perfect joy, and of the honor you have bestowed on us by joining our family. . .

*Insert names for the Divine most meaningful to the honored family.

"We create this covenant as your parents:
To love you unconditionally,
To teach you the Love of the Spirit who gives you Life,
To love and respect each other as partners that you may feel
strength and security within our bond.

"We promise to give you a happy childhood,
To protect you and be your advocate,
To guide you and stand beside you as you meet Life's adventures
and opportunities, creating a life that is uniquely yours.

"We promise to enfold you in our family traditions, old and new,
To teach you compassion and respect for yourself and all others,
Wonder for the holiness of all life, Gratitude for the gifts
of the Earth & the Spirit world.
To keep sacred the story of your birth and to respect it as
your birthright.

"We promise to parent you with intention, and to nurture your
Spirit, mind, and body through our daily lives."

Lighting a candle, someone says:

"I light this candle in honor of the New Covenant."

Blessings Conferred on the Honored Child

Participants are invited, one by one, to share their charm symbol for
the honored child and give a brief blessing or explanation. (Before
anyone shares, you may want to ask folks to keep it brief so the ceremony doesn't get too long and tedious for the little ones. Longer written blessings can be given to the family for the child's memory book.)

After each blessing, the charm is given and displayed in a special place
(by the child if s/he is old enough). Participants gently blow bubbles
over the honored child to celebrate the love and wisdom bestowed
with each blessing. (Be sure to shield the eyes of an infant from bubbles
popping near the face.)

The final candle is lit and someone says:

"I light this candle in honor of New Life."

All: (in unison) *"Fielding,* the world is forever changed by the new life
forces you bring. Each of us is forever changed by your presence, and
by the gifts you bestow upon our circle of Love and Family."

Grandmother's Blessing by Andrea Alban Gosline*

A Welcoming World

And the child came gently
to the warm embrace of family
and they kissed the child and sang
a welcome song, promising
to nurture, guide, and celebrate
this precious new life.
And their joyful song was heard
in every grateful home,
by sunlight and twilight,
in this moment and all moments:
We are glad you're alive.
You belong here with us.
Welcome home, *Fielding*.

Benediction: (a leader speaks one line at a time and everyone repeats)

From all that dwell below the skies,
Let faith and hope with joy arise,
Let beauty, truth, and good be sung
Through every land, by every tongue.

(Adapted from a hymn by Isaac Watts)

Final Blessing Song: Love Grows One by One
by Carol Johnson**

Love grows
One by one,
Two by two,
And four by four.

Love grows
Round like a circle
And comes back knocking
At your front door.

* Excerpted from the book *Welcoming Ways*, available at www.ambledance.com

** Music for "Love Grows One by One" by Carol Johnson from her recording
"Might As Well Make It Love," available at www.caroljohnsonmusic.com

Reclaiming a Passage of Birth & Arrival

Each of us has a birth story, a name, and the need to belong to a family. Sometimes we're fortunate enough to know the significance of our name and our birth from an early age. Sometimes we're fortunate enough to know a profound sense of belonging in our family. However, all of us, no matter what our biography or ancestry, can gain clarity from understanding the events of our birth, deciphering the deeper meaning of our name, being reminded that, whether or not our *blood* family is our *true* family, such intimate kinship is not restricted to the family into which we were born.

If you feel a need for greater clarity, understanding, or healing of your own birth and arrival, or the birth and arrival of another family member, consider celebrating in one of the following ways:

- **Create a Birth Story:** Whatever events surround one's birth, and whatever details have been forgotten or lost, everyone needs a strong and loving birth story. A birth story can include factual details of the birth, embellished with the anticipation and waiting welcome of loved ones. It can also be a symbolic or soulful rendering of the birth event. To weave a new birth story for yourself or a loved one, you may want to contact family and friends who were present at the birth. Ask each person to share their memories of the birth in person, in writing, or in an audio or video recording. Weave the details together into a meaningful story. For an adopted child, the story might include their adoption journey and welcoming into their new family. Birthdays or the anniversary of an adoption can be potent times to bring a birth or adoption story back to life. Telling the story by heart and with particular turns of phrase can be especially memorable. Take a look at the children's books, *Knots on a Counting Rope* by Bill Martin, Jr., *On the Day You Were Born* by Debra Frasier, or *I Love You Like Crazy Cakes* by Rose Lewis. A symbolic birth story that you create or adopt for yourself or a loved one can bring profound meaning and impart a deep sense of welcoming and belonging. Such a story might be especially helpful when the facts and details of a birth are unknown.

- **Create a Nameplate:** One's name is an integral part of one's identity. Most names have myriad meanings historically. Knowing the origins of a given name, and why our parent/s chose a particular birth name for us can be enlightening. As we grow and change with the cycles of life, we may choose to derive new meaning from a name. We may also choose to change the given name/s by which others know us. Reflect on your name or the name of a loved one. Look at it from many different perspectives and traditions. Once you choose the meaning most empowering and significant to you, consider designing a nameplate with text and graphics. You may want to print your nameplate on cardstock and frame it for display; create a laminated bookmark or refrigerator magnet; or engrave the name's meaning on a key chain, watch, "dog tags," or necklace charm. It's never too late to draw greater meaning and strength from a name.

⚜ **Adopt a Family Member:** Throughout our lives, sometimes we encounter a surrogate parent, sibling, or grandparent who is not related to us by blood. The choice of adoption shouldn't be reserved for parents only. Find ways to acknowledge, honor, and celebrate such adoptions of the heart. Andrew and I have adopted grandparents, aunts, uncles, brothers, sisters, and cousins for ourselves and our children. After my father's death, my two grown brothers adopted a good friend of my father's as their honorary dad. They presented George, their adopted dad, with a certificate of adoption that was both touching and humorous. Likewise, a godparent need not always be chosen at birth. Such supportive relationships may be affirmed and sought out at any age or stage of life.

⚜ **Swaddling Cloths:** Just as newborns are swaddled in blankets to give them a feeling of warmth and security, no matter our age, the experience of being lovingly held and supported can be transformational. In my immediate family, we are not shy about letting one another know when we need to be held and cuddled. I feel fortunate that my children (who are now young adults) are insightful and bold enough to ask for physical nurture when they need it. After my father died, a friend of mine sent me a knitted prayer shawl as a symbol of comfort for me in my grieving process. I was surprised how nurturing that simple gesture of being swaddled in my prayer shawl could be. A special quilt or blanket can work just as well to allow one to feel held physically and spiritually, especially in the absence of loved ones.

~~ **Rocking Chairs & Lullabies:** Comfort gestures aren't just for babies. Take time each day to create soothing moments for yourself, perhaps rocking on a porch swing or rocking chair. Imagine being held in the arms of Divine Spirit (by whatever name you cherish). Sing lullabies to yourself and practice holding yourself in a gesture of unconditional love.

~~ **Homecoming Welcome:** Birth and adoption are not the only occasions to bubble over with anticipation and gratitude for one another's presence in our lives. When a family member has been away for an extended period – at school or camp, on a personal retreat, in the hospital or a recovery clinic, at war, on an extended work-related trip or lengthy vacation – their homecoming can be a grand opportunity to welcome the person back into the family circle and remind them how greatly they're appreciated, supported, and loved. To celebrate the occasion, you may want to write a heartfelt letter composed by the whole family and plan a special dinner, or, if the homecoming occurs at a significant life passage, consider creating a ceremony to honor the occasion. An example can be found on page 253, "Returning Home Again." Also, take a look at the song "Welcome Home" from my book *Sanctuaries of Childhood* available through Gilead Press (www.gileadpress.net).

Songs for Birth & Arrival

Kum Ba Yah, My Child

African, Angola
(text revised)

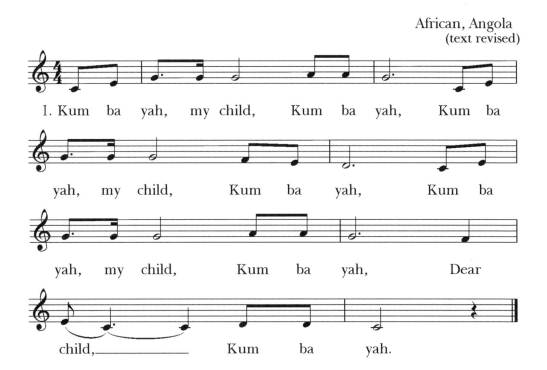

1. Kum ba yah, my child, Kum ba yah, Kum ba yah, my child, Kum ba yah, Kum ba yah, my child, Kum ba yah, Dear child,_____ Kum ba yah.

Choose from these verses or create your own. . .

2. We are waiting, child, Kum ba yah. . .
3. We are praying, child, Kum ba yah. . .
4. We are dancing, child, Kum ba yah. . .
5. We are laughing, child, Kum ba yah. . .
6. We embrace you, child, Kum ba yah. . .

*"Kum ba yah" is translated "come by here."

A New Parent's Prayer

Shea Darian

El - ders who walk be - fore me, Bless me with your wis - dom, Friends__ who walk be - side me, Bless me with your love.____ Child__ yearn - ing to be free, Child,__ come and learn with me How we may grow in - creas - ing - ly com - pas - sion - ate and strong.____

Health, Joy and Love

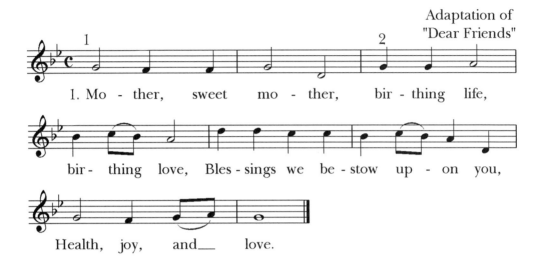

Adaptation of
"Dear Friends"

1. Mo - ther, sweet mo - ther, bir - thing life,
bir - thing love, Bles - sings we be - stow up - on you,
Health, joy, and— love.

2. Father, dear father. . .
3. Child, growing child. . .
4. Fam'ly, loving fam'ly. . .

* The first verse of this song was offered by Sonika Tinker and Dinyah Rein. The original version of "Dear Friends" and other rounds sung to this melody can be found under the title "Peace Song" in *Rise Up Singing*, edited by Peter Blood-Patterson. (Bethlehem, PA: Sing Out Corporation, 1988)

Child of My Heart

Freely

Shea Darian

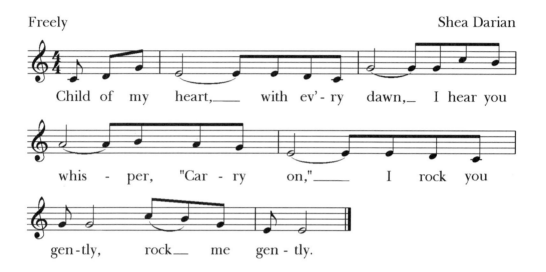

Child of my heart,____ with ev' - ry dawn,_ I hear you

whis - per, "Car - ry on,"____ I rock you

gen -tly, rock___ me gen - tly.

2. Child of my seed, my little dove,
   How you define the name of Love,
   I rock you gently, rock me gently.

3. Child of my womb, your warm caress
   Fills my soul with tenderness,
   I rock you gently, rock me gently.

Blessed Child

Shea Darian

Bless-ed child, you came from a - far, as full as the

moon and bright as a star; Shine your light, love,___

— Shine your light,___ love, Shine on, dear

child, shine on.

The Dew of Your Birth

Shea Darian

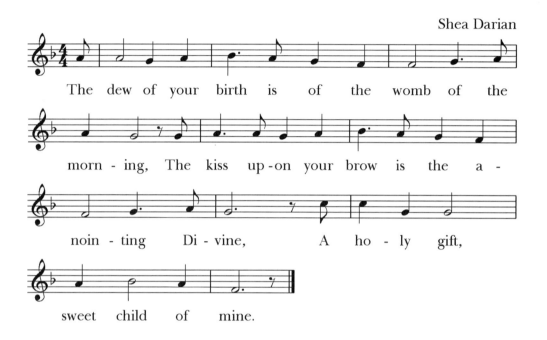

The dew of your birth is of the womb of the

morn - ing, The kiss up - on your brow is the a -

noin - ting Di - vine, A ho - ly gift,

sweet child of mine.

"The dew of thy birth is of the womb of the morning."

~ Psalm 110:3b

2 ⁊ The Wonder Years
Rites of Passage for the Growing Child

It is with people as it is with trees –
One must grow slowly to last long.

~ Henry David Thoreau

Celebrating Childhood

We parents are a funny breed, hanging on a baby's every facial expression, every gurgle. Recounting over and over again, for anyone who will listen, the first halfway coherent word, the first wobbly step, the oh-so-simple and wondrous daily discoveries a young child uncovers in their little world.

There's something about becoming a parent that turns our souls inside out, lures most of us to free fall into the abyss of unconditional, absolute love. From the center of that love, we rediscover the world as if for the first time.

This overwhelming love serves us and our children well because when a child comes into the world as an infant, they do so without a sense of individual "selfhood." The infant experiences others, especially the infant's primary caregivers, as an extension of the infant's own being. This is one significant reason why Andrew and I chose to rearrange our lives and our family budget when we decided to have children. *We* wanted to be the ones to share such an intimate encounter with our children in their early years. Granted, not all parents have the inner or outer resources or the opportunity to do so. However, what's important to remember in providing genuine care for the infant and young child is that their primary caregivers are not simply *caring* for the child. Their primary caregivers *are* the child, in the sense of being an integrated element of the child's being. Perhaps this is why it's so easy for parents to fall lovingly into our baby's eyes. We are surely part of them, as they are us.

Yet, there's an excruciating paradox we encounter often on this parenting journey. I encountered it in a profound way when I was eight months pregnant with Willa and serving as full-time, at-home mom to our 21-month-old, Morgan. Morgan had just gone through a week of teething, cutting some new molars. A week during which I didn't know what else to do, except sit with her through three-hour crying spells, pain, frustration. I was exhausted from concurrent sleepless nights, days when I truly felt I didn't have enough love to give her, couldn't open myself wide enough. But in the midst of the struggle to see those molars emerge, I realized that being with her through her pain was enough. It was enough to hold her and tell her that I love her. Before I knew it, the storm was over.

One morning, Morgan rose with a smile. We shared a leisurely breakfast, washed dishes, did chores, played in the yard. Then, after lunch, Morgan dozed for nearly three hours. Later that afternoon, watching Morgan play from my perch on the backyard deck, I suddenly caught a clear glimpse of her as an individual being, apart from me, fulfilling her own unique life destiny. This was a picture I expected to glimpse when she went off to kindergarten for the first time, at her eighth grade graduation, or when she moved away from home to go to college. But here I was, beholding a startling picture of my 21-month-old as a unique and complete being, apart from myself. It suddenly dawned on me that Morgan's life was much less about me than I imagined, and that my work as Morgan's parent was much less about Morgan than it was about me developing my own inner capacities for love.

There is something absolutely transformative about holding a space for a child in the world. Especially in the early years when a child's vulnerability requires so much of us – body, soul, and spirit. There is something utterly life-changing about merging into an infant's being and holding them secure, so that the child in them may emerge. Step by step, word by word, tooth by tooth, the child emerges out of the other and into the self. And we parents have the privilege to stand by as a witness when a child takes their first step, rides a bicycle for the first time, experiences their first great sorrow, or tells their first hilarious joke.

Mysteriously, as a parent nurtures a child toward wholeness, a parent experiences an expanding sense of wholeness from within. It's as if some mystical transformation occurs in parenting in which the loving parental attention a parent gives a child reflects itself back into a parent's soul, reaching into every crevice that's ever been void of a parent's caring touch. So, as we parent a child, we parent ourselves. Herein lies the truth of the old adage, "it *is* in giving that we receive." May we parents bask leisurely in our love for our children, so we may fully know the wonder of parenthood, the wonder of childhood.

Rites of Passage for the Growing Child

In recent years, a small bounty of much-needed work has been done around adolescent rites of passage that communicate the significance of a youth's transition from childhood to adulthood. However, we live in a culture in which we are quickly burying childhood under a fast-paced, competitive, profit-driven reality – a practice coined by David Elkind, in his book *The Hurried Child: Growing Up Too Fast Too Soon,* as the "hurried child syndrome." Given this reality, rites of passage that focus on childhood transitions are every bit as formative and potentially life-affirming as the later adolescent rites. Childhood rites of passage not only encourage us to honor and preserve childhood, they lay the foundation for a child to "come of age" gradually, one transitional life passage at a time.

During the first two to three years, children grow at such a lively rate that if we were to create a rite of passage for every significant developmental change, we could easily become overwhelmed with the possibilities. The first three years of a child's development are potently and continually transitional. It can be helpful to think of these early years of a child's life as an intense initiation period – for the child as well as the parent. Although simple acts of celebration can be created along the way, planning a rite of passage to coincide with the completion of a child's first three years can be an effective way to acknowledge this three-year cycle of initiation and celebrate the myriad learnings and accomplishments of these years. (See "In the 'I' of the Beholder" and "Celebrating the Third Year Passage" on pages 92 and 93.)

A family's priorities, life situations, faith perspective, and a parent's understanding of child development will greatly determine the significant life passages that a family chooses to celebrate in a child's life. Because I chose to breast-feed my children and because Andrew and I shared a bed with our children for the first several months of their lives, rites for weaning and receiving a new sleeping space were significant to our family. We also found potty training to be a significant passage of these early years, as well as losing baby teeth and attending the first day of kindergarten and grade school.

In addition to the childhood passages presented in this chapter, you may identify passages your child is experiencing that aren't reflected here. Adapt or create rites of passage that reflect the uniqueness of your child's journey and your family's identity. Keep your eyes and ears open for those moments that cry out for encouragement, acknowledgment, and ceremony.

A Ceremony of Weaning

Just as the decision to breast-feed can be monumental for a mother, so too can the decision to end a mother's and child's nursing relationship. With Morgan, because she was my first, the decision was more difficult. Being a voracious reader, I discovered a bounty of literature on the subject, most of it suggesting that the first several months (until a baby's nutritional needs are being provided by solid foods) are the most crucial time for a child to receive the exceptional nourishment healthy breast milk provides. I read books and articles that suggested six months, nine months, or twelve months as the ideal time to wean a child. One popular perspective promoted weaning a child only when the child initiates it, which, for some children, may not happen until the child is three or four, or sometimes even later. No wonder the decision was a difficult one for me as a new mother.

Ultimately, Andrew and I conversed about the possibilities. We considered a child's need for the kind of intense nurturing and nourishment breast-feeding provides. We considered, as well, a toddler's developmental need to loosen such intense ties to the mother as the child becomes a bit more independent and learns to stand and walk about in the world. We contemplated what was right for me and what was right for our family. We took into account other major life transitions we were experiencing, such as the birth of a new sibling and moving to a new home, so we could time weaning around these events. We considered health issues for me and our children. We recognized that weaning is a process that can be honored in stages as nighttime nursing or public nursing is discontinued, or as breast milk is offered to the child less frequently.

Ultimately, Andrew and I chose to complete weaning with Morgan when she was two years old, after she had grown comfortable with the idea of sharing mom and dad with a new sibling. We completed Willa's weaning at 20 months, a few months after our family moved from Citrus Heights, California to Cincinnati, Ohio and we were well settled into our new home.

For Morgan and Willa, the weaning transition happened easily. I'm sure their comfort with this passage was closely related to my inner confidence that each of them was being weaned at the appropriate time, and that the change in our relationship was a change to be celebrated.

The following weaning ceremony is similar to one we shared with Willa on that momentous day when, after nearly 3-1/2 consecutive years of nursing my children, I could claim my breasts as my own once again! Though the following ceremony lasted only a few minutes and was celebrated in the privacy of our immediate family circle, the confidence and joy Willa experienced through this rite was tangible. We have photographs of Willa after the ceremony, holding her new drinking cup, sitting tall and proud, nearly bursting with enthusiasm over her newly found independence. It was surely a potent ceremony, for Willa never asked to nurse again.

Tools ✖ We sat in a circle on floor pillows. In the center of the circle was a beautiful cloth upon which we set three symbols to be given to the child being weaned: a small, round pebble (which can be placed in a little, transparent case for safety purposes), a small ceramic figurine of a baby sleeping, and a silver cup with the honored child's name engraved on it. Other tools included a small pitcher of rice milk (a favorite drink of Willa's), three drinking cups for the rest of us, a candle, and matches.

Gathering

As the family sits quietly together, someone lights the center candle. The mother invites the child to nurse one last time. As the child nurses, the father or other family member reads or recites the following poem:

> Child, suckling at your mother's breast,
> Lay in that bed of roses one last time;
> Among those creamy and crimson petals
> Remember the tiny babe you were
> When first you opened your lips
> To that river of gold.

> Child, suckling at your mother's breast,
> Taste that milk and honey one last time;
> It is enough, it is surely enough.
> Behold, now, the child you are,
> No longer needing to open your lips
> To that river of gold.

Child, suckling at your mother's breast,
Rise now – you have been nourished well.
Rise now – you have been made strong.
Rise now – knowing life courses through you,
And the Source of that golden river
Gives you direct access to the mother lode.

Gift-Giving

After the poem is read or recited, the mother invites the child to sit on the pillow next to her to receive some gifts.

Mother: (handing the child the small, round pebble)

"From the time you were a tiny seed inside me,
 you were fed from my body."

(handing the child a small figurine of a baby)
"When you were born into this world as a baby,
 you were fed from my breasts."

(handing the child the new drinking cup)
"Now, I give you this cup, so you can feed yourself."

Blessing

Song: Take Your Cup (page 105)

Take your cup, fill it up and drink of its goodness,
Take your cup, fill it up and drink of its joy,
Take your cup, fill it up and drink deep and long,
For the life within your cup will make you strong.

Communing

The father or another family member pours the chosen beverage into the cups. Family members sip the beverage and share conversation. When everyone is through drinking, family members gather around the honored child who is holding the new drinking cup. Family members gently place a hand on the child and sing the above blessing song again. Afterward, the cup is kept in a special place and brought out when the child needs to drink.

Blessing a Child's New Sleeping Space

Dusk is a sacred time. A time that calls us home, calls us to the circle of a family reunited. The evening hours are a vulnerable time. A time that calls us into the dark shadows of our lives, calls us to grow familiar with endings. And before we can embrace the possibilities that arise with a new day, we must be willing to give ourselves over to that dreammaker known as sleep.

Whether a child sleeps in bed with their parents in the first months or years of life, or in a nearby crib or bassinet, the eventual move to their own sleeping space or a "big child's bed" can be a significant rite of passage for the child and their parents.

From the time our children were infants, Andrew and I knew that a nightly rhythm of restful sleep would be one of the most significant family practices we could develop to foster healthy, joyful family life. So, when when we gave birth to each of our children, imagine us dedicating ourselves to sharing a bed with each of them for the first several months of their lives! For those who have never experienced such an arrangement, it may come as a surprise that family sleeping can provide a profound sense of comfort and protection for our children, and allow the whole family – yes, even mom and dad – to sleep more soundly and for longer stretches through the night. I was able to tend to nighttime nursing and soothing without ever getting out of bed, and Andrew could easily change nighttime diapers on the changing table he had set up bedside.

When Morgan was 18 months old, I was five months pregnant with Willa, and even though we had a king-sized bed, sleep became more challenging as Morgan and my belly steadily grew. So Andrew and I decided to redecorate Morgan's room with a "big child's" bed, and I made some simple rose-colored curtains that filled the room with a rich, warm glow when the sun shone through. Morgan was delighted with her freshly decorated room; all the more when we blessed her new sleeping space and created a new bedtime ritual. For the nighttime ritual, we enjoyed a brief story time, lit a candle, sang a song, and spoke a verse of prayer. Morgan basked in the magic of it all, but her favorite part was blowing out the candle – an act that signified the dark had come and with it, a time to rest.

When a child moves to a new sleeping space, whether from a crib or family bed, or due to a geographical move or the rearranging of family bedrooms, the child can be greatly comforted by your attention to make the child's new sleeping space a haven of peace and comfort. To inspire a child to come to their new bed with a sense of anticipation and ease, consider the gift of a new comforter or new soft flannel sheets, new pajamas, a dream pillow (see page 287), soothing lavender oil to dab on a pillowcase or favorite doll, a chime to ring or a candle to extinguish to signify the day's end, a picture of a guardian angel watching over a child, or a music box to lull a child to relax into the nighttime silence. Of course, the most important gift of all will be the intimate moments you share with the child at bedtime.

Before blessing your child's new sleeping space, consider creating a predictable nightly routine for the child (if you haven't already) that includes donning pajamas, brushing teeth, and, for the toilet trained, going potty. After bedtime preparations are complete, use the following blessing (or create one of your own). Continue to use the blessing each night, so the child can depend upon it at bedtime. As a child grows, you'll be able to sense when the blessing needs to be altered. Remember, it makes the bedtime blessing more effective when elements, such as ringing a chime, telling a story, or winding a music box, are experienced only once each night. In this way, the child knows that begging for more is not an option, and they can settle more easily into a peaceful rest. For the young child, a rhythmic, comforting bedtime blessing serves as a reminder that (at least in the child's own little corner of the universe) all is right with the world. Every child deserves such a moment before they give themselves over to that dreammaker known as sleep.

> **Tools** ✒ A candle in a safe, sturdy candleholder, matches or a candlelighter (to be stored away from curious little hands), a wind chime, a story to read or tell from memory, a music box, and (for blessing the new sleeping space the first evening) essential oil of lavender which is known for its relaxing, healing qualities.

Lighting the Nighttime Candle

The nighttime candle can be lit after the bedroom light is turned off, or light the candle in the bathroom after teeth are brushed and carry it into the darkened bedroom.

Welcoming the Night

The child rings the wind chime one time, and when the tones have faded, the parent recites the following verse. Depending on the child's age, they may join in speaking this verse with you after hearing it several nights in a row. It's a verse that can be used with children of all ages, even those grown old and tall.

> Wrap 'round me soft blanket of darkness,
> Sing to me, sweet music of silence,
> Move me to rest, rest in me still,
> Still me to rest in your peace.

Story Time

Storytelling by candlelight can be magical for both the teller and the listener. The first night, to help bless the sleeping space, a parent can tell the story of the child first sleeping in the mother's womb, being born and sleeping in a bassinet, crib or family bed, and finally growing big enough to sleep in a big bed of their own. This story can be repeated for several nights because young children thrive on repetition.

When it's time for a new story, consider the repertoire of stories you already have stored in your memory. Tell simple stories of yourself at your child's age, happenings you witness in nature (such as ants gathering food or a butterfly emerging from its cocoon), or stories you were told as a child – "Goldilocks and the Three Bears" or "The Three Little Pigs." Young children thrive on hearing such stories several nights in a row and revisiting them from time to time. In this way, the story library in your head can more easily grow along with your child.

Blessing Song: All is Well (page 106)

> All is truly well in the world tonight,
> All is truly well 'neath the starlit sky,
> All is truly well in this moment in time,
> All is well, all is well, all is well.

Blessing the New Sleeping Space

As the following poem is spoken, parent and child bless the bed with little drops of lavender oil. (Change italicized words accordingly for the child being blessed.)

We bless *Dylan's* bed with lavender sweet,
The pillow for *his* head, the blanket for *his* feet,
The four strong corners that hold *him* while *he* dreams
By twilight and starlight and moonbeams.

We bless *Dylan's* bed and know angels abide,
His spiritual keepers who ne'er leave *his* side,
They wing through the night and guide *him* to wake
When the sun paints the sky at daybreak.

We bless *Dylan's* bed with lavender sweet,
The pillow for *his* head, the blanket for *his* feet,
The four strong corners that hold *him* while *he* dreams
By twilight and starlight and moonbeams.

Being Tucked into Bed (a blessing offered by Brit Reis)

(Change italicized words as needed.)

"And then the *boy's mommy* tucked *him* into bed,
pulling up the covers to *his* chin.
The *boy* rested peacefully beneath the roof of the house,
beneath the sky of the night
with the moon and the stars in all their glory.
And as the *boy's* body rested,
the *boy's* soul traveled the earth,
and angels watched over *him*,
letting *him* know all is truly well in the world.
All is truly well. . ."

Blessing Song: All is Well (page 106)

(After the song, allow the child to blow the candle out or extinguish it with a candle snuffer.)

---

*For more bedtime resources see the bedtime and sleep chapters in *Seven Times the Sun: Guiding Your Child Through the Rhythms of the Day* and *Sanctuaries of Childhood: Nurturing a Child's Spiritual Life*. (www.gileadpress.net)

Celebrating Toilet Training

Perhaps to parents in the midst of it, *celebrating toilet training* is an oxymoron. Dealing with body wastes and fluids isn't the most glorious parenting task, and toilet training can be one of the most frustrating passages for parents and children. In today's workaday world, there's a great deal of pressure on parents and children for the child to be toilet trained before they begin daycare or nursery school. As with other aspects of child development, we sometimes want to hurry our children along out of a sense of convenience. We sometimes forget to allow the passage of toilet training to unfold with a sense of wonder and gratitude for the life-giving functions of these miraculous human bodies we inhabit.

At the same time, the disposable-diaper industry has encouraged parents to keep young children in diapers for longer and longer periods of time. Unfortunately, disposable diapers are filling up our landfills at an alarming rate, and with the fast-paced tempo of life today, more and more parents are justifying the convenience of disposables. Such environmental concerns prompted Julie Fellom to take action. Julie, who is now a successful potty-training consultant in San Francisco, has helped over 1200 families toilet train their children in a matter of days by becoming aware of a child's toilet training readiness, usually between 15-27 months. According to Julie, many children are toilet trained at the time gender identity is being established, between 27-39 months – ironically, a time of development when it becomes more difficult for a parent to influence a child's choices. Around the age of three, a child also develops a stronger sense of shame around potty accidents and may actually *prefer* diapers. In her upcoming book, *Diaper Free Toddlers*, Julie promotes a parent-initiated, child-led, and child-friendly approach to this passage. (Order her book at www.diaperfreetoddlers.com.)

Toilet training is a key event in the life of the young child. Messages a child receives during toilet training can greatly affect a child's self-esteem, healthy perceptions of their body, and even their sexuality, particularly the way they approach their intimate sexual relationships as adults. If we desire to lay the foundation for our children to celebrate their bodies – to experience their bodies as a wondrous aspect of human existence – there's no better place to deepen this understanding than at the potty. And, as with all significant life lessons, this one must be timed intentionally, given a child's stage of development and readiness.

Making toilet training a fun event rather than an anxiety-producing chore can go a long way in encouraging a child during this significant life passage of the early years. As Rahima Baldwin suggests in her book, *You Are Your Child's First Teacher*, when a child is approaching readiness for toilet training, buy a child's potty chair and give it to the child as a special gift. Consider other ways you can make potty training pleasurable for a child. In addition to giving the potty chair, you might want to make or buy a transparent bar of soap with a toy or nature gift in the middle of it. (See www.bodygreat.com.) Allow your child to use the soap to wash their hands each time they use the potty. After several trips to the bathroom, the child will wear the soap down to retrieve the little prize.

A verse or song to share with a child as they wash up afterward can also make potty time more pleasurable. The first stanza of the following song, found in *The Book of a Thousand Poems*, works well for washing hands; I added the second stanza for drying.

Washing Song (page 107)

Wash, hands, wash,
(Farmer's) gone to plough,
Splash, hands, splash,
They're all washed now.

Wet in the puddle,
Wet in the sea,
Wet in the (potty),
But not on me!

Acknowledge successful potty training with a simple gesture of celebration. Morgan still remembers how proud she felt the day we went shopping for her first "big girl underwear" because she had learned to use the toilet regularly. Since Andrew and I chose to use cloth diapers when our children were young, and provided at-home childcare, we didn't feel the pressure many parents feel today to rush through the passage of toilet training. We simply focused our efforts on patience and fun. Sure enough, Willa and Morgan both learned to use the toilet and, miraculously, are still using it to this day.

In the "I" of the Beholder

There was never any doubt, from the time Willa was two months old, that we had aptly named her; Willa was one of the most willful children Andrew or I had ever experienced. In Willa's younger years, this willfulness lent itself to nap-time tantrums of stellar magnitude and episodes in which she imagined herself to be royal sovereign over the Darian family. Willa's inner fire and passion also expresses itself with an intense joy for life and relationships that is irresistible. Andrew and I see Willa's strength and intensity as a gift that has demanded a certain courage and wisdom from each of us – courage and wisdom we may never have discovered without Willa's presence to challenge and guide us.

When our children were young, Andrew and I became aware of the developmental change that occurs for a child around the age of 2-1/2. Around this time, the child first gets a glimpse of themselves as an individual in the world. Before this time, a child sees the world as an extension of themselves, and although this perspective doesn't fade completely until around the age of nine, at 2-1/2, or thereabout, a child begins to see that he or she is an individual person, apart from mom, dad, sister, brother, grandpa, grandma, or any intimate caregiver. Beautifully, this change in a child's perspective can be heard in their word use, as they move from referring to themselves by name or the pronoun "me" to referring to themselves as "I." For example, before this change, a child might say, "*Evan* want a hug," or "*Me* want a hug;" after this developmental shift in consciousness occurs, a child says "*I* want a hug."

As we witnessed Willa moving through this developmental passage, we became aware of her need and *our* need to acknowledge the significance of this vulnerable juncture in her young life. So Andrew and I decided for Willa's third birthday to create a rite of passage that would honor Willa's growth and budding sense of self. We planned a ceremony to celebrate the significant accomplishments of her first three years of life – standing, talking, walking, and communicating, among others. It was clear that Willa had moved out of toddlerhood and was a child in her own right. We also wanted the ceremony to reflect Willa's expanding circle of caregivers and friends who were assisting us in protecting and supporting Willa as she became more independent.

For the ceremony, we invited 14 or 15 intimate friends and family members who were able to attend – people who served as Willa's intimate community of encouragers and supporters (beyond the circle of our immediate family). In the invitations, we included a brief explanation of the ceremony and our purpose for having it. We asked everyone to bring a written blessing for Willa and a simple nature gift for her – a rock, shell, crystal, feather, etc. In the invitation, we let folks know they would have the opportunity to share a brief blessing with Willa during the ceremony.

In the Christian tradition, a water blessing is often used as a way of "remembering one's baptism," that is, remembering the Divine gift of spiritual rebirth. In many traditions, water is a symbol for the renewal of life. Andrew and I chose to use the water blessing for Willa's ceremony as a symbol for her being "reborn," in a sense, into a growing consciousness of her individual selfhood. This ceremony was a significant rite of passage not only for Willa, but for us as parents learning what it means to encourage a child to grow fully into the cycle of life at hand.

Celebrating the Third Year Passage

Tools ✍ In our dining room, we removed all the chairs from around our dining room table except for the raised chair Willa used for mealtime. On the table we set a large ceramic bowl, a pitcher filled with water, scented oil, a candle to represent Willa's life, two "parent candles" (lit during the first song), matches, and a basket of small gifts wrapped in various colors of tissue paper for Willa to give to each guest. Before the ceremony began, we gathered in the living room to teach everyone the song we planned to sing together. Then we moved into the dining room and stood in a circle around the dining room table with Willa in her chair of honor, Andrew, Morgan, and me beside her.

Coming Together

Gathering Song: Gratitude (page 108)

"Parent candles" are lit by the parents during the singing.

> We must laugh and we must sing,
> We are blest by everything,
> (Gratitude, our welcome guest,)
> Everything we look upon is blest.

> Excerpts from "A Dialogue of Self and Soul"
> by William Butler Yeats (added lyrics in parentheses)

Statement of Purpose

Though it's helpful to explain the purpose of a ceremony in the written invitation, revisiting the purpose at the beginning of a ceremony can inspire a unified vision. At Willa's ceremony, we began thus:

"Today we celebrate Willa's third birthday. Willa has graced our lives in these three years with her joy, love, beauty, and energy. In three years, she has learned and accomplished much. In her first year, she learned to stand on her own two feet, and then to walk. In her second year of life, she learned to talk a blue streak, and in her third year, she first came to see herself as a person of her own. Now that Willa is getting bigger and older, she's supported in her daily life not only by her mother, father, and sister, who love her deeply, she's also loved and supported by her larger circle of family and friends, represented by the family members and friends standing here in this circle. We want to thank each of you for coming to show your encouragement to Willa as she grows and begins to walk a little further out into the world, protected and supported by your love."

Preparation for the Blessing

Lighting the Child's Life Candle

Together, the parents light the child's candle from the parent candles, and a parent or grandparent tells a brief biography of the child's life.

Father: "On November 5th, 1989, at 5:55 p.m., a child was born. We named her Willa Andi Darian – 'Willa,' meaning 'brave will,' 'Andi,' meaning 'of your father, Andrew,' and 'Darian,' meaning 'heart of wisdom, compassion, and grace.' The child grew strong, like her name..." (Andrew continued by telling a few brief stories about Willa in her first three years.)

Pouring the Blessing Water

Willa's older sister, Morgan, who was 4-1/2 at the time, had the honor of pouring the blessing water from the pitcher into the bowl and anointing the water with a few drops of scented oil. (We had practiced ahead of time so Morgan could take part with confidence.)

The Blessings

Parenting Covenant (spoken by the child's parents)

"Willa, we create this covenant as your parents.
We promise to love you with a transforming love,
a love that accepts you as you are unconditionally.
We promise to comfort you in your pain and vulnerability,
and to celebrate with you in your joy and discovery.
We promise to teach you what we believe it means to be strong and
humane, and to seek peace in our family and in our world.
We promise to share with you our insights of Life,
realizing that you will grow into your own insights,
choices, and unique ways of being.
We respect the person you are forever becoming
and promise to learn from you all you have to teach us.
We promise to play with you, to work side-by-side with you,
to cry with you and laugh with you.
And as we learn to parent and love you,
we dedicate ourselves to learning, more fully,
what it means to parent and to love ourselves and each other."*

*Originally published in *Seven Times the Sun: Guiding Your Child Through the Rhythms of the Day* by Shea Darian (www.gileadpress.net)

Anointing and Individual Blessings

Willa sat in the circle on the raised chair she used for mealtime. Andrew and I blessed Willa first by dipping our fingertips in the water, touching her gently on the head or hand, and speaking a blessing. Then Andrew held the bowl of water as the circle moved clockwise, a person at a time, so each person could anoint Willa and share their blessing. The blessings were brief. Some were written out and others were spoken spontaneously. Willa was quite comfortable having her friends – adults and children – touch her and speak to her. *Other children may be more comfortable having guests speak their blessings from where they stand in the circle.*

Sending Forth

Willa's Gifts to Her Friends

Willa helped to choose friendship bracelets to give as gifts for each person present at the celebration. She also helped to wrap them. At this time, Willa walked around the circle with the basket of gifts, and each person helped Willa find the gift she had chosen for them, which had their name written on the gift tag. Participants waited to open the gifts until everyone had theirs in hand. With the gift, we included a copy of the following poetry excerpt so everyone had the words before them when we spoke the verse in unison.

Blessing Verse: Excerpt from "I Am Cherry Alive!"
by Delmore Schwartz

"I am cherry alive," the little girl sang,
"Each morning, I am something new. . .
I am red, I am gold, I am green, I am blue,
I will always be me, I will always be new."

Blessing Song: Gratitude (page 108)

We must laugh and we must sing,
We are blest by everything,
(Gratitude, our welcome guest,)
Everything we look upon is blest.

Excerpt from "A Dialogue of Self and Soul"
by William Butler Yeats (added lyrics in parentheses)

Putting Faith in the Tooth Fairy

I've often wondered who the genius was who invented the tooth fairy – this magical creature that allows a child to see the loss of one's baby teeth as a good and necessary change. Losing a tooth can be unsettling and scary for an adult, let alone a child. The tooth fairy is depended upon to bring comfort and point a child toward the reality of divine beings who minister to us in our losses. The tooth fairy's visits give children a picture of themselves being cared for by beings greater than ourselves.

For a child meeting this passage, the coin or gift found beneath the pillow is no small token. Each exchange represents an acknowledgment that loss is at the core of personal growth and rebirth. Loss always comes to us with a gift in her hands.

The significance of a child losing their baby teeth came home to me when Morgan lost her first tooth in kindergarten. The day before the tooth came out, she drew an elaborate picture of a magnificent bush with vibrant, multi-colored leaves. The leaves were falling from the bush and scattered over the ground. To me, it was a picture of the vibrant beauty and joy we may find in our losses if we're willing to celebrate the changes that come with them.

When Willa and Morgan were young, they loved to write the tooth fairy notes of inspiration and thanks for her hard work. They placed the lost tooth in a seashell beneath their pillow and sometimes left her other special gifts — a beautiful bead, a crystal, a feather. I know one mother who made a special little pouch in which her child could place a lost tooth to slip beneath her pillow. In the morning, the tooth was gone and the pouch contained a small surprise. There's also a delightful little tooth fairy puppet (with a pocket to hold a child's tooth) available from Folkmanis Puppets. (Check their website at folkmanis.com.)

With the loss of a child's first tooth, you may want to acknowledge it with the touching celebration on the following pages, created by my sister, Rebecca, for her daughter, Fielding. With each subsequent tooth a child loses, simple preparations for each tooth fairy visit and a song at bedtime may be all the added magic that's needed.

Celebration for a Child's First Lost Tooth

Written by Rebecca Danica

> **Tools** ❧ A little tooth fairy with a pocket in her dress is hanging from the ceiling above the child's bed. A low table is set up in the living room and covered with a cloth. On the table is a white candle to represent the tooth, and matches are handy. The child's tooth is placed in a small, clear bottle. To begin, the family sits on the floor around the table.

Poppa: (lights candle) "Tooth Fairies, we welcome you to our home and invite you to join us now in celebrating *Fielding's* first lost tooth. Dance with us!"

All Sing: (to the tune of "Brother, Come and Dance With Me" from Englebert Humperdinck's opera, *Hansel and Gretel;* everyone dances with scarves around the table)

> Tonight the fairies dance with me
> For magic's in the air, you see,
> We'll dance with joy, Please take my hand,
> We'll journey to tooth fairy land!

Momma: (edit this section for the child being honored)

> *"Fielding*, today you lost your first tooth while eating a piece of corn on the cob! We see you growing in so many ways and losing your baby teeth is one sign of that. We also celebrate:
>
> ❧ how you can cross the monkey bars and drop seven feet
> ❧ teaching your sister, Zady, new songs and poems you learn
> ❧ the ways you comfort Savanah when she misses momma at preschool
> ❧ learning our phone number
> ❧ hitting line drives off the baseball tee
> ❧ learning to write new letters of the alphabet. . ."

Poem: "From the Tooth Fairy" by Rebecca Danica

> I see you've lost your little tooth,
> The pearly one that's been so loose,
> I'll fly tonight on fairy wings
> And come to you while soft you dream.
>
> I'll take your tiny gift in hand
> And fly away to fairy land
> Where fairies all rejoice with you
> And marvel at how fast you grew!
>
> In exchange I'll leave a treasure
> To amuse and bring you pleasure
> And to remind you as you grow
> To claim the magic that makes you bold!

Procession: The candle is carried into the darkened bedroom, and the honored child places the tooth into the pocket of the tooth fairy hanging above her bed.

Story: The children's book, *Charming Opal,* by Holly Hobbie (told or read by candlelight or a reading light)

Song: Fairy Blessing (page 109)

> Fairy light in the night,
> Come to me while I rest,
> Fairy light in the night,
> May your travels be blest.

Blow out the candle and await the magic!

In the morning, the child might find a special coin or some other little gift in the tooth's place. For this first tooth, Fielding was given a tooth fairy charm to add to the charm bracelet she received on her adoption day.

Celebrating the First Day of School

At whatever age, when a child goes off to school or daycare for the first time, it can be cause for celebration as well as a source of great anxiety for both child and parent. A simple rite of passage to honor and celebrate this event can be a profound source of encouragement and comfort for the whole family.

Throughout our children's kindergarten years, when they were three to five years old, the first day of a new school year was celebrated with a simple acknowledgment – a new school bag, a new outfit, a special breakfast, or a new morning blessing to send them off to their first day of the new school year with a sense of joy and encouragement. We viewed these early school years as an extension of our home life and chose their kindergarten experiences with this in mind. The Waldorf school kindergartens they attended emphasized free play time, rather than children being drilled on their ABC's, and included storytelling, puppet plays, visual arts, growing and grinding wheat to make bread, preparing snacks, and caring for one's environment.

In the Waldorf grade school, students continue to be taught through the fine arts and practical endeavors, in addition to more traditional educational methods. Even so, the transition from the Waldorf kindergarten to first grade is seen as a dramatic step. A child is assessed as being ready to take on the more "academic" work of mathematics, reading, and writing. The child transitions from the more homelike environment of the kindergarten to a first grade classroom that usually includes individual desks or work tables, and chalkboards.

When our daughter, Willa, began first grade, we planned a simple family ceremony for the morning of her first day. We gave her a turtle-shaped bank and I shared with her an image from a Native American legend that speaks of the world being created on Old Mother Turtle's shell. I told Willa that a whole new world was awaiting her as she began first grade, and mentioned many things she would be experiencing as a first grade student. Andrew then told her the story of the tortoise and the hare, emphasizing the patience and perseverance the tortoise displayed in winning the race against the overconfident hare. (The story was chosen especially for Willa who, in those days, was almost always on "fast forward.") After the story, we blessed Willa with "fairy dust"* (fine, sparkling glitter), as we spoke our hopes and visions for her in the coming school year.

Fortunately, the faculty at Willa's school also created a ceremony to celebrate and welcome the new first grade students. Family members were invited to attend the celebration which took place at the very beginning of the school day. As parents and siblings gathered, we formed two lines that extended from the first grade classroom door toward the kindergarten wing of the school.

We held freshly cut boughs overhead, creating an archway for the children to walk through. One by one, each child was escorted through the archway of boughs by their kindergarten teacher. Outside the first grade classroom door, each student stood before their first grade teacher. The door was covered by a silken cloth. At the threshold of the doorway was a two-sided step unit with two steps on each side.

Tears easily swelled in my eyes as Willa walked purposefully through the archway, her heels firmly planted with each step, so eager to greet her new first grade teacher. Willa's kindergarten teacher spoke first, saying, "Ms. Corby, Willa Andi Darian is now ready for the first grade." Ms. Corby shook Willa's hand and said to her:

> "Willa, welcome to our class,
> Now through the threshold you must pass."

Willa released her kindergarten teacher's hand and entered her first grade classroom with confidence and joy, ready to meet the challenges and adventures unfolding before her.

The Waldorf school our children attended also celebrates a yearly tradition of the eighth grade students giving the new first graders a rose at the first all-school assembly of the year to welcome them into the grade school. At the end-of-the-year assembly, the first graders reciprocate by giving the eighth graders a rose in celebration of their eighth grade graduation. In this way, in addition to family and teacher support, the students experience encouragement from one another.

* When our children were young, we often used "fairy dust" as a fun, magical tool of blessing. You should be able to find fine, iridescent glitter at your local craft store. Put it in a little bottle or pouch to keep for special blessings and birthdays.

Reclaiming a Passage of Childhood

You may or may not remember your own childhood passages of weaning, potty training, moving to a new sleeping space, losing your first tooth, or going to school for the first time, but perhaps you can recall vivid memories of other childhood passages. These passages may or may not have inspired you to celebrate the miracle of your physical growth or served as catalysts for a growing sense of confidence and courage. Your childhood passages may or may not have provided you with an emerging knowledge of yourself as a uniquely cherished human being.

Because childhood is teeming with growth and newness, it's a time we grow familiar with rebirth and new beginnings. It's a time when we need to be surrounded by loved ones who encourage us through these numerous transformations. However, even when we've received the most attentive care as children, as adults we sometimes identify childhood transitions from the past that need attention.

As parents, when we support a child's need to breast-feed, we recognize our own need for intense nourishment and nurturing. When we support a child through an intentional weaning process, we recognize the importance of weaning *ourselves* from unnecessary dependence in relationships. When we guide a child to trust the solace of nighttime and sleep, we somehow heal our own fears of being alone in the night. In celebrating the process of potty training with a child, we learn to accept the wonder and goodness of our own bodies. When we experience a child's wonder at the prospect of a visit from the tooth fairy, we're reminded to consider the beginnings of our own faith in powers and mysteries greater than ourselves.

Call forth memories from your childhood. Identify a life passage that was celebrated or lovingly acknowledged by a parent, grandparent, caregiver, teacher, or other loved one. You may want to write the memory in a journal or tell the story to a loved one, highlighting why this life passage and its acknowledgment was significant to you.

For me, one such memory is the day my mother taught me to roller-skate. I was four. She surprised me with a gift of those hard plastic skates that attached to the bottoms of my tennis shoes. We must have spent a good hour at it — my mother giving me instruction, then standing back as I wobbled up and down the sidewalk in front of our house. Her words of encouragement propped me up, egged me on, until I fully overcame my fears of stumbling, falling. Finally, I could drop my arms and confidently glide the length of our sidewalk. The real moment of triumph, though, came afterward.

After I unscrewed the skates from the bottoms of my tennis shoes, my mother told me how I was getting "so big" and that she had a special job for me. I devoured every word, imagining from the tone of her voice that she was giving me a special mission only I could accomplish. She handed me a letter that needed mailing and asked me to walk the few blocks to a nearby street-side mailbox. She said to get there I would, of course, have to cross the street by myself. She said she trusted that I would remember to stop and look both ways to watch for cars.

Suddenly, I felt ten feet tall. With every step to the mailbox, and *especially* when I stopped to look both ways, I wanted the whole world to know I was growing up. When I arrived back home, successful from my mailbox mission, my mother gave me two shiny dimes for my effort. I immediately asked to run down the street to a friend's house to relay my earth-shattering news. Somehow, my friend's four-year-old mind didn't grasp the magnitude of the situation, but I celebrated with her anyway by giving her half of my first "paycheck."

Sometimes, simply telling the story of a significant passage in our lives can deepen its meaning. Moreover, the storytelling itself becomes the rite that affirms the growth, courage, or awareness we gained from that moment in our life's journey.

In addition to calling forth memories of a childhood passage that was celebrated or acknowledged by a loved one, recall memories of a childhood passage that was overlooked or may have become an obstacle to your growth and well-being. Consider how you can transform the memory by addressing your desire for wholeness and healing.

One such passage for my brother Jim took place the summer he was five. Dad took Jim and our brother, Roger, down to the lake to teach them how to swim. While our dad was focused on Roger, he hadn't noticed Jim sinking to the bottom of the lake. Although Jim was rescued that day, the experience left my brother with an intense fear of water and swimming.

When he was a youth, my mother coaxed Jim to attend swimming classes, but on the first day of class, when the swimmers-to-be were asked to sit underwater and hold their breath, the old fear gripped him. Jim had just built up the courage to join his classmates underwater and was taking a big breath to sustain himself when a teenage helper assisting the instructor came up behind him and dunked his head underwater. Sputtering and choking, Jim literally climbed up and over the young man to get to the side of the pool. Screaming and crying, he made his way to the dressing room and refused to go back to class.

As a teenager, Jim made the habit of driving himself to a public pool (where he knew no one) to try to teach himself to swim, but again whenever he came close to going underwater, the old fear clawed at his sensibilities. Many years passed, and finally, for his fiftieth birthday, Jim enlisted the services of an able swimming instructor and, in a matter of months, transformed his fear. Jim says that his trepidation of water isn't completely gone, but in the presence of his swimming instructor, Jim was able to swim in deep water by himself. Such a powerful allegory for his life.

The years of childhood are a gold mine for us to uncover treasures that help us understand the ways we live and breathe and function in the world. If we come to these memories and experiences like an artist with a pallet of colors, we learn that we can mix and remix the hues and tones to attain the desired color we wish to place on our canvas. Despite our culture's fixed concepts of time, the essence and meaning of our childhood experiences can be altered. We can revisit the children we were then. They have much to teach us, and we have gifts to bestow upon them still.

Songs for Celebrating Childhood

Take Your Cup

Shea Darian

Take your cup, fill it up and drink of its good-ness,___ Take your cup, fill it up and drink of its joy,_____ Take your cup, fill it up and drink deep and long, For the life with-in your cup will make you strong.

"God gave to every people a cup of clay,
and from this cup they drank their life."

~ Ancient Proverb

All is Well

Shea Darian
Inspired by Brit Reis

Washing Song

Anonymous
Additional Lyrics, Shea Darian

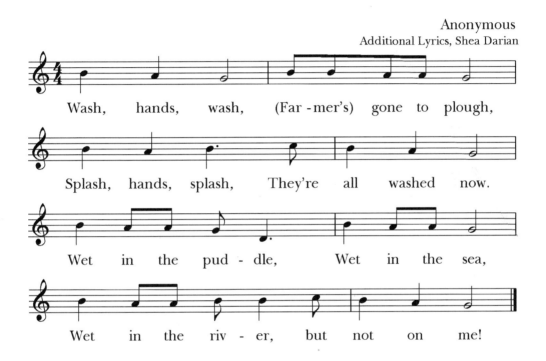

Wash, hands, wash, (Far-mer's) gone to plough,

Splash, hands, splash, They're all washed now.

Wet in the pud - dle, Wet in the sea,

Wet in the riv - er, but not on me!

When using this song during potty training, you may want
to replace the word "river" with "potty."

Gratitude

William Butler Yeats*   Shea Darian

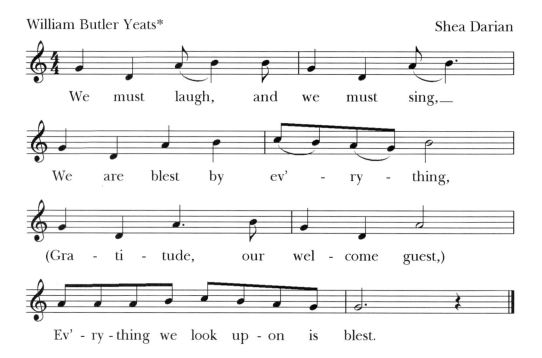

We must laugh, and we must sing,—

We are blest by ev' - ry - thing,

(Gra - ti - tude, our wel - come guest,)

Ev' - ry - thing we look up - on is blest.

*Lyrics are excerpted from "Dialogue of Self and Soul" by William Butler Yeats.
Additional lyrics in parentheses by Shea Darian.

Fairy Blessing

Shea Darian

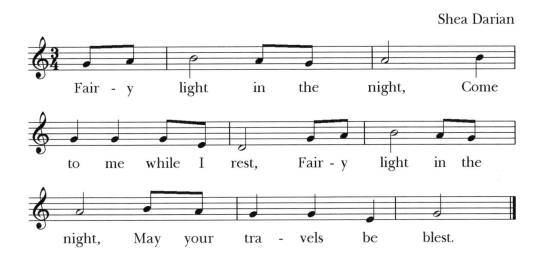

Fair - y light in the night, Come

to me while I rest, Fair - y light in the

night, May your tra - vels be blest.

3 ✍ The Awakening
Rites of Passage for the Growing Youth

Prince, I warn you, under the rose,
Time is the thief you cannot banish.
These are my daughters, I suppose.
But where in the world did the children vanish?

~ Phyllis McGinley

Celebrating Youthhood

When is a child no longer a child? Is it when childhood fantasies fade? Or when a young person sees clearly that a parent inhabits not a throne but feet of clay? Is it when a child has their first romantic "crush" or accomplishes their first challenging feat single-handedly? Or when a child recognizes their personal power to stand as a unique individual in the world and the potential aloneness that comes with that recognition? Is it when the finality of death is comprehended by a child's expanding mind? Is it when a boy's voice changes pitch? When a child grows pubic hair? When a boy has his first wet dream, or a girl her first orgasm? Yes. Yes to all of it and more, for a child doesn't suddenly don the skin of the youth. It happens gradually. The youth *becomes* a little at a time.

Youthhood, with all its complexities of human development, is commonly known as a vulnerable and awkward time of transition; yet, culturally, we consider youths to be some of the most threatening members of our society. The fears that lurk in our minds and imaginations are well documented in the book, *Framing Youth: 10 Myths About the Next Generation*, by Mike A. Males. The author clarifies with revealing statistic after revealing statistic how youth of today have been unfairly and erroneously labeled as a generation of violent drug abusers who are reckless, suicidal, "at risk," and suffering from a "moral meltdown."

When I reflect on such negative cultural attitudes toward the youth of today, I imagine it isn't the youths *personally* that we so fear. I imagine it's youthhood itself. Because, whatever else the transition from childhood to adulthood is about, it's mostly about power. The fading power of magic and the potential power of faith. The power of hormones, sex, emotions. The power of the individual and the power of community. The power of life and death. The power of the parent and the power of the youth. Being empowered. Being overpowered. Fear of having power, asserting power, and losing one's power. When we consider the unresolved issues concerning power that most of us carry from our own youthhood, is it any wonder that, as a culture, we target youths as a menace to society? Is it any wonder that some parents come to these years in a young person's life with a sense of trepidation? Is it any wonder that many young people are simultaneously thrilled and frightened at the intensifying announcement they hear from within: "No longer a child! I am no longer a child!"

Parenting a youth and staying awake to their significant life passages – passages that in their vulnerability and awkwardness they may attempt to hide from us – requires a great deal of courage. Parenting a youth requires one to look long and often at one's own unresolved issues surrounding gender and sexuality, the potential for public success and failure, disillusionments about magic and belief, fears of power (asserting it or having it taken away), fears of death, balancing autonomy with interdependence, and asserting individual identity in light of family and community values and expectations.

When I was twelve, smoking was one of the risk-taking activities among my middle school friends. One day when I was home alone, I grabbed one of my father's cigarettes to have a quick smoke in the bathroom. Suddenly, I heard my father's car in the driveway. I quickly put the cigarette out, opened the bathroom window to fan the smoke away, and sprayed deodorizer to cover the smell. Before my father walked into the house, I ran to my bedroom and sprawled on my bed with a book. Despite my cover-up, a few moments later my dad walked into my bedroom, smiled and said, "Was the cigarette good?" I was speechless. I wasn't prepared for his response. I expected fireworks. Consequences. A grounding. Not a smiling acknowledgment.

Later that evening, when I kissed my dad good-night, he told me (in a loving but matter-of-fact tone) of his concern about my smoking. He said he started smoking at the age of twelve and didn't know then of the addictive consequences of his decision. He repeatedly attempted to break the habit, but found it overwhelmingly difficult. He said he cared about me and my health and didn't want to see the same thing happen to me. That's all he said before he kissed me good-night. It was enough. My dad knew he couldn't patrol all of my 12-year-old leisure time. He knew if I chose to smoke, I could find a way. So instead of attempting to control my behavior, he admitted his own weakness and promoted a vision of something better for me. He also inspired me with the knowledge that I had the power to choose and that the responsibility of the decision was mine to make. I can't say I never smoked another cigarette. But I can say I never enjoyed it after that and soon became an anti-smoking advocate myself.

Over the past two decades, in observing and mentoring parents, I've seen adults repeatedly lose sight of a fundamental principle that is key to creating a successful relationship with a youth. The principle is this: when we allow a youth to express and utilize their personal power, it doesn't mean giving ours away to them. Youthhood is not a time for an adult to fully relinquish power to a youth or unyieldingly wield power over them. It's a time for adults – parents, grandparents, teachers, counselors, and caregivers – to guide a process for *the redistribution of power* between the adult and the youth.

Many parents display an obvious discomfort in knowing how to address this redistribution of power. Young children act like precocious teenagers, and adults nervously laugh and call it "cute." Teenagers pretend to be comfortable assuming adult vices and choices, and some parents use it as an excuse to withdraw supervision. Conversely, those of us with a strong hand of control err on the side of believing that control is power, only to have that control backfire the moment a young person discovers they need not submit to the control of *anyone*, not even a parent or teacher they revere. Furthermore, in attempting to control youths, we deprive them of the opportunity to become more responsible, capable human beings.

Youth of today yearn to be lovingly guided by their elders. They yearn for adults who are interested in their lives, their successes, the unique struggles and joys they face as youths of the 21st century. No matter how cool and independent a youth may appear, most young people yearn to be nurtured physically, emotionally, socially, and spiritually. They're looking for adults who are strong and loving enough to traverse with them the dark valleys, the mountain tops, the seemingly never-ending, barren plains of their life experiences. As a young person learns to navigate the geography of youthhood on their own, there will be times a youth grasps for a parent's hand, just as there will be times a youth may want only to glimpse the hearthfires shining in our window from afar. Yet, as distant or rebellious as some youths may become toward the significant adults in their lives, they do not *ever* desire to be strangers to us.

Encouraging a young person to express personal power and growing independence in the context of respectful, committed relationships is a crucial aspect of development during youthhood. As parents, grandparents, teachers, counselors, and caregivers, may we hold this truth before us with each new dawn. There is nothing our culture needs as desperately as hope in today's youth. And it is *we*, as much as the youth of today, who are the torchbearers of that hope.

Rites of Passage for the Growing Youth

Graham Greene once wrote, "There is always one moment in childhood when the door opens to let the future in." There was in my own childhood that moment, and many more than one, when I felt the hand of the woman I am now reach through time to take the hand of the girl I was then. Youthhood is full of such mystical encounters in which the child and adult within each of us meet one another face-to-face. For me, some of these youthful life passages were celebrated with others. I recall my parents buying me a shiny red Schwinn bicycle after my older brother taught me to ride his bike (several sizes too big). Suddenly, the whole neighborhood was my domain. I also remember my friend David letting me watch him pee, so I could see how boys "do it." I was devilishly delighted; not so my mother, who burst into the bathroom in the middle of the demonstration. Even so, I was grateful to David for the education. I recall, as well, my mother helping me hang blue ribbons above my bed after running in my first track meet. I remember writing and performing a comedic monologue that had the whole middle school in stitches; thus, I proved to myself that I could stand alone in front of my peers and reveal at least one face of my inner being. And I remember the affirmation and soulful sense of metamorphosis I felt when my parents gave me permission to pierce my ears after beginning my menses.

There were other moments of youthful passage, however, that I acknowledged silently in my own soul, with only the woman I would become as witness: the Christmas season that Santa Claus appeared as a strange, old man in a red costume; changing schools in third grade and feeling the need to prove myself friend-worthy; writing my first outstanding poem in fourth grade and being accused of plagiarism by my teacher (in front of the whole class); thrilling over the new sensations of a body transformed by hormones; shaming myself for fondling my own body in bed at night; experiencing acne as an enemy to my self-esteem; and maturing into the power of an athletic body grown strong and lean. Youthhood overflows with such life passages – passages that call for attention, understanding, support, nurturing, celebration, and love.

We parents do well to keep our eyes and ears open, our hearts and minds alert during the years of youth. What appears as the son or daughter who was the same today as yesterday could be a whole new creation standing before you. Youthhood has a way of changing everything.

Becoming a Keeper of the Magic

An especially tender youthful passage occurs when a child penetrates the veil of magic surrounding such childhood characters as the tooth fairy, Santa Claus and the Easter bunny. I remember well the morning in second grade (before the meaning of cultural diversity was made clearer), when my beloved teacher, Mrs. Powell, asked each of us to compose a Christmas "wish list" addressed to (none other than) Santa Claus. My heart skipped a beat as I hurried to get out pencil and paper, but my eagerness was abruptly halted with the protest of a freckle-faced, pigtailed classmate who blurted out, "Who still believes in that (bleep)!"

Of course, the culprit was immediately shushed by dear Mrs. Powell, but, for me, the damage was done. While most of my classmates continued to scrawl their Christmas visions with enthusiasm, I sat in a stupor, knowing in my heart of hearts that what my classmate proposed was true. There was no such powerful magic as Santa Claus.

That Christmas season was a lonely one for me. I grieved soulfully for my childhood belief. The idea of receiving Christmas gifts lost its lustre. When I saw Santa at the department store, I stared at the now all-too-obvious costume and the ordinary man who inhabited it, amazed that I hadn't recognized it before.

I still played along on Christmas Eve when my father insisted I better hurry to bed. He said he could hear Santa's sleigh bells from afar. I longed to hear those bells with my own ears, but when I looked out the window to scan the darkened sky, there was only silence. That silence spoke of the magic of Christmas being swept from my imagination forever – or so I thought.

Almost two decades later, when I became a parent, I discovered the deeper meaning in the magic of Santa Claus, as well as the tooth fairy and the Easter bunny. I realized such magical mainstays of childhood serve the monumental purpose of guiding a child toward soulful realities that the child may not otherwise be able to see or touch. The tooth fairy soothes the potentially frightening loss of one's baby teeth and guides a child toward the idea that change and loss can be positive, necessary elements of life. Likewise, the Easter bunny announces with delight that death is *not* stronger than life, laughter, and love, and Santa Claus appears in many homes and communities, reminding us that the spirit of generosity and compassion knows no economic or ethnic boundaries. Santa Claus travels the world over and models a spirit of giving that reaches beyond family circles and territories.

When Morgan was in second grade, she and her peers had a heated, ongoing debate about the reality of Santa Claus. The debate began before Christmas and lasted until spring. Morgan brought home details of her arguments and conversations with classmates. I quietly listened and when she asked if I believed Santa Claus (or the Easter bunny or the tooth fairy) was real, I reflected the question back to her by asking what she felt or thought about it. She responded each time with conviction of her faith in the magic, but in lessening degrees as the days cycled on.

Finally, on a March afternoon, as Morgan continued to debate with herself, she turned, looked me square in the eyes and asked, "Mom, I want to know: do *you* believe Santa Claus is real?" I knew the moment of truth had come. I drew Morgan up into my lap and after she had settled in, I responded, "I'll tell you what I believe...I believe that long, long ago, there lived a man named Nicholas whose spirit of giving was so strong that, after he died, in his memory, people all over the world found ways to keep his "spirit of giving" alive. That man became known as St. Nicholas and, later, Santa Claus."

Morgan looked at me a bit crestfallen; the light seemed to fade momentarily from her eyes. After a thoughtful pause, she queried, "Does that mean you and Dad fill our stockings?" I hugged her and smiled, then said gently, "Yes. Yes, it does." After a brief silence, to allow her discovery of the past three months to be more fully absorbed, I added, "You know what else it means?" Morgan shook her head, and I continued, "It means you're old enough and wise enough to become a Keeper of the Magic." I then shared with Morgan the essence of a rite of passage Andrew and I were planning for her. A week or so after Morgan completed her discovery, Andrew and I snuck into Morgan and Willa's bedroom after Willa was asleep. We invited Morgan (who was eagerly awaiting our arrival) to the following ceremony. The next day was Easter and to our delight, Morgan proved to be the most enthusiastic and wily Easter bunny of all.

> **Tools** ❧ If there are younger siblings in the home, create the celebration space behind closed doors, away from sleeping children. You'll need a transparent cloth veil, a candle and matches, fairy dust (fine, sparkling glitter), and a symbolic gift, such as a pendant, necklace, ring, charm, or other symbol to serve as a reminder of the youth's commitment to be a keeper of the magic. In the celebration space, sitting pillows or chairs are set in a circle for all participants.

Gathering

With the transparent cloth draped over the youth's head and face, s/he is led by a family member to the celebration room. When the door is opened to let the youth in, someone lights the candle, which is placed in the center of the circle. The following Shel Silverstein poem is recited to the youth as s/he is brought in and invited to sit in the circle:

Poem: "Invitation" by Shel Silverstein*

Song: Magic Is Everywhere (page 163)

> Magic, magic is everywhere,
> It's hidden in the earth,
> It's streaming through the air,
> It's in the candle dancing bright,
> It's in the fountain's flight.
>
> Magic, magic is everywhere,
> In our hearts and in our minds,
> Binding all of humankind,
> True magic is faith to believe
> In the things we cannot see.
>
> Magic, magic is everywhere,
> Now you can let it live
> In the joy that's yours to give
> to young and old who dare to see
> Magic is faith's golden key.

* "Invitation" can be found in Shel Silverstein's poetry collection *Where the Sidewalk Ends*.

Story: Becoming a Keeper of the Magic

A parent or various loved ones tell stories of the magical childhood characters that have been close to the youth's heart and experience. Conclude the telling with a story of the youth penetrating the magic of these characters and, in so doing, becoming old enough and wise enough to be a "keeper of the magic." After the storytelling is complete, a parent or other elder removes the transparent veil from the youth's head and face.

Keeper of the Magic Vow

Adapt the following for the youth being honored, inserting appropriate names and references. Speak the vow below a phrase at a time, so the youth can repeat it easily.

Parent says:

"Morgan DeShea Darian, you have been richly blessed by the magical characters of your childhood. They brought you many moments of joy and celebration. Now comes the time for you to create the magic for others. *Morgan*, if you choose to become a 'keeper of the magic,' repeat this vow after me:

"In the name of the *Easter Bunny, St. Nicholas and his horse, Santa Claus and his reindeer, the Advent Gnomes,* and the Tooth Fairy*, I, *Morgan DeShea Darian*, vow on this day, *April 6, 1996,* to share the magic that has been so generously given to me. I promise to be a keeper of the magic for: *my little sister, Willa; Patrick Cassidy; Ivan Imes; Shanna Webb;* and all the children everywhere who continue to believe.

"As my *mother and father* before me, I promise to keep alive the spirit of *the Easter Bunny, St. Nicholas, Santa Claus, the Advent Gnomes, and the Tooth Fairy*. I will carry the spirit of giving and magic within me, and promise to faithfully serve."

---

*When our children were young, the Advent Gnomes appeared at our house one at a time on the four Sundays of Advent, announcing the coming of Christmas and bringing a simple gift, such as new mittens or a family board game to enjoy together.

Blessing

The youth is invited to repeat three times:

"I am a Keeper of the Magic."

All participants sprinkle the youth with fairy dust (fine, sparkling glitter) as a sign that the magic continues. Then the youth is given a gift, such as a piece of jewelry or a symbol of magic. The gift serves as a reminder of the youth's vow to be a Keeper of the Magic.

Sending Forth

Song: Keeper of the Magic (page 164)

Good Keeper of the Magic,
We place our trust in you –
The magic lives within you
In what you say and do
To boldly serve faith's infant,
The babe that grows to be
Our belief in the more
Invisible truths we cannot see.

(Invite the new Keeper of the Magic to extinguish the candle.)

Breeching a Boy's Confidence

In earlier centuries, there wasn't much distinction between girls' and boys' clothing in our culture. Until the early 1900's, both genders wore dresses and skirts up to a certain age. Boys wore lacy collars and curls just like their sisters. Usually at the discretion of the mother, when a boy was perceived as moving out of childhood, he was dressed in trousers or "breeches" for the first time. The event was a major rite of passage as the boy took a step toward manhood, and the occasion was often celebrated with a party and a professional photograph.* There was no such rite of passage for girls since their dress essentially remained the same.

Although times and fashion have changed considerably, we parents can easily create similar rites of passage for our sons that involve a change in dress. As a boy enters youthhood, he might be given his first formal suit, or his first tie tack and real tie (as opposed to the clip-on variety). The youth's father or another male elder can take time to show the youth how to properly knot a tie. Such a rite can be timed with a birthday or another special event in the boy's life. Enlist an able photographer to capture a visual reminder of the passage. A formal family dinner or a "dress-up" party can be planned so the boy can don his new attire with pride.

A rite of passage centered on a change in clothing can also be honored when a youth transitions into young adulthood. An ancient Greek tradition involved a male of 16 or 17 shedding his boyhood tunic and having his father dress him in an adult toga for the first time. Likewise, a young man receiving or buying his first quality suit or wearing his first tuxedo can be a memorable life passage to honor in our contemporary culture.

Consider other clothing rites of passage for males and females alike: donning a team uniform or performance costume for the first time, dressing for a first formal dance, or donning attire for a sacred religious rite. Clothing can speak volumes about one's changing identity, alliances, and stages of growth. Savor such moments with care; they so swiftly pass.

*For more information on breeching, see Historical Boys Clothing (www.histclo.com).

The Nine-Year Change

A life passage often overlooked by parents and caregivers – except for the emotional turbulence it usually causes – is one that commonly occurs in the months leading up to (or after) the ninth birthday. Around the age of nine, a youth gains an inner picture of themselves as a unique and independent person, standing apart from others. With this recognition comes a surge of personal power and a desire to express one's unique, individual self. Simultaneously, however, the youth experiences a sense of loss, grappling with the human condition of being utterly alone within one's own skin.

Interestingly, this life passage is a time when many young people (even those abiding with their birth parents) sense that they *must be* adopted. The youth imagines that the parent, long called "Mom" or "Dad," must be some alien member of society who stole them from the cradle at birth. This potentially volatile time of life also brings a fuller comprehension of the finality of death. Many youths making this passage inwardly grieve for the simpler world of childhood in which death is not final, good appears to reign supreme, and happily-ever-after endings are easily accepted.

Fortunately, youths experiencing this passage are ripe for believing in the power of their own inner courage and their ability to overcome adversity and injustice. It's a time when parents, grandparents, and caregivers do well to support a youth in meeting age-appropriate challenges and making an effort to help themselves and others understand and overcome injustice in their immediate environments. It's also a crucial time to direct a youth toward a family's chosen faith, so that childhood magic can mature into a deeper understanding of spiritual and soulful realities. A youth thus empowered may transcend the impotence often experienced when the magic of childhood fades.

Despite my naive parental doubts, my easygoing, eldest daughter, Morgan, met the nine-year-change like a fire-breathing dragon. Somehow, Andrew and I imagined that the resilience and balance Morgan displayed in her first eight years might deem her exempt from such a turbulent metamorphosis. Not so, we found out in a surprise announcement that came days into Morgan bringing eight-year-old crankiness to an exhaustively heightened level. One evening, after a particularly grumpy display,

Andrew sat Morgan on his lap to help calm her. However, instead of settling into her papa's lap as we expected, Morgan vehemently fought Andrew's embrace and screamed at the top of her lungs, "You're not my Daddy! You're not my Daddy!"

In retrospect, we should have expected fireworks from Morgan during the nine-year passage because she was the child who lived so comfortably in the world of fantasy. She was the one who could fly like Peter Pan and took nightly trips out her bedroom window to Never-Never Land. She was the one who coerced her little sister, Willa, to build fairy houses in the backyard and dressed the two of them with leaf costumes so they could dwell among the fairies. Willa remembers playing along with Morgan's fantasies for her sister's sake, but she didn't relish Morgan's imaginative adventures with the same gusto.

When Morgan began to emerge from the magical realm of childhood, it shouldn't have shocked us that she would come from that world kicking and screaming. She had piled up a mother lode of magical treasures there and had a great deal to lose by leaving it all behind.

Of course, each youth will come to the nine-year passage in their own way, according to their temperament and life circumstances. Some journeys will be more turbulent than others. One youth may become belligerent, another withdrawn or clingy, and yet another may attempt to hide their vulnerability and self-doubt by asserting a tough, calm exterior. As parents and caregivers, we do well to look beneath the surface to a youth's need for nurture and empowerment during this life-changing transition. Depending on the youth's needs and family circumstances, this life passage may be celebrated with a simple acknowledgment, such as gifting the youth with a "power song" created or chosen especially for them (see page 133), or the youth's family may plan a more elaborate celebration, such as the knighting event on pages 124-132. However your family chooses to celebrate this passage, let it be a reminder to the youth that despite their perceptions of separateness, they are held eternally in a loving community of support.

A Youth's Knighting Celebration

When Morgan screamed her parents awake to her life-changing needs a few months before her ninth birthday, we were prompted to create for her a knighting ceremony to honor her emerging sense of personal power and heightened responsibility. We wanted Morgan to experience this rite of passage in the context of a caring, supportive community. We also thought knighthood would be a compelling image for Morgan and her friends to experience as a picture for their youthful striving to live with courage and compassion. The knighting celebration (also used to honor Willa's nine-year passage two years later) combined reflective, prayerful elements with engaging, festive activities and fun. It was greatly enjoyed by young and old alike!

Setup ❧ The invitation to the knighting celebration includes a request for the youth participants to wear knight costumes. Parents, grandparents, or other significant adult mentors of the youth being knighted can play the parts of King Arthur and Queen Guinevere. Ideally, able singers and instrumentalists can serve as court musicians, and other friends and relatives can play the roles of servants and pages. Simple medieval garb can be made or assembled, or more elaborate costumes can be borrowed or rented from a costume collection. Planning ahead allows everyone to relax and enjoy the occasion as it unfolds, so plan logistics well in advance, and a day or two before the celebration, set up all the rooms and activities needed: a quiet room with a prayer altar for the honored youth's prayer vigil; clues and treasures for the grail search; plans and materials for the sword-making workshop; a room setup and decorated as the feast hall, and food prepared. Key players with speaking parts can gather a day or two in advance to practice (although scripts can also be used), and those helping with food or activities may arrive at the celebration early to review their plan of action and help with setup. Suggested tools are listed in italics in each section of the celebration.

The Knight's Preparation

Cleansing Bath

In the tradition of knighting ceremonies of old, a bath is drawn for the youth the evening before the ceremony. *Scented oil or bath salts* may be added to the water. Set *candles* safely around the bathroom, turn off the overhead light, and play a *recording of relaxing Medieval music*. Set out a *towel and nightclothes* for the youth, and a *hand towel* for the one who will bathe the young person. After the bath has been prepared, the youth is invited to soak in the tub. After a few minutes, a parent or grandparent with whom the youth feels comfortable may enter quietly. The adult pours water over the youth with a *conch shell, bowl, cup, or pitcher*. Although much of the bath can be given in silence, the adult can briefly explain to the youth that squires of old who were preparing to be knighted would take a cleansing bath. The bath was a symbol for purifying oneself for beginning a new life as a knight. Also, the adult can speak about the meaning of knighthood for the youth and name the youth's personal gifts and noble qualities that reflect their readiness for knighthood. When the bath is complete, the adult says:

"You are no longer a little child. Now, you journey into the years of your youth."

The adult invites the youth to lean their head back and then pours water over the youth's head three times. Afterward, the youth is left to relax, dry off, and put on their nightclothes. If you choose, a family prayer vigil can take place with the knight-to-be before bedtime. The rest of the knighting celebration takes place the following day.

Gathering of Knights

The Arrival

The entryway is decorated regally. The *greeting party* may include a *page*, a *musician* (on trumpet, cornet, or even kazoo), and *Queen Guinevere*. Upon entry, each guest is greeted by the royal page who opens the door and says:

Page: "Welcome to Camelot!"

The page takes coats and gifts from the guests. Guinevere refers to a *prepared guest list* so she can receive each youth by the knight's name chosen for them, or the guest list can be prepared as guests arrive and each youth is invited to choose one of a *collection of name cards*. The name cards can include a picture of the legendary knight chosen and a brief accounting of the knight's deeds. The youth's own first name is used as the place from which the knight comes. For example, a youth named "Drew" might be called "Sir Galahad of Drew." (Parcival* is the knight's name reserved for the youth of honor.) After the youth is greeted, Guinevere says to the youth:

Queen Guinevere: *"(Name of knight)*, we will present you to the King."

The page goes to call the King who is supervising in the sword-making workshop. Upon return, the page and musician take their places on either side of the entryway where the knight being presented stands.

Presentation to the King

The musician "trumpets" a call to signal the presentation. The king appears and takes his place at the far end of the entryway, facing the knight being presented.

Queen Guinevere: "King Arthur, I present *(name of knight)*."

* Parcival is a legendary knight who went in search of the Holy Grail, which is a metaphor for spiritual enlightenment.

King Arthur: (*Name of knight*), do you pledge to serve your King and Queen as a good and faithful knight? If so, say, "yes."

Knight: Yes.

King Arthur: Do you pledge to honor our newest knight, Parcival of (*honored youth's name*), and to be Parcival's true and constant companion? If so, say, "yes."

Knight: Yes.

King Arthur: Then come into our castle and join me in our workshop where we have swords to forge!

If guests arrive together, more than one knight may be presented at a time. After being presented, knights follow the king to the workshop.

Making the Swords

The king and his assistants are in charge of the sword-making. A *snack table* and a *table for sword-making materials* are set up. You may also want to have quiet games or activities for youths to enjoy when they complete their sword and are waiting for the others to finish the task. Materials for the sword-making include: *pre-cut wooden swords* (heavy cardboard can also work); *sandpaper;* an array of water-based *craft paints and brushes*; and *cloth or leather strips or duct tape* for wrapping the handles of the swords. The knights sand their wooden swords and paint them with their own unique design. Arthur and his assistants help each knight wrap the handle of their sword with leather, cloth, or duct tape. After a knight's sword is complete, the youth stands in front of King Arthur who holds the sword, puts a hand on the youth's shoulder and says:

King Arthur: "May this sword bring no harm. May it point the way to goodness, beauty, and truth."

King Arthur hands the sword to the youth and gives clear rules for appropriate swordplay. To avoid injury, the swords can be put away during the grail search or other lively activities.

Knight's Prayer Vigil

After the swords are made, the youth being honored goes outside and comes to the front door to make a grand entrance. All other participants (except King Arthur) gather inside at the entryway. The page and Guinevere greet Parcival as they greeted the other youths upon arrival (page 126). When King Arthur appears, he says:

Arthur: Parcival of (*youth's name*), do you come seeking knighthood? If so, say "yes."

Parcival: Yes.

Arthur: Then come, enter the place prepared for your knighting vigil. Go to pray and reflect on your new life as a knight.

Someone leads Parcival into the room already prepared for a time of quiet reflection. The prayer room includes an *altar table* with a *sheet of instructions* to guide the youth through the prayer vigil. Various *symbols and readings* for the youth to consider can be included. Choose these based on the youth's religious life, spiritual understanding, and reading level. Consider the youth's favorite poems, prayers, stories, and symbols, and include those that are most meaningful for the occasion. As the youth prays and reflects, Arthur and Guinevere lead the other participants through the logistics of the knighting ceremony. Songs are taught and instructions given so everyone feels ready to participate in the knighting.

Knighting Ceremony

When it's time for the knighting, youth participants create a path for Parcival to walk by standing in two lines facing each other. The path leads from the place Parcival will stand to Arthur and Guinevere who guide the ceremony. Youth participants hold their *swords* in hand, with the tips toward the floor. The page stands next to Guinevere, holding a *small bowl of water* for blessing Parcival's sword and shield. There is a *cushion* on the floor in front of Arthur and Guinevere, where Parcival will kneel for the knighting. When all is ready, Parcival is invited to stand at the foot of the path with *sword and shield* in hand.

Preparing the Path

Guinevere: Noble Knights, pass to us the sword belonging to Parcival of (*youth's name*). (One line passes sword.)

Arthur: Noble knights, pass to us the shield belonging to Parcival of (*youth's name*). (Other line passes shield.)

Guinevere: Noble Knights, lift your swords in honor of Parcival of (*youth's name*).

The youths lift their swords over the path, creating an inverted V archway through which Parcival will walk.

The Knight's Pledge

Arthur: Parcival, if you are prepared to become a knight, come and stand before us now as we sing. (Singing begins and the honored youth walks the path to the king and queen.)

Song: Journey Forth (page 165)

We bless you with good health,
We bless you with good cheer,
We bless you with courage for your spirit,
Journey forth in love on this special day,
Journey forth with courage for your spirit.

Parcival stands before the king and queen.

Guinevere: (dips her fingers in the blessing bowl and blesses Parcival's sword) "Parcival of (*youth's name*), this sword is not a sword to hurt or maim. It is a sword to point you in the direction of goodness, beauty, and truth." (dips her fingers in the blessing bowl and blesses shield) "Parcival of (*youth's name*), this shield is not a shield to protect you from life, for you must never run away from that which you must face. Let this shield remind you to protect yourself from needless harm and to protect, in your heart, mind, and soul, the powers of faith, hope, and love."

Arthur: "Parcival of (*youth's name*), kneel before me now (youth kneels on cushion). You are no longer a little child. You are entering the years of your youth – years that will be filled with much growth and adventure.

"To show that you come in good faith to be dubbed a knight, repeat after me this oath of knighthood:

Arthur speaks a phrase at a time and Parcival repeats:

"I, Parcival of (*youth's name*), do pledge:
to be gentle to the weak,
and courageous with the strong.
To the best of my ability,
I will defend the helpless,
serve *God** and love my family.
I will strive to be noble of deed,
strong in compassion,
and true in friendship.
To the best of my ability,
I will strive to uphold and protect
goodness and beauty,
faith, hope, and love.

"I, Parcival of (*youth's name*),
pledge to be a true and noble knight."

Arthur: (holding the sword) "I dub you, Knight Parcival of (*youth's name*)." (Arthur touches the sword to one shoulder, then the other.) "May your light and honor shine."

As singing begins, Parcival stands and receives the sword and shield.

Song: Rise Up, O Knight
(to the tune of "Rise Up, O Flame," page 274)

Rise up, O noble knight, the
Fire of your life glowing,
Shine forth with deeds of courage,
Shine with wisdom and love.

*Insert name for the Divine most meaningful to the youth being honored.

Guinevere: "One and all, repeat after me, as we bestow upon Parcival this blessing:" (Guinevere speaks one line at a time in a call and response pattern.*)

"Parcival of (*youth's name*), go forth!
There is 'a world to be born under your footsteps!'"**

Grail Search

Arthur: "Parcival, your first task for your king is to take this band of noble knights out into the wilderness to search for the holy grail."

Arthur explains that the grail search will take place outdoors and is a *series of riddles to be solved*. The final riddle will lead to the grail cup and other treasures. Arthur sets out the rules and boundaries of the game, including the rule that all knights must work together to solve each riddle. Arthur and his assistants supervise the grail search. Meanwhile, those hosting the feast can do last-minute preparations. After the knights find and enjoy their treasures (*small gift bags* for everyone, labeled with their names, and a *grail goblet* for Parcival), they are called into the feast with an *outdoor bell, trumpet, or other instrument*. Gift bags are "checked at the door" to avoid chaos in the feast hall.

The Feast

Depending on the size of your group, strive to create a *long feast table*, so everyone can see one another and interact during the meal. King Arthur and Queen Guinevere sit at the far ends of the table so they can oversee the festivities. Parcival sits next to the king. You may want to have a *wash basin and towels* set up for handwashing before the meal. At our feast, we used finger foods common to Medieval times and had a *small, wooden water bowl at each place setting* for rinsing hands during the meal. We borrowed long benches from a school to create more intimate seating around our four-leaf dining room table, and we borrowed enough *earthy-looking plates and goblets* from friends and acquaintances that we were able to create fairly authentic place settings for the feast. If you don't have earthy-looking serving dishes, borrow from a friend or try a local resale shop.

* Call and response involves a leader speaking or singing one line of a verse or song at a time so those gathered can repeat it.
** Quote by Saint-John Perse

Grail Blessing & Toast

If musicians are available, begin the feast with music while someone circles the table and fills each goblet (except the "grail cup") with juice or cider.

Arthur: (fills the grail cup and lifts it up) "We bless this holy grail and ask that the one who drinks from it this day, the honorable Parcival of (*youth's name*), will be blessed with a long and happy life. . ."

(Arthur gives grail to Parcival, then lifts his own goblet.)

"Lift your cups for a toast to Parcival: noble knight of King Arthur's court!"

Arthur invites everyone to speak the following blessing in a call and response pattern one line at a time:

Meal Blessing: Cup of Clay

God gives to us a cup of clay,
And from this cup we drink our lives.
~ adapted from an ancient proverb

Arthur: "Parcival of (*youth's name*), may your life be blessed!"
(everyone drinks)

The Meal

Food for the meal may be offered by servants or passed around the table. If guests bring gifts to the celebration, throughout the meal Arthur calls one guest at a time to offer their gift to Parcival. In this way, the gifts are not the center of the celebration, and the honored youth has an opportunity to appreciate each gift apart from the others. Conclude the meal with dessert and one of the songs from the celebration, such as "Journey Forth" (page 165) or "Rise Up, O Knight" (page 274), or, if the knighting coincides with the honored youth's birthday, choose a song from the birthday chapter.

Power Song

A song that speaks powerfully to a youth's life circumstances is a profound gift to offer a young person, especially during significant life passages or when the youth faces obstacles to overcome. The song can be an original or chosen from the repertoire of a more well-known songwriter.

Early in his life, my godson experienced his parents' marital strife first-hand, even witnessing physical abuse. Although his mom filed for divorce soon after that and she and her son made a new life for themselves, I wondered how closely my godson continued to identify with the anger and violence he witnessed. Since the nine-year change is one of recognizing oneself as a unique individual in the world, I wrote a song for my godson's ninth birthday, focusing on his ability to heal and differentiate himself from the violent behavior he witnessed as a young child. Since we lived miles apart, I recorded the song and mailed it off in time for his big day. His mother reported that he carried the recording with him for days and shared it proudly with his teacher and classmates at school.

The song, called "The Boy With the Dancing Eyes," begins with an excerpt of a Walt Whitman poem from my godson's birth announcement:

"There was a child went forth every day,
And the first object he looked upon, that object he became,
And that object became part of him for the day or a certain
   part of the day
Or for many years or stretching cycle of years." (Walt Whitman)

Come join the circle, I'll tell you a tale
Of a boy who was friends with the earth and the sky,
Come gather 'round and I'll tell you a story of a lad
Called "the boy with the dancing eyes."

He walked with the mountains and meadows,
He spoke with the birds and the whales and the sea,
He embraced all he saw with his dancing eyes,
And said, "I am the world and the world is me."

The boy looked upon every object
As a beautiful joy to proclaim;
So, each day, the first thing that he looked upon
Was the thing that the boy became.

He walked with the mountains and meadows,
He spoke with the birds and the whales and the sea,
He embraced all he saw with his dancing eyes,
And said, "I am the world and the world is me."

The boy lived with parents who loved him,
His mother was priestess and friend,
But his father and she always spoke angrily,
And the boy thought the anger was him.

He saw the tight fists of his father,
And his mother fall under the blow,
And the hate it flashed down like a bolt from the sky,
And inside him it started to grow. . .

So, he ran to the mountains and meadows,
He screamed to the birds and the whales and the sea,
He spoke out to them what he'd seen with his eyes,
And said, "I'm not the world and the world's not me."

The boy sat for hours in silence,
Alone with his questioning tears,
And as silence can will, the boy started to heal,
Rising up to the challenge of answering his fears.

The boy grew in wisdom and stature,
And he learned what it means to be free –
To envision a life of one's own design
And the things in the world that he wanted to be.

He walked with the mountains and meadows,
He spoke with the birds and the whales and the sea,
He beheld the great gift of his dancing eyes,
And said, "I'm in the world, and the world's in me,
I'm in the world, and the world's in me."

Alexander Pope once wrote: "What will a child learn sooner than a song?" Yet, not only a child. A song can work on us at any age – to permeate one's inner being with wisdom and healing.

Celebrating Puberty

Oh, the adventures and trials of puberty, when it seems (almost overnight) the child diminishes and the youth emerges in a body that unmistakably speaks of sex. Puberty abounds with transformations: the appearance of pubic, facial, and body hair; the hidden joy and guilt of self-pleasure and sexual play; developing breasts and penises; the mystery of erections, orgasms, wet dreams, and menses; the lowering pitch of a male's voice; and surging hormones that cause a youth to feel different, look different, smell different, and even think differently. No wonder puberty can be an emotional rollercoaster! What makes puberty even more challenging is the fact that most parents know how vital a healthy sense of sex and sexuality is to adult life, but many of us are immobilized by our own questions and unresolved issues and find it difficult to impart sexual wisdom, knowledge, and healthy expectations to those of younger generations.

Culturally, we create conflicting messages about sexuality. We ask young people to repress sexual feelings, thoughts, and habits; then, as they mature, we communicate vastly different expectations for males and females. As a culture, we can be obsessive about keeping secrets from young people concerning the opposite gender; then, when we do inform them, we tend to impart only scientific, sterile information that reflects little about the whole human being. At the same time, youths are absorbing repeated images from the media that depict sophisticated teenagers (usually played by much older actors) who are incredibly at ease with sexual relationships. No doubt, as a culture we are a sexually-confused people, at once idolizing *and* fearing the power of sexuality. Ironically, this is the same confusion youths often feel as they enter puberty: intrigued by the mystery and power of their maturing bodies and potent sexual feelings, while fearing these changes.

If we hope to empower a youth with a healthy sense of their own sexuality, we have no choice but to begin in the family. For if we relegate "sex education" to a youth's peers, the movie screen, or even "qualified sex education instructors," our own silence on the subject teaches a youth volumes. Parents who desire to celebrate the gifts and challenges of puberty, and guide a youth toward a healthier understanding of themselves as sexual beings, may find inspiration on the following pages.

The Book of Knowledge

In my workshops on rites of passage, some adults tell me that the only "sex talk" they had with their parents when they were growing up was hurriedly being handed a book on the "birds and the bees" and being told to read it in their spare time. These were some of the lucky ones. Other adults remember being reprimanded for sexual behavior, but never being told clearly what healthy sexual behavior looks like. Still others remember silence and embarrassment whenever a sexual topic surfaced from the pool-of-the-unspeakable.

A friend of mine remembers painfully his entrance into puberty. He was at the beach with his mother and her friend, lying on his beach towel, when a beautiful young woman passed by and set in motion an unfamiliar bodily sensation. No one made it clear to my friend that he would experience his first erection one day, and in his questioning and fear of that moment for which no one prepared him, he quickly brought his concerns to the attention of his mother and her friend. They laughed. Right there at the beach, in front of God and the whole world. They laughed and engraved in my friend's body, heart, mind, and soul that horrifying moment when he awoke to the power of his sexual feelings – and was immediately *dis*empowered.

Puberty is a passage that calls for our loving attention. It can be awkward enough for a youth to assimilate the myriad changes of puberty without parents and caregivers adding to the embarrassment and confusion. One way for adults to transform our unresolved issues and unhealthy attitudes about puberty is to explore our own youthful memories about sexuality and body image and to identify lingering topics of discomfort we need to process. In an Interpersonal Communications class I took in college, the professor asked the class to name what we imagined to be the "cleanest parts" of our bodies. Tentatively, we named hands and faces. The daring ventured to say "our torsos" or "the insides of our arms." Not a single student named the more hidden and probably cleaner body parts: breasts, butt cheeks and, yes, the self-cleaning vagina. This exercise demonstrated to our class our repressive tendencies on topics construed as "sexual." We couldn't name intimate body parts as being *clean*, because, culturally, we'd learned they were *dirty*. Our professor assured us that any body part is not *dirty* or *clean* – it is, simply, a body part.

I grew up in a family where sex and sexuality was, for the most part, a taboo subject. As an adult, I continued to find it difficult to speak with my parents about sex-related issues. Old habits die hard. But it was different with my children. As I experienced pregnancy and childbirth, changing diapers, breast-feeding, guiding children in their potty training, naked toddlers fully delighting in their nakedness, and incidences of sexual play among children, I was given opportunities to offer my children healthy, positive perspectives of their bodies. Moreover, I was able to transform some of the limiting attitudes about sexuality and the human body I learned as a child.

Even so, the day one of my children recounted for me her first experience of orgasmic self-pleasure, I was bowled over by her candid description! I was simultaneously panicked and thrilled that she felt comfortable enough to share with me the details of this intimate experience and ask me questions about it. Soon after that, when Andrew and I witnessed both our daughters (who were two years apart) simultaneously experiencing the physical changes of puberty, I was the one diving into library and bookstore shelves for a book on "the birds and the bees." But, it wasn't one I'd throw at my children and run. Andrew and I had a different plan.

After days of searching, I found two gems written by Lynda and Area Madaras called *My Body, My Self for Girls* and *My Body, My Self for Boys*. Though only about 120 pages, these books are chockfull of information, quizzes, checklists, and journal exercises. They also include inter-generational activities to inspire dialogue. Andrew and I gave a personal copy of the book to both Morgan and Willa. Morgan was eleven, and absolutely devoured the book from front to back within a few hours. She flew down the stairs from her bedroom with the book in hand, bursting with enthusiasm about her new knowledge: "Oh, thank you! You'll never know how much I needed this!" Willa, who was only nine and developing ahead of the majority of her peers, took weeks to saunter leisurely through the book. Whenever Willa asked, she and I would read one small section – whatever topic inspired her curiosity or enthusiasm. Occasionally, the whole family worked through some of the more family-oriented pages, using them as effective ice breakers for approaching topics one family member or another found uncomfortable to consider together. The family conversations that resulted were full of energy and humor, and inspired greater family intimacy. Remember, no matter what other "book of knowledge" you may give a youth, the youth will be inclined to read *you* more.

The Art of Puberty

Living as we do in an informational, scientific age, our souls crave the healing presence of the arts – arts that can nourish our whole selves – body, heart, mind, soul, and spirit. Art guides us toward creative mysteries and insights that a more linear approach to life might well miss. Puberty is no exception. Some "sex educators" do far more than impart information on their students. Two such educators I know guide groups of girls-becoming-women through a course on their emerging feminine power as they begin their menstrual cycle. The final project, designed by Tamara Slayton and Robin White, involves creating a womb out of vibrant cloth, pearls, stars, silk flowers and ribbons. The youths immerse themselves in this creation in ways that filling out a workbook diagram can't replicate, and the results are spectacular to behold (see www.mwt.net/~womankind).

In our contemporary culture, although we often experience sexuality and the human body as a commodity being peddled, it's still possible to witness the miracle of the human body in a variety of art forms today: painting, drawing, photography, sculpture, music, and poetry, to name a few. Parents and educators can guide youths toward creating and admiring art that celebrates the human body, not as an object of sexual lust (as is too often the case in our contemporary culture), but as a subject of miraculous mystery and beauty. Consider Walt Whitman's poem, "The Body Electric," in which Whitman praises every part of the male and female form, deeming them each perfect – and perfect in a variety of manifestations. Whitman sings: "If anything is sacred, the human body is sacred." Lucille Clifton, in her poem, "Homage to my Hips," speaks of the goodness of hips that "don't fit into little petty places," and in her "Poem in Praise of Menstruation," reflects upon a woman's monthly cycle of bleeding as a "beautiful," "faithful," "brave," "ancient" river. Such poetry draws us into a place of gratitude and awe for the gift of the human body. A comforting place to be, especially for a youth experiencing puberty.

Several years ago, I began a tradition of writing each of my family members a poem on Valentine's Day. At the time, Willa was in fifth grade, and going through an awkward, gangly stage; at the same time, her elder sister was receiving more than a little attention for her external beauty. However, to a mother's eyes, there was no more awesome sight than Willa's lean awkwardness, stretching toward womanhood. I celebrated the vision in the first Valentine poem I wrote for her:

> Radiant, your beauty,
> As if Love seeps through
> The pores of your skin
> To shape its own face.
>
> Agile and long, your beauty,
> As if Love creeps through
> Your arms and legs
> To stretch its muscles lean.
>
> Love delights in its own strength,
> In its unencumbered purity,
> To be nothing less than Love.
>
> Love delights in You.

Upon being gifted with these words, Willa glowed in the light of this simple acknowledgment – an acknowledgment that her physical growth could be experienced as Love's movement and delight.

Whether you share original art with a beloved youth, or offer creations by more well-known artists, such images of reverence for the human body may prompt a youth to reframe more positively their perceptions of puberty, their own sexuality, and the unique and changing shape of their physical form.

Sexual Self-Knowledge

With the onset of puberty, I told each of my children, "The first person you have a sexual relationship with is yourself." There's no getting around the fact that, for most youths, puberty brings powerful sexual feelings to assimilate. Encouraging youths to respond to their own sexual yearnings in appropriate, private moments through self-pleasure can help a young person develop a healthy body image and foster positive attitudes about puberty and the sexual feelings it arouses. Furthermore, encouraging a youth to set appropriate boundaries with oneself by practicing self-pleasure privately and by not allowing it to interfere with other aspects of daily life is a first step in learning what it means to set appropriate sexual boundaries with others. Youthhood is a potent time for gaining knowledge of one's own sexual yearnings, hormonal rhythms, and bodily appetites. Parents and educators who affirm self-pleasure as a positive, healthy choice assist a youth in feeling free to touch, know, and look at their own body as one way of gaining important self-knowledge and understanding themselves more fully as a human being.

Although the religious views of some parents discourage it, there are a multitude of reasons to help youths dispel the negative mythology around self-pleasure. Pleasuring oneself is a sensual art that helps to release the pressure of surging hormones, relieves stress, relaxes the body for sleep, and prepares us to be better lovers when the time is right. It can energize us, elevate our mood, and help us to focus more productively. Significantly for youths and young adults, self-pleasure can also be an effective means of delaying sexual relationships with others.

How freely a parent talks with a youth about the gifts of self-pleasure will depend upon the youth and parent, and their relationship. Whether you share a reading on the subject, transfer knowledge through conversation and stories, or offer a self-pleasure gift bag (with massage oil, ideas for self-touch, guidance on hygiene and safety issues, and positive artistic images of sensuality and self-pleasure), the youth will get the message that their sexual yearnings are not something of which to be ashamed, but a call to explore and celebrate oneself as a sexual being. Self-pleasure can also be a significant path of healing for a youth recovering from sexual abuse or inappropriate touch. Pleasurable self-touch can coax a person to reclaim one's body as one's own and embrace the gifts of one's sexuality.

Sexuality and spirituality are intimately connected. Puberty is a significant time to help youths foster this recognition and claim sexuality as a sacred aspect of human existence. Simple, poetic affirmations can be catalysts for ongoing conversations and deepening understanding:

Self-Pleasure

Made of earth and spirit,
My body is a sacred gift.
To touch it and feel it sing
Allows me to drift
In the Mystery. . .

I journey to a place
Where earth and spirit meet.
Rivers merge into the waterfall.
My being surrenders,
is made complete
In the Mystery. . .

Even if a youth doesn't fully comprehend the meaning of such a poem, the essence will be understood, and the youth can build on that understanding over time.

Body Alterations

When I was in fifth grade, my underarm hair grew in full force and the hair on my legs darkened. I asked my mom if I could shave. The request elicited teasing remarks from the entire family. Being the youngest of four siblings, I often battled what me growing up meant to everyone else's self-image, and I sometimes fought to prove my growing maturity. In this particular instance, I felt that I had a right to care for my body in the way I chose, and being more than a little angry about the teasing that transpired, I decided to throw caution to the wind and shave without permission. Unfortunately, I knew little about shaving and proceeded on my secret mission with only a determined heart and a dry razor at my disposal. Of course, I paid for my rebellious act with scraped legs and stinging armpits. I also felt liberated by the gesture, and given my physical discomfort, my parents weren't overly punitive. They figured I'd suffered enough.

Youths experiencing the changes of puberty often have questions and concerns about body and facial hair, the unique aromas of puberty, and body image. Females may have concerns and questions about bras and menstrual-care products, and male athletes and dancers about jock straps, cups, and dance belts. A youth may desire to engage in certain fashion trends that alter their body and appearance including hairstyles, body piercing, and tattooing. They may also desire to use makeup. Wading through such youthful questions, concerns, and requests can be confusing for a parent. While many parents don't desire for a youth to grow up too fast too soon, we also need to be careful not to give a youth the message that we parents are the sole authorities over their bodies. Youthhood is a time to empower young people with the information they need to care for their bodies knowledgeably and thoughtfully.

Although Andrew and I decided to wait until our children entered young adulthood to grant them such freedoms as body piercing and tattooing, we felt it was important for them to be able to assert authority and make significant choices concerning their own bodies and appearance during the years of their youth. When each of our daughters experienced the changes in body hair that come with puberty and requested permission to shave their legs and underarms, I had a conversation with each of them at the time about the idea of shaving. We talked about our culture's differing expectations for men and women. I shared with them my perceptions of the advantages and disadvantages of shaving. I told them of times in my life I chose not to shave and times I experienced shaving as a liberating act of self-care. They were each invited to share their perceptions, stories, and reflections on the subject. Ultimately, I made it clear that shaving was a personal choice, and that their dad and I had decided they were old enough to make that choice for themselves.

On the day the privilege of shaving was granted to each of them, Andrew and I gifted the one experiencing the rite of passage with their own personal razor and shaving gel, and I drew them a relaxing bath. I set up a CD player with soft music and strategically placed candles around the bathroom for ambiance. After the honored one settled into her bath, I entered the bathroom and gave a brief lesson on shaving technique and safety. When my shaving student felt confident enough to proceed on her own, I left her alone to finish shaving in solitude. Of course, I was close at hand to deal with any little nicks and scrapes that accompanied the learning process. Each daughter felt greatly supported and empowered in taking on this new privilege.

Of course, a similar rite of passage can be created between father and son, or, if there's no father in the household, with some other male mentor in the young person's life. Standing at the bathroom mirror side-by-side can be an effective way for a father or other mentor to demonstrate shaving techniques for the various contours of the face and neck. Although some dads teach their sons how to shave before their facial hair appears, it can be especially meaningful to share this rite of passage in response to the actual physical changes taking place in the young person's life.

In addition to shaving legs and underarms, makeup use is a significant passage of enculturation for females in our society. Andrew and I found that granting such a privilege at an age when the parent still has sufficient influence can temper a youth's choices and teach moderation. Because Andrew and I granted the privilege of makeup use on Morgan's and Willa's respective twelfth birthdays, we could easily stipulate that makeup use be "parent approved." One of their birthday gifts that year was a collection of lip gloss and subtle eye shadows. Even though I seldom wear makeup and use it sparingly when I do, our daughters felt empowered by being granted the privilege. Because of our strategic timing, they were also willing to follow the guidelines we set.

Of course, puberty often brings with it a youth's desire to make bodily changes that are more about fashion trends than deeply rooted societal norms such as shaving and wearing makeup. Sometimes a youth is relentless in their requests to embody fashion choices that appear foreign to older generations and are not options we would choose for them. One way Andrew and I dealt with such requests from our children was to grant a privilege on a *future* birthday or at a significant time of passage yet to come. This practice can be a delayed way of saying "yes," heightening the youth's anticipation of receiving the desired privilege, and allowing momentary whims to pass.

As a new teenager, our eldest daughter, Morgan, was enamored with body piercings and tattoos. After many requests from Morgan, Andrew and I finally agreed to give our permission for one body piercing at the age of 16 and a small tattoo at the age of 17. (However, we required that she do some research on the dangers of tattoos and the potentially poisonous effect of certain inks.) Being granted these privileges momentarily satisfied Morgan. By the time she became a legal adult and could decide such issues for herself, her attraction to such body art was more moderate. Granting children new privileges and giving them greater authority to make choices for themselves isn't a now-or-never proposition. If now is not the time, the time will surely come. As parents, we need to remember that we don't *give* a youth such authority over their bodies, we help prepare them for such authority to emerge from within.

Middle School Friendship Celebration

Who among us did not experience a life-changing passage of friendship in our youth? Friendship passages are especially potent around the age of twelve, when one-on-one friendships take on new meaning and a youth becomes aware of the profound effect their attitudes and actions can have on their peers. Helping a youth to consider the value and meaning of friendship and deepen friendship bonds can assist them in navigating the sometimes tumultuous waters of social life in the older elementary and middle school years.

Experiencing challenging physical feats together can be especially bonding for older youths: ropes courses or physical challenges in nature (canoe trips, wilderness adventures, rock climbing, etc.). Even navigating a cross-city trip on the bus system or subway can draw youths together in an absorbing, cooperative effort to overcome the obstacles in front of them.

When Morgan was in sixth grade, she was a member of a sixth grade class that had been together since first grade. Although the social dynamics of the class were fairly healthy, toward the end of fifth grade, some of the girls in the class developed competitive, spiteful behavior toward one another that carried into the sixth grade year. As Morgan's twelfth birthday approached midway through the school year, Morgan expressed a desire to invite all the girls from her class to attend a birthday party we were planning for her. So Andrew and I planned the party around themes of friendship and working and playing cooperatively with others.

Morgan's party included dinner, making friendship bracelets, reflecting on significant qualities of friendship, enduring "friendship trials," playing games that incorporated friendship themes, and a sleepover. The high point for me came at breakfast the next day when one of Morgan's friends said, "I'm so glad we did this! Sometimes we forget how much we mean to each other."

A few years later after our family had relocated to a new town, Willa's friendship celebration took place with a group of new friends. Even though the youths Willa invited weren't as intimate as the group at Morgan's party, the celebration was every bit as meaningful, as Willa's new friends worked and played cooperatively and reflected on the meaning of friendship.

> **Tools** ✎ In the invitation to the party, ask each participant to write about a cherished memory of the birthday person and be prepared to share it at the party. Also, ask the youth being honored to prepare a simple gift or memory to share with each friend invited. For "Reflections on Friendship," you'll need materials for a craft project to prompt participants to express artistically a personal quality they always look for in a friend. The craft could be friendship bracelets, friendship stones (described below), origami, or whatever seems appropriate. For the "Friendship Trials" (pages 147-150), you'll need written clues, materials to accomplish each trial, and the treasure that the group finds upon completing the trials successfully. You'll need materials for each "Friendship Game" chosen (pages 151-153). For the "Friendship Ceremony" (pages 153-155), you'll need one candle for each participant (including the honored youth), matches or a candle-lighter, a bag or basket to hold the crafts made earlier, and a crystal singing bowl, chime, or other resonant instrument.

Reflections on Friendship

To prepare for the friendship ceremony, participants create an art or craft project as a symbol of friendship. Before participants begin their creations, talk about the importance of friendship and how each of us tends to look for certain qualities in a friend. Perhaps one person thinks loyalty is the most important quality a friend can have, while another person values love, humor, respect, or honesty. Ask the youths to reflect on the friendship quality they cherish and make their craft with that quality in mind. If you choose a project that uses the symbolism of color, animals, or other images, have a chart available for the youths to refer to that shows the qualities associated with each symbol. For Morgan's celebration, we chose to make color-coded friendship bracelets and had several patterns from easy to advanced. Adults and youths who were skilled at making the bracelets helped beginners. Another simple art project I've used with people of all ages is painting friendship rocks. Acquire some smooth, flat stones and have each youth paint a word, animal, or other symbol on the rock with craft paints and brushes or paint pens. These friendship symbols will be exchanged during the "Friendship Ceremony" (page 153).

The Friendship Trials

The "Friendship Trials" are a series of challenging tasks that the youths must accomplish together. You may want to make this portion of the celebration a surprise, so the trials can be shrouded in mystery. A priority in planning these trials is to create tasks that will require courage, teamwork, and trust. The specific trials you plan will depend on your setting; the needs, abilities, and social relationships of the youths and adults involved; and the time of day.

Since we planned for the "Friendship Trials" at Morgan's celebration to be outside in our wooded lot after dark, we timed dinner and the craft project accordingly. Our trials included searching among the trees after dark for an intimidating figure we called the "Dark King," building a fire with flint and steel, obstacle jumping, and a blindfold group trust walk.

Materials needed for each trial were prepared before the party and placed in their appropriate hiding places while the youths worked on their craft project. The adult playing the part of the Dark King donned his costume in secret. When the youths completed the craft project and were cleaning up, another adult strategically lured two of them to discover the first message left by the Dark King, which was scrawled on the outside of an envelope that held the clue to the first trial. Once the message was discovered, the group was called together and the message read aloud. Revise the following clues according to your setting and the specific trials you plan:

A Message from the Dark King:

> O young friends now gathered here,
> Listen with your inner ear:
> Your friendship true, 'tis time to prove,
> Thus, past four trials you must move,
> NOT one by one, but as a tribe
> Decipher now what I transcribe. . .

Before reading the first clue, ask the youths to clarify the meaning of the message together. Make sure they understand the instruction that they are to work as a group. Then, the first clue can be read:

The First Trial: The Trial of Courage

> The first trial will require courage,
> Let not the darkened wood discourage,
> For in the dark, I hide the key. . .
> To find the second trial, find me.
> Approach me as you would a king
> And speak out boldly, DO NOT CLING,
> Each stands upright, all say as one:
> "Dark King, give up the trial! YOU ARE UNDONE!"

Guide the youths toward consensus about what they think the clue means. Encourage them to come up with a plan of action, and if the plan doesn't work, to retreat to a lighted place to decipher the clue again. The clue, as written here, requires the youths to find the Dark King, and when they do, to bow to him. After the bow, they stand up tall and speak their demand to the Dark King boldly and in unison.

> **Dark King:** (after the task is completed, holds up next clue)
> "I give you here the tiny spark
> to build that which transforms the dark;
> Who will take it from my hand? (points at the most fearful youth)
> YOU! You are the one that I command!"

The clue to the second trial is wrapped around a piece of flint for starting a fire. After the chosen youth takes the clue from the Dark King, the Dark King disappears and is not seen again. (Of course, the one playing the Dark King may rejoin the group in his/her own clothing and identity.)

The Second Trial: The Trial of Will

> You have been strong, you have been swift,
> To face the Dark King has its gift:
> Where dead trunks rest, help does abide,
> A basket of tools I provide.
> After you build that which I ask,
> You'll eat your way to the third task.

The second clue, as written here, guides the youths to the wood pile, where they find a basket which holds a flashlight and materials needed to start a fire with flint and steel rather than a match. In the bottom of the basket is a box with a message on it: "After your second task is complete, return here for a toasty treat."

At Morgan's party, the group was closely supervised as they worked over our outdoor firepit to figure out how to start a flint and steel fire. (Depending on the resourcefulness of the group, materials for such a trial could include written instructions.) When the task of fire-building is complete, the youths open the "toasty treat" box to find a bag of marshmallows. Invite them to toast the marshmallows over their fire. The clue to the third trial is at the bottom of the marshmallow bag.

The Third Trial: The Trial of Risk

> The third trial now requires risk,
> You must have strength, you must be brisk,
> Circle yourselves around a pile
> Where the dead have been laid to rest awhile.
> If you can all jump it, receive the token
> that is the key to the next trial spoken.
> Fly from the North, South, East, then West,
> The final jumper will do it best;
> From that direction, if you journey on
> You'll come to the last test to be undergone.

The third clue, as written here, guides the youths to gather by the wood pile. They are to jump over it one at a time from the various directions (which they must figure out). If this trial is used, make the wood pile high enough for the task to be a challenge for the daring, and low enough at the edges that the more timid can still accomplish the feat with a bit of effort. If a member of the group has difficulty with this task, encourage the group to figure out ways they can assist the one having trouble. After everyone jumps the pile, the youths are given a key (or combination) to a lock they will open in the final task to retrieve their treasure. As written here, the final jumper (who "flies" from the West) continues straight ahead twenty or thirty feet and finds a bag hanging from tree branches overhead. The bag contains a blindfold for each youth (with the exception of the birthday youth) and the following clue:

The Final Trial: The Trial of Trust

> Accomplished much, you have this night
> To bring your friends into the light,
> The treasure that awaits you near
> Demands that you give up your fear.
> Go blind, but one who knows this place
> Will lead you with uncovered face.
> All hands on shoulders; s/he'll beam the light.
> Listen well, for s/he is your sight
> To low-hanging branches and where to tread lightly;
> Each one to have treasure must hang on tightly.
> S/he knows the end to this overgrown place,
> Where you finally end this treasure chase.

The final clue, as written here, instructs the group to put on the blind-folds and line up one behind the other with their hands on the shoulders of the person in front of them. The honored youth is not blind-folded, and stands at the front of the line with flashlight in hand. At Morgan's celebration, she led the group through a section of our lot that was overgrown with tall grass and wildflowers. At the end of the lot was a treasure chest. The chest can be one that locks, or a box or tub tightly wrapped shut with a padlocked chain or rope. The key or combination the youths received during the third trial gives them entry to the treasure box, which might include individual gifts or treasure bags, a gift for the birthday person that all the youths can enjoy together (such as a fun, large-group board game), an invitation for a future group outing, or an edible treat.

In the top or bottom of the treasure box, place a final message:

> Well done, true friends, through the night you came,
> You conquered great fear your prize to claim,
> Friends falter not when the sun sinks to set,
> Friends hold a candle when darkness is met,
> Be a light for each other – a beacon, a spark
> That shines from your heart to conquer the dark.

Friendship Games

The "Friendship Games" emphasize various aspects of friendship: teamwork, cooperation, listening, observation, etc., and can be used in place of the "Friendship Trials." Choose games that will work best for your setting, time frame, and the participants invited. It may be helpful for the social dynamics of the party to intersperse active games with quieter activities. If team games are played, teams can be strategically selected before the party so participants have an opportunity to team up with a different combination of people for each game. If prizes are given, you may want to create a point system for each game. After all the games are completed, the points can be tallied and youths can choose their prize one at a time in the order determined by point totals. Include enough prizes so the final person selecting still has a choice. Remember, game prizes need not be expensive. Such prizes as edible treats and like-new youth novels from the resale shop can be enjoyed as much as more expensive loot. At Morgan's and Willa's parties, the youths were highly invested in the fun and competition of the games – and in the end, everyone earned prizes they selected enthusiastically without feeling left out.

Knowing Who Our Friends Are

For this photo identity game, youths will need to bring to the party photos of themselves as babies and preschoolers. In the invitation to the party, include the following note: "Please bring two photos of yourself to the party *that none of the people coming to the party have seen before* and seal them in an envelope. If possible, include a photo of yourself as a baby and another photo when you were two or three. Don't show them to anyone!"

Collect the photographs from each youth as they arrive at the party. Behind closed doors, mount the pictures carefully on a poster board with a number beside each, or lay them out on a flat surface and place a numbered sticky note on the edge of each photo. For this game, each youth is given an answer sheet to write down the name of the person they believe is represented by each photo. After everyone turns in their written guesses, let the group guess aloud the photo identities one at a time. Then ask each photo subject to reveal the correct answer and share any personal information about the picture they wish to divulge.

Scavenger Hunt

Most young people today haven't had the pleasure of participating in an old-fashioned, door-to-door scavenger hunt to beg neighbors and strangers for small household items. At Willa's friendship celebration, this was a highlight of our evening together. We split the participants into teams of four or five and assigned an adult to each group. We assigned each team to a different section of the neighborhood and gave the youths clear rules for the game, including staying together (in sight of the adult team member) and waiting outside each home when collecting items. Each team received the same list of items to collect and a bag in which to carry them. Items on the list were divided into categories of one, three, and five points. The one-point items were fairly common: a rubber band, a barrette, an empty matchbox, an empty spice container, etc. Three and five point items were more novel: a photograph of your family pet, a Mug's root beer can, a cash receipt from the grocery store, birthday confetti, etc. Although the youths came across a few people that didn't want to be bothered, the majority of folks solicited were delighted to see a group of young people having some good, old-fashioned fun and were happy to play along.

Friendship Poems

A set of magnetized words for creating refrigerator poetry or a set of words cut out of magazines is all you'll need for this game. Each team is given a 10 or 12 minute time-limit to use the words in front of them to create a poem about friendship. After the poem is composed, the team shows it to the gamekeeper, and the gamekeeper records it before scrambling the words for the next team. You may be as pleasantly surprised by the outcome of this game as I was when one of the teams at Willa's party produced the following poem:

> You inspire the heart
> I am lonely in the dark
> Cry a tear from my soul
> But when I am with you
> You show me hope and love
> A friend - An angel in the sky

(by Kerstyn Perrett, Jenny Peterson, Megan Sutkay, and Willa Darian)

Group Listening Games

Friendship games can include a fun, large-group board game that re-quires group listening skills. One of my family's favorites is Catch Phrase® – a game in which the group is split into two teams that take turns getting their own team members to say a particular word or phrase by giving descriptive clues. Nonverbal charade-type games, such as Guesstures®, can also work well for a group-listening challenge.

Friendship Ceremony

After the more raucous activities of the friendship trials and/or games, you may want to lead the group into a more mellow time of reflection and ceremony.

> **Tools** ∾ For the "Friendship Ceremony" participants bring their memories to share (described in the tool box on page 146). The youths sit in a circle on chairs, sitting pillows, or on the floor. On a table or mantel at the edge of the circle, a display of votive or tea light candles are safely set; the number of candles correlate with the number of youths present. Have matches or a candlelighter on hand. In the center of the circle, set a bag or basket filled with the crafted friendship symbols made earlier, and a resonant instrument, such as a chime, bell, gong, or crystal singing bowl (an instrument thought to evolve from a Tibetan tradition, used as a tool to promote inner harmony and soulful cleansing.

Giving Gifts of Friendship

To begin the ceremony, the birthday youth lights a candle from the display, and all are invited to speak the friendship vow. (Participants can be given a printed copy of the vow to read, or asked to recite it after an adult leader or the honored youth, line by line:)

Friendship Vow

Friends no matter what the weather,
Each trial we meet, we meet together,
True friends can face the dark of night,
Transform it with our love and light.

Adult leader says:

"Each of you has created a *(name the craft made)* that represents what you believe is the most important quality a friend can have. Now, someone in this circle will receive your creation as a reminder of what it means to be a true friend." (The adult asks a youth in the circle to close their eyes and draw an item from the basket.)

After each youth chooses a crafted item from the bag or basket, the one who created the selected item explains the quality they cherish most in a friend and how that quality is reflected in their creation. If the group made friendship bracelets, the creator of the item ties the bracelet on the receiver's wrist after their explanation. To avoid youths drawing their own creation, ask the youth whose gift was chosen to be the next person to select an item.

Friendship Blessings

Song: Dear Friends (page 166)

Dear friends, dear friends,
Let me tell you how I feel,
You have given me such treasures,
Circle 'round again.

One at a time, each friend comes to sit in front of the birthday youth and shares a cherished memory of the one being celebrated. This memory (written down ahead of time) can be read or shared spontaneously. After the friend shares, the youth being honored offers the friend a simple gift, friendship symbol, or memory of their own – also prepared ahead of time. After both youths have spoken, they hold right hands and place their left palm over the other's heart. Then, everyone reads or recites this Druid pledge of friendship (which can be memorized ahead of time):

> "We pledge by peace and love to stand
> Heart to heart and hand to hand."

After a handshake or hug, the friend stands, lights a candle from the display, and returns to their place in the circle.

A Final Blessing

Once all the friends share memories with the youth of honor and receive their gift, symbol, or remembrance in return, everyone stands to read or recite the "Friendship Vow" again:

Friendship Vow

> Friends no matter what the weather,
> Each trial we meet, we meet together,
> True friends can face the dark of night,
> Transform it with our love and light.

To end the ceremony, the birthday youth is invited to stand in the center of the circle while everyone sings "One More Year" (page 314). Then, the birthday youth can ring in their new year on a crystal singing bowl, chime, or other resonant instrument – one ring for each year and one for the year to come. (Be sure to extinguish the candles.)

Rules of Friendship

Not long after Morgan's friendship celebration, she posted a list on her bedroom wall called "Fifty Rules of Friendship." She only listed five or six directives and planned to add rules as she learned from and contemplated her friendships and interactions with others. Encouraging a youth to create their own friendship covenant, creed, or rules can help a youth to comprehend the personal power and responsibility they have in shaping healthy relationships with their peers and friends of all ages. It's also a proactive way to inspire a youth to consider relationships that are worthy of their attention, time, and energy. Written reflections on friendship can provide a foundation on which to stand when a youth encounters unhealthy or hurtful behavior directed at themselves or others.

You may want to consider the ins and outs of friendship with a youth one-on-one or as a family. To begin, each family member can write down the three guidelines or rules they feel are most important in being a friend to others, and the three most significant qualities they look for in a friend. Each time you come together to consider what it means to create genuine friendships, consider a different aspect of friendship, such as listening, gratitude, conflict, communication, empathy, attraction, loyalty, compassion, betrayal, disappointment, social pressures, popularity, kindness, jealousy, trust, etc. – whatever issue of friendship seems most relevant or timely. As family members gain clarity about their approach to friendship, each family member can express their personal values, beliefs, and desires concerning friendship in a written creed, covenant, or list of rules.

When a conflict or problem arises among friends or peers, family members will be able to refer to their friendship conversations and their own recorded wisdom. As each family member continues to learn about friendship and makes intentional commitments to be a friend, covenants and creeds can be amended, and rules added or changed. This way, all friendship experiences – positive and negative – can be reflected upon as a gift to help family members create healthier, more satisfying relationships with others.

Reclaiming a Passage of Youthhood

When we dig deep into the memories of our own youthhood, we may discover a mother lode of inspiration for our personal growth and transformation. Because, no matter how grown up we may *appear* to be, most of us continue to wrestle with the same life themes so prominent during youthhood:

- What does it mean to be (or have) a true friend?
- Who am I as a sexual being?
- How powerful am I?

These are some of the massive youthful questions we carry within us – questions that usually get buried under the diversions and weightiness of our adult lives, as we focus on family life, goals, careers, and financial responsibilities. It's easy for us to lose sight of our soulful needs for friendship, romance, and healthy relational partnerships. Yet, these questions will not be put down. They arise in us again and again, whether we give them our undivided attention, or not.

So, as some of us used to say in our younger years, I dare you. I double-dog dare you to start asking these questions again. Take a journey back into the years of your youth, not only to remember who you were then, but to remember how you asked these massive questions that lived right beneath the surface of your youthful skin.

What does it mean to be (or have) a true friend?

It's been said that to have a friend, a person must first be a friend. Yet, it is equally true that to be a friend, one must have a friend willing to receive the gift of one's friendship. For some of us, youthhood was filled with the companionship of bosom friends. For others, it was a time of searching for friendship or a rollercoaster ride through the ups and downs of relational complexities. But, whatever friendships we enjoyed or not, for most of us in our youth, friendship was the gold mine we sought.

With our busy daily schedules and geographic mobility, it's difficult for many of us to make true friendship a priority, even when we find a person with whom we strongly resonate. So from time-to-time, we youths grown old and tall need to revisit that gold mine we sought in our younger years. We need to remember the potential healing, adventure, and camaraderie that await us in the presence of a true friend.

Consider your "best friends," past and present. Not necessarily the friends with whom you are most intimate, but the friends who serve/d to bring out the best in you, those who inspire/d you to be your truest self. List the name of each friend and the personal qualities they exude that drew you to be their friend in the first place. As you look at the lists, notice if there is any overlap in personal attributes, or if there are personal qualities that all of your "best friends" exude. Sometimes, looking for key qualities that we value in a friend can help us to identify the type of person with whom we are most likely to cultivate strong and lasting friendships.

It's never too late to become the friend you can be or to have the kind of bosom friend that you had or dreamed about in your youth. It's never too late to build strong bonds of friendship through the kinds of adventures youths are known for. Catching frogs on a summer afternoon, going on an old-fashioned scavenger hunt, playing board games, blowing bubbles, stargazing, rock climbing, sledding, water balloon fights, a trip to the water park, basking in the wild of nature, or bungee jumping can inspire a sense of fun and deepen intimacy in ways we adults sometimes neglect to experience. A bonding gesture, as well, can be to honor a covenant of friendship with an intimate friend or circle of friends. Several years ago, my friend Maggie and I created a friendship ceremony when our relationship was in need of healing and attention. We created a friendship covenant from the section "On Friendship" in *The Prophet* by Kahlil Gibran (listed on page 333 of the resource section), and made symbolic gifts for one another. At a time when we were both parenting young children, the friendship celebration reminded us to keep the bonds of our friendship alive.

As adults, we sometimes bury our desire for friendship under the serious considerations and responsibilities of adult life. It can be transformative for us to remember the healing power of friendship, laughter, and play. And it's good to remember that to be a friend and to have a friend requires time and attention. Time and attention.

Who Am I As a Sexual Being?

Living, as we do, in a culture that is more than a little confused about sexuality and the human body, it can be growth-inspiring to nurture a sense of wonder and curiosity about our own sexuality and to romance and nurture our sexual selves. An effective tool for understanding ourselves as sexual beings is to review our biography from birth to the present as it relates to body image and living in our physical body – our feelings and experiences during puberty; our moments of sexual enlightenment; experiences of sexual play with peers or siblings; incidences of sexual abuse or having our sexual boundaries crossed; first intimate sexual encounters; romantic partners; guidance we received from others; sexual guidance we imparted ourselves; sexual hang-ups we had (or still have); curiosities about our own bodies or the opposite gender; fears or fantasies we have about sex or sexuality; how we care for our bodies; insight into our monthly rhythms related to hormones; or whatever seems pertinent.

Write and reflect. Ask a marriage partner or intimate friend to commit to do the same. Set aside time to share your sexual biographies with one another. After you share your biographies, future conversations can include reflections on the following questions:

- Throughout my life, how have I learned to express my sexuality in positive ways? How have I misused it or expressed my sexuality in harmful ways?

- In my youth, how did I feel about my body and sexual feelings/sensations that arose? How does that differ from the way I view my body and sexual feelings/sensations now?

- What aspects of my sexuality are in need of healing?

- How can I better express love and care for my body?

- What is "romance?" How can I create a greater sense of romance in my life? With my sexual partner? With myself? In relationships that don't include sexual intimacy?

- How can I more fully embrace my sexuality as a sacred gift?

- Imagine the possibilities. . .

How Powerful Am I?

When I was a youth, there was one place in the world I felt invincible. It was on the track, running like the wind. There was something about racing and crossing a finish line that made me feel I could do anything I set my mind to. Back then, I was sure I would grow up to win a gold medal in the Olympic Games. A gold medal wasn't in the cards, not even close, but that feeling of accomplishment, that sense of fiery vigor I felt in my gut every time I stepped onto the track is something I never forgot. Now, my family teases me whenever we attend a track meet because I'm prone to vocal outbursts of encouragement to the runners at every turn and to shedding tears for no reason at all. No reason, except the overwhelming gratitude I feel for a sport that infused me with an experience of being able to fly on winged feet. My middle-aged knees won't let me run much anymore, but that feeling of invincibility still lives in my runner's soul.

Where was that place for you? That place you knew you could accomplish anything you set your mind to? Where did you know you could make an important contribution, and didn't fear someone coming along and making you feel small? Was it on the baseball diamond, in the art studio, abiding in the presence of someone who knew how to make you believe in yourself? Was it while studying a subject that thrilled your mind and imagination, participating in religious services or spiritual ceremonies, basking in the grandeur of nature? Was it in accomplishing some challenging physical feat, such as horseback riding or rock climbing? Wherever that place was, that place that filled you up with a great sense of your own personal power, remember it. Remember how it made you feel. Remember who celebrated your youthful sense of personal power and who rejected it. Reflect on ways you claimed your personal power in positive, life-giving ways.

Consider, as well, a place in your youth where you felt *dis*empowered. A place where you felt your personal power being sucked out of you. Perhaps a person in your life had a knack for diminishing your sense of self, or a subject in school caused you to feel ignorant or incapable. Perhaps you experienced an embarrassing public moment or failure, or you faced a devastating life event or circumstance, such as being the victim of a violent crime, enduring a parent's unemployment, or poverty. Whatever that place of disempowerment was, remember it. Remember how you felt and how you responded to the situation. Did you lash out or withdraw? Remember who was there. Who added to your pain and who affirmed you in that place of vulnerability? Who did you confide in about the experience, if anyone?

I can remember visiting the dermatologist when I was in sixth grade. As if my acne problems weren't enough of a challenge to my self-esteem, one day I was tended to by an older female nurse who intentionally rubbed her breasts across my upper body as she addressed my skin problems. I was mortified, but immobilized. I didn't have any idea what to do or say. My mother and father didn't speak to me of sexual issues, so I didn't feel comfortable telling them what had happened. I was so unsure of myself sexually that, as I pondered the incident, I began to imagine that it was something I had made up in my head. However, the next time I went back to the dermatologist's office, the nurse was there again, using her same old body-bumping tactics. After my appointment that day, I was still unable to tell my parents what had happened, but I did inform my mother, in no uncertain terms, that I would not go back to that doctor's office again. She honored my request.

One of our greatest challenges as adults is learning to create healthy, caring relationships in which the personal power of one is not diminished by the other. One reason it's so difficult for some of us to learn this lesson with one another as adults is because, in our youth, we experienced damaging incidences in which adults managed to wheedle our power away from us, leaving us feeling impotent and incapable. Sometimes, as adults, we establish entire relationships on attempting to take our power back. Sometimes, we treat any self-possessing adult as if they're a threat to our intrapersonal security. Marriage partners are notorious for waging power wars with one another, both publicly and privately. When Andrew and I decided to marry, our family track records on resolving marital power struggles weren't at all impressive. At the time, 70% of all the marriages in our birth families had ended in divorce or long-term separation.

Early in our relationship, Andrew and I committed ourselves to an intentional partnership in which power and responsibility would be equally shared. Before we got married, we went to a counselor for several months to uncover relational issues that needed tending. We learned in those months how to articulate to one another the ways in which we felt empowered or disempowered in our relationship. Additionally, we allowed ourselves to think outside the box in terms of power asserted within the family and in our work lives; inspired by such reflections, we created various parenting and work arrangements through the years. We each had the opportunity to serve as primary caregiver to our children when they were young. We also each had the opportunity to serve as primary wage earner for our family. There was a time when our children were young when we each worked part-time and shared parenting, and there were times when they were older when we both worked full-time outside the home. Our flexibility to consider nontraditional family arrangements allowed each of us to feel supported in our more public work and in our parenting.

Through the years, Andrew and I have created rites of passage that further define and honor the mutual partnership that we're striving to create with one another. When we decided to marry, we took on a new family name that we chose for ourselves (by joining two Hebrew names), which means "heart of wisdom, compassion, and grace" – qualities we strive to uphold in our marriage and family life. We celebrate an anniversary ceremony each year in which we reflect on the marriage vows we wrote for our wedding, and recommit ourselves to our marriage covenant. We celebrate an intimate "wedding ceremony" with our children every seven years to acknowledge the growth cycles of our relationship. We celebrate rites of passage for birthdays and life transitions that articulate our mutual support and caring for one another. Learning to assert our personal power with one another in our marriage (without diminishing the power of the other) has fostered a relationship in which intimacy continues to deepen after 21 years. Our relationship is a living being in which new life springs forth on a frequent basis:

> Is our love pregnant again?
> I feel it here in the hollow of my belly.
> New life kicking.
> I smile, remembering
> The tender fire in your eyes
> that placed it there.
> Yes, we are giving birth again.
> Faint not.
> This baby's name is Soul.

Songs for Celebrating Youthhood

Magic Is Everywhere

Shea Darian

Ma - gic, ma - gic is ev' - ry - where,___ It's hid - den in the earth,___ It's stream - ing through the air, It's in the can - dle danc - ing bright, It's in the foun - tain's flight. _____

2. Magic, magic is everywhere,
   In our hearts and in our minds,
   Binding all of humankind.
   True magic is faith to believe
   In the things we cannot see.

3. Magic, magic is everywhere,
   Now you can let it live
   In the joy that's yours to give
   to young and old who dare to see
   Magic is faith's golden key.

Keeper of the Magic

Shea Darian

Good keep - er of the ma - gic, We

place our trust in you,_____ The

ma - gic lives with - in you In

what you say and do_____ To

bold - ly serve faith's in - fant, The

babe that grows to be_____ Our be -

lief in the more in - vi - si - ble truths we

can - not see.____

Journey Forth

Shea Darian

We bless you with good health, We

bless you with good cheer, We

bless you with cou - rage for your

spi - rit,_____ Jour - ney

forth in love on this spe - cial

day, Jour - ney forth with

cou - rage for your spi - rit.___

Dear Friends

4-part round

Adaptation*

Dear friends, dear friends, Let me tell you how I___ feel, You have gi - ven me such_ trea - sures, Cir - cle 'round a - gain.

* "Dear Friends" and other rounds sung to this melody can be found in the *Rise Up Singing* Songbook, edited by Peter Blood-Patterson, (A Sing Out Publication, 1988).

4 ⚬ At the Crossroads
Rites of Passage for Coming of Age

You have to do your own growing
no matter how tall your grandfather was.

~ Abraham Lincoln

Celebrating Coming of Age

Coming of age. We adults often refer to it as if it's a once-and-for-all event in a young person's life. But take note of the term – it isn't "come of age" – it's *coming*. In the human life cycle, coming of age is a process, a becoming, an evolution that takes place over a number of years. When we diminish our understanding of coming of age to a singular legal, religious, physical, or social event, we fail to acknowledge multiple aspects of growth required to become a healthy, whole, mature adult person.

For most youths in our culture today, the transition into adulthood isn't celebrated in one decisive ceremony, but is pieced together a little at a time, as a young person experiences myriad initiations. Oftentimes, from the beginnings of puberty to the age of 21 (and beyond), various events in a young person's life announce that youthhood is fading and adulthood is coming to the fore. Through a series of life passages, adulthood is gradually conferred upon a young person by their family, faith community, the legal system, educational institutions, civic groups, and, ultimately, by their own inner recognition of the adult self.

When we imagine meaningful rites of passage for the transition from youthhood to adulthood, it's important to remember that, although a girl's menarche (first menses) or a boy's first ejaculation may announce that a youth's body is becoming capable of procreation, few in our society correlate these events with adult maturity. Likewise, youths of 12, 13, or 14 who are initiated through religious rites as members of their faith are seldom treated as mature adults, even by members of their faith community.

Like all other cycles of human growth, coming of age is a gradual unfolding, a cycle of life I call the woman-becoming and the man-becoming. It's a time when the young person stands at the crossroads where youthhood and adulthood intersect. On any given day, depending on life circumstances, the young person may find one road more inviting or familiar than the other. As parents and mentors, we do well to help youths and young adults create coming of age rites that affirm this dual perspective.

I once heard of a teenager who barely endured the well-meaning coming of age celebration his parents planned for him. The ceremony was based on a rite of passage extracted from an ancient culture. During the celebration, the young man lay in bed with his mother, cuddling and conversing. Suddenly, a group of men burst through the door to rip the youth out of his mother's arms. The experience was highly disconcerting for the youth as his mother wailed and carried on, attempting to *save* her son from his abduction into the world of manhood. Ultimately, the male "kidnappers" were successful in stealing the youth away from his mother and the realm of childhood, but the next day, the youth's social status and the family structure remained unchanged. The youth would continue to live in the same household with his mother for years yet, and she would continue to be an authority figure and nurturer in the young man's daily life. So, while the dramatic event of a boy being ripped from his mother's arms to join the ranks of manhood may have been greatly relevant to the youth living in the culture from which this rite emerged, it's doubtful that a youth in our society will find the rite especially meaningful or relevant.

As we create and re-create coming of age celebrations with youths and young adults of today, we do well to utilize language, images, and rituals that speak to a young person's life experiences. We do well to celebrate rites that authentically reflect the passage being experienced at any given moment. Even so, one enriching aspect of traditional tribal rites that can be incorporated in contemporary coming of age rites of passage is the deep connection such rites often foster with the earth and the natural world. Communing with creation is a soulful gesture that fades in many young people as they move toward the complexities of young adulthood. Yet, the natural world is one of our most accessible sanctuaries to experience powers and realities greater than ourselves, powers and realities that give us breath and a foundation upon which to stand. Consider celebrating coming of age rites that allow a young person to cultivate a sense of awe and wonder for creation and for their own body as one miraculous aspect of creation.

Ultimately, through consciously honoring a young person's myriad coming of age passages in simple or elaborate celebrations, we parents witness a young person's growing ability to walk down the path into young adulthood without having to be carried away by their elders. And we parents – mothers *and* fathers – may gradually loosen the hold we have on our children. Rather than grasping and wailing our discontent as they fly from the nest, we may send them off with the song of our blessings.

Rites of Passage for Coming of Age

Celebrating Menarche

When my eldest daughter, Morgan, began her menses at the age of twelve, I was delighted to take up the task of helping to guide her through this passage of budding womanhood. However, when her ten-year-old sister's menarche arrived a month later, I was bowled over by the fact that both of my children were well into the transition of womanhood. No doubt, such dramatic moments of growth for our children can produce conflicting emotions in us. Looking back, this life transition when my daughters took a giant step toward womanhood at the same time was, for me, the most emotionally turbulent of all.

It wasn't that I wanted to hold back the turning of time or pull Willa and Morgan back into the innocence of childhood. It was simply that I didn't have a role model to show me the way. And suddenly, I was being called upon to provide for my children what I never received myself.

During my own menarche transition, my mother guided me as lovingly as she knew how. She prepared me for the day my menstrual cycle would begin, which was far more information than she received from her mother. My mom made sure I knew the ins and outs of menstrual care products, and a few weeks after I was initiated into my monthly bleeding, she took me to get my ears pierced. My mom never said that the two events were connected, but I intuited that she looked at me with different eyes. For me, that ear piercing was a profound initiation into womanhood, so when Morgan and Willa began pleading to pierce their ears at an early age, Andrew and I chose to reserve ear piercing for their coming-of-menses passage. This way, Willa and Morgan could look forward to the transition with great anticipation, and we could preserve a significant rite of passage passed on from my youth.

For Willa and Morgan, the ear piercing was a highlight of their coming-of-menses. A somewhat painful highlight, but they each had the whole family present to support them. Each could also look forward to the celebration dinner we enjoyed as a family after the ear-piercing was complete. To strengthen the father-daughter bond through the menarche passage, we established the tradition of Andrew taking each daughter on a father-daughter dinner date on their half-birthdays. This tradition continues to be a cherished annual event for each of them. Andrew plans the evening and buys his date a single rose. Father and daughter usually dress up to enjoy an evening of dining and conversation.

As powerful as the ear-piercing ritual was and as bonding as the father-daughter dinner dates became, Andrew and I felt this coming of age transition in our daughters' lives called for something more. We desired for Morgan and Willa to clearly experience menses as an empowering affirmation of their strength, creativity, and life-giving power as women. We desired for them to embrace their monthly bleeding, not as an inconvenience or liability, but as a cyclical reminder of the miracle of their physical bodies and the emerging potency of their sexual selves.

As a way of empowering Willa and Morgan during this transition, Andrew and I decided to include them each in planning a ceremony in their honor. We desired for them to be involved in the decision-making concerning who would be invited, the setting, the elements of the ceremony that would be included, and the timing of the celebration. Ultimately, they both chose to celebrate with a small circle of intimates. Although Morgan's initiation ceremony (page 174) was celebrated in connection with Morgan's menarche, it can be edited and used anytime a girl takes a significant step towards womanhood.

Willa chose to focus her coming-of-menses celebration around the ear piercing ritual and family dinner. After several conversations with Willa and one another, Andrew and I recognized that, while Willa was thrilled to begin her menstrual cycle, she didn't feel prepared to be initiated as a woman-becoming. Willa was still strongly rooted in the world of youth-hood, and the idea of an elaborate coming of age ceremony seemed to all of us (most significantly, Willa) to be out of sync with Willa's own process of maturity. Thus, we chose to reserve Willa's more elaborate coming of age ceremony for the teenage transition at thirteen. I was not the only one bowled over by Willa's early physical maturing. She also needed time to catch up with herself.

A Menarche Ceremony

In Judith Duerk's book, *Circle of Stones*, she writes: "How might your life have been different if there had been a place for you. . . a place of women, to help you learn the ways of woman. . . a place where you were nurtured with an ancient flow sustaining you and steadying you as you sought to become yourself."

My friend, Susan, created a simple, beautiful ceremony for her daughter after Kate's menstrual cycle began. Susan chose five "women of wisdom" for Kate and invited them to participate in a Sunday afternoon ceremony to initiate Kate at this important passage in her life. In the invitation, Susan asked each woman to bring to the celebration their own story about menstruation; she also asked the women to bring a symbol for Kate that reflected their own identity as a woman of wisdom. Susan prepared a sacred space for the gathering, which included a picture of Susan's mother (who died Susan's senior year of college), a large platter of stones with smaller red pebbles running through it, a candle, and a bouquet of red roses. Kate, the honored one, chose to prepare hors d'oeuvres for the gathering herself.

Kate's menarche ceremony was simply a circle of women gathered to tell stories and share wisdom. As each woman shared, she spoke directly to Kate, and Kate was richly blessed by the tender care she received. At the end of the ceremony, Kate gave each woman a red rose as a way of saying "thank you." And I imagine as Kate went to sleep that night, with the wisdom of her menarche blessing dancing in her heart and mind, her soul may have whispered, "My life will be different because there is a place for me. . . a place where I am being nurtured with an ancient flow sustaining me and steadying me. . . a place of women . . ."

Menses Bath

A monthly cleansing bath is symbolic of the cleansing that occurs during menstruation as toxins are released with the menstrual blood. It is also reminiscent of women of other times and cultures visiting the women's lodge each month to practice self-nurture and affirm menstruation as a time of being spiritually blessed and open to Divine wisdom.

A simple, nurturing acknowledgment for the menarche passage is to gift the woman-becoming with a basket of natural bath oils, salts, and skin moisturizer, a recording of soothing music, and a journal. In the front pages of the journal, write a poem, story, or inspirational passage about menstruation, and invite the woman-becoming to create for herself a relaxing ritual bath each month during her menses. Before or after each bath, she can add to her journal a reflection, insight, question, poem, or story of inspiration about menses or the journey into womanhood.

A Woman-Becoming Celebration

Tools ◈ Depending on the preparation rituals you choose, gather materials for the cleansing bath, massage, and/or adornment (below). As written here, the tools you'll need for the initiation ceremony are a full moon (if you can time an outdoor celebration accordingly); a campfire; fire irons; lawn chairs or blankets for sitting; luminaries (small paper bags with sand at the bottom to hold a tea light); lighter/s for the luminaries; dried cedar branches, sweet-smelling herbs, or incense; a hand drum or other resounding instrument; a pail of water; and "gifts of red" to be given to the initiate. For the final blessing, you'll need any gifts to be given by the father and/or other male elder/s, red roses, and musical instruments, including an array of percussion instruments.

The Preparations

In the days and weeks leading up to the celebration, the one being initiated as a woman-becoming prepares an artistic offering or meditation to share with her circle of women. She also commits to memory a poem, story, or prose piece to recite for the final blessing on pages 178-179. The day of the celebration, consider the following gestures of nurturing and preparation for the initiate.

Cleansing Bath

Create a relaxing bath for the woman-becoming (page 173).

Massage

If the woman-becoming chooses, one or more significant female elders can give her a full body massage. (For ideas, check out a book on massage at your local library. One of my favorite massage reference books is *The Massage Book* by George Downing.)

Adornment

The female participants or a small group of intimates can help adorn the woman-becoming for the ceremony, and/or they can adorn themselves for the celebration with hair braiding and styling, fingernail and/or toenail painting, painting the skin with henna body paint or stage makeup, using henna tattoos, making a head garland with flowers, or whatever adornments the honored one prefers.

Celebration Meal

Male participants and younger, uninitiated females can prepare the celebration meal while older female participants prepare and/or initiate the woman-becoming. The feast can be enjoyed before or after the initiation ceremony.

The Ceremony

Outdoors, create a lighted path with luminaries for the initiate to walk to the circle of women. The path can lead from the back door of the house to the celebration space around an outdoor firepit, if available. Leave the final luminary on one side of the path unlit. Build the fire and set all the props: cedar branches, herbs, or incense; a hand drum; "gifts of red;" and a pail of water. Invite someone to beat the hand drum to signal to the honored one that it's time to emerge from the house and walk the lighted "path of womanhood."

Journey to the Circle of Women

The drum continues to beat as the journey to the circle is made. This walk to the circle of women may be taken by the honored initiate alone, or it can be a procession that includes significant female elders, such as the grandmothers, godmother, and mother. In situations of blended families, if the initiate chooses to include both mother and stepmother in the ceremony and the two women feel comfortable participating with one another, both can be included. (Amend the ceremony as needed to allow the initiate's elders who are present to feel honored and welcome.) If the initiate's elders walk the path in a procession before her, they can enter the path a few steps apart, with the eldest leading the way. All of them can already be standing in the circle of women when the honored initiate begins her journey on the path. Allowing the initiate to make this journey alone can be a profound visual experience for the elders and a significant act of autonomy for the honored one as she walks alone to join her significant female community. When the honored one arrives at the end of the path and is asked to identify herself (see page 176), she can use symbolic names (as shown) or given names. This matriarchal genealogy can be memorized and traced as far back as the initiate chooses.

Women: You, who walk this path to womanhood, what is your name?

Woman-Becoming: I am *Great Brightness,* daughter of *Strong Woman of Grace,* goddaughter of *Priestess of the Morning Light,* granddaughter of *Music Charmer.* I walk this path to womanhood.

Women: *Great Brightness,* add your light to this path. We who have journeyed before you welcome you here. We welcome you to the Circle of Women.

The woman-becoming is handed the lighter to ignite the final luminary placed in the path. She takes her place in the circle of women.

Words of Welcome and Purpose

The mother or another significant elder offers words of welcome to those gathered and offers reflections about the meaning of the event for the one being honored and for herself.

Blessing the Circle of Women

Woman-Becoming: (taking a cedar branch, a handful of herbs, or bit of incense, she throws it into the fire)

"I, the maiden, bless this circle with youthful exuberance and the promise of new beginnings."

Mother: (taking a cedar branch, a handful of herbs, or bit of incense, she throws it into the fire)

"I, the mother, bless this circle with fertility and life."

Godmother: (taking a cedar branch, a handful of herbs, or bit of incense, she throws it into the fire)

"I, the godmother, bless this circle with enchantment and Divine Insight."

Grandmother: (taking a cedar branch, a handful of herbs, or bit of incense, she throws it into the fire)

"I, the grandmother, bless this circle with the gift of endings and the Spirit of Wisdom."

Song: Mensi Com Ni by Rebecca Danica (page 204)

A beautiful menarche song written in pidgin English and based on the menstrual mythology of various cultures.

Bestowing Words of Wisdom

One by one, participants share with the initiate what each wishes they would have known when they experienced the menarche passage into womanhood. Women can share stories and reflections on menses, living in a woman's body, or other insights about walking the path to womanhood.

Blessing the Woman-Becoming

The honored one is given gifts of red. Participants can each be asked to bring a gift, or the group can gift the woman-becoming collectively. Consider what gifts of red would be most meaningful for the one being honored: a red shirt, dress, skirt, shoes, or scarf; a necklace or earrings with red stones; a red candle; an artistic creation that utilizes or highlights the color red; or whatever you choose. The gifts can be worn, used, and appreciated as reminders to claim the goodness, creativity, and strength of menses and womanhood. Following the gifting, this blessing may be read or recited:

> **All:** Claim the power of blood - life blood,
> **Mothers:** red flame burning strong,
> **Grandmothers:** red angel ready to bless.
> **All:** Claim the power of blood - life blood,
> **Maidens:** speak your truth and live your truth,
> **Mothers:** like a red flame burning strong,
> **Grandmothers:** like a red angel ready to bless.
> **All:** Claim the power of blood - life blood.

Song: Woman Becoming (page 203)

> Woman becoming, flowering red,
> Life pouring through as the child is shed,
> River flowing, Spirit bestowing
> Wisdom you seek at the source of All-Knowing.

Woman-Becoming Shares Her Gift

The honored one shares an artistic creation she prepared for the ceremony. This could be anything from reading a letter she wrote to her "circle of women," giving each participant an edible treat or craft she made, sharing meditations on a photograph, or performing a dance. The gift can reflect the initiate's own interests and creativity.

Litany of Affirmations

After the initiate shares her artistic creation, the circle of women gather around the woman-becoming and gently place a hand on her. After a moment of silence, the women spontaneously share one-word or one-phrase affirmations that reflect the gifts and personal qualities they witness in the woman-becoming: "dancing free," "courageous," "poetic," "swift runner," "compassionate friend," "voice of an angel," etc.

Emerging from the Circle of Women

When the litany has quieted down, these words are spoken:

Leader: *(Name of initiate)*, as you put out this ceremonial fire,

    All: The red flame burns strong in you!

The initiate separates the logs of the fire with the fire poker and douses the flames with the water. The women walk down the luminary path together to join the men and young ones for the final blessing.

A Final Blessing

A Gift From the Men

The initiate's father, grandfather, and/or other male mentor may have a special gift or symbol of womanhood to give the initiate. Before or after this gift-giving, each adult male present places a red rose in a vase and speaks a word of blessing to the honored one.

Musical Improvisation

After the men offer gifts to the woman-becoming, musicians can bring out their chosen instruments, and small percussion instruments can be passed out to others. (If there aren't enough to go around, be creative – wooden blocks and small yogurt containers with beans inside can work well.) At this time, instructions are given for the musical improvisation, described below.

Father or another significant male mentor says:

"(*Name of initiate*), may you always stay true to your own life rhythms, may you always sing to the tune of your own heartsong, may you always speak your truth in love,
and may you walk the journey of womanhood with joy."

The woman-becoming begins to play her instrument. After a time, one more person joins in, then another and another, until all are playing together. Everyone must listen closely for the initiate's lead to play loudly, softly, slowly, quickly. The song continues for a time until the initiate gradually leads the group back into silence. In the silence, the honored one stands to recite an appropriate story, prose piece, or poem (such as my poem "Red River") selected or written by the initiate and memorized for the occasion.

Poem: Red River

Do not ask me to take up this power quietly,
This ripe, red power of womanhood,
Flowing river of creation's delight
Running through my veins.
For, it is life, the very life of life,
Red river of the Spirit's power is
Calling me by name:
"Behold the woman, my beloved,
with whom I am well-pleased."

Conclude the ceremony with a blessing song, such as "Woman Becoming" (page 203) or "Journey Forth" (page 165). The ceremony can be followed by the feast, or if dinner has already been enjoyed, finish off the evening with dessert.

A Journal Journey

When Willa was experiencing all the changes of a woman-becoming, she sometimes found it hard to divulge her inner thoughts and questions to me face-to-face, so she came up with the idea of writing to one another in a spiral notebook we passed back and forth. Many times, the entry was simply a question we'd never asked the other before. Nothing of particular consequence, just something we wondered about the other. Our conversation journal was a fun way to know one another better and share intimate thoughts and feelings.

Such a journal can, of course, include a wide variety of subjects about life, information, personal experiences, opinions, beliefs, etc. You'll want to be clear with one another about how private the journal is and whether or not it's all right to show it to other family members. Agree on a safe place to keep the journal. You may even decide to destroy some pages afterward, if they contain confidential information that you don't choose to share with other family members or friends.

A "Journal Journey" can be an effective way to broach topics around sexuality and sexual intimacy that a parent or youth feels uncomfortable speaking about in person. Somehow, writing in a journal can feel safer than a face-to-face conversation because there's no need to respond immediately and words can be measured more carefully. For example, if a parent wants to begin a conversation with a young person about the joys and challenges of surging hormones and sexual desire, the parent might begin by writing a story or poem in the journal as a conversation starter:

Sexual Desire

This fire in me is beauty and light,
And a mother lode of dynamite.
Will it give birth to love or destroy it?
Will it open the soul or consume it?
Will it be a blessing or a curse?
Will it obliterate or illumine the universe?
This fire in me is beauty and light,
And a mother lode of dynamite.

Along with the poem, a parent might tell a story about a time during their own coming of age when sexual desire felt like a blessing, and another story of a time it felt like a curse. The parent might ask how the young person perceives others acting upon sexual desire in positive or negative ways. The back-and-forth journal conversation can continue with questions, stories, and reflections about aspects of sexuality and sexual desire the young person experiences as pleasurable, confusing, or frightening.

Coming of Age Stories

Another catalyst for sharing thoughts and feelings during puberty is enjoying a great coming of age novel or movie together. Conversing about someone else's coming of age story can dissolve the awkward silence that sometimes builds up between a parent and youth and can prompt the sharing of personal reflections and experiences more freely. Some of my family's favorite coming of age novels about boys include: *The Moves Make the Man* by Bruce Brooks, *Holes* by Louis Sachar, and *Maniac McGee* by Jerry Spinelli. Great coming of age stories about girls include: *Walk Two Moons* by Sharon Creech, *The Music of Dolphins* by Karen Hesse, and *The Diary of Anne Frank*. All of these stories include a sense of mystery and legendary appeal, yet speak to the real obstacles encountered in youthhood. Be sure to choose a book that corresponds with the youth's interests and reading level. Read the book aloud, or silently, chapter by chapter, so you can reflect on the story together as it unfolds.

A coming of age film can also inspire deeper conversation. Some of my family's favorite films about boys coming of age include *Simon Birch* (PG, 1998), *Rudy* (PG, 1993), and *October Sky* (PG, 1999). Enlightening movies about girls coming of age include *Whale Rider* (PG-13, 2003), *Tumbleweeds* (PG-13, 1999), *Little Women* (PG 1994), and *Anne of Green Gables* (Not Rated, 1985). Choose a movie that will speak to the unique joys and challenges of life for a particular youth. Afterward, take time to journal your responses about the film to spark a conversation. Ask yourselves: What character in the movie is most like me? How is my life similar or different from this character's? If I knew this person intimately, what would I want to say to him/her? If I were this person what would I most desire to change about my life? For what would I be most grateful? Of course, the possibilities for reflection are endless.

Thirteen

To be 13 today. What does it mean? What does it mean to be initiated into the "teenage years?" To be sure, the passage of 13 in our culture is a potent status symbol of a young person's growing independence and personal power. It's an age that causes some parents anxiety, others, relief – prompting us to withdraw supervision or tighten our parental grasp in such a way that invites rebellion. Granted, 13 (and the middle school years in general) can be confusing and turbulent for youths and parents alike.

Andrew and I found that when Willa and Morgan were coming into 13, we were called to be ever more vigilant in our parenting. We constantly reassessed the balance between giving Morgan and Willa new freedoms and responsibilities that correlated with their growing maturity and offering firm boundaries and clear expectations. Unsupervised mixers at the homes of friends and proposed trips to hang out at the mall became opportunities for us to practice the push-pull dance of interdependence so common between teenagers and their parents. During this passage, Willa and Morgan learned that we wouldn't be persuaded to change our expectations of them based on what their friends were allowed to do. Andrew and I learned that, no matter how explosive the fireworks became when the answer was an unequivocal "no," Morgan and Willa were often grateful for the boundaries we set. These boundaries allowed them to learn the dance of interdependence not only with *us, as their parents*, but just as importantly, with their *peers*. They came to appreciate having our support when faced with questionable choices and expectations their peers presented to them.

If we look closely at the lives of today's 13-year-olds, we see that they're making wiser choices than teenagers of past generations. According to a recent *Time* magazine report, 13-year-olds today are "less likely to smoke, drink, do drugs, get pregnant, commit a crime or drop out of school than those of their parents' generation . . ." A majority of the 13-year-olds who participated in the *Time* magazine poll that accompanied the report said that sex should be reserved for marriage, and a third of the youths polled didn't even know what oral sex was. A markedly different picture of today's youth than is commonly peddled to us by the media.

No doubt, being thirteen today carries with it unique challenges. The usual identity crisis at thirteen (when a youth tends to have one foot lingering in childhood and the other racing toward adulthood) is exacerbated today by unrealistic, over-sexualized, sophisticated images of teenagers in the media. These images often encourage youths to become fixated on their own self-image and their perceived shortcomings in light of cultural perceptions of beauty, sexuality, popularity, fashion trends, and the latest, coolest consumer products. Thus, 13 is a notorious age for a youth to stand gazing in the mirror. What better time to encourage a young person to look past their own reflection to the landscape of the soul?

Thirteen can be an especially meaningful time for a youth in our culture to celebrate a coming of age initiation. A young person surrounded by elders and loved ones encouraging them on their journey toward adulthood reminds a youth who they are and who they're choosing to become, apart from what pop culture is luring them to be.

The summer after Willa turned 13, we celebrated her woman-becoming ceremony, which was similar to Morgan's (page 174). However, since Willa's menses cycle began when she was ten, her celebration at 13 focused on the goodness of living in a woman's body (particularly as the able dancer Willa had become) and claiming her inner wisdom as a woman. Willa chose five elders, including Andrew, to initiate her. For the ceremony, Willa's five elders each shared a blessing and gifted her with a necklace charm that symbolized the wisdom each elder desired to impart as Willa continued to make her passage into womanhood. Her godmother wrote a song for the occasion ("Circle of Life," page 207) and I wrote and recited for her the poem "Dancin' Feet" to celebrate the awesome way Willa inhabits her female form:

> Girl, you were born with dancin' feet
> Dancin' feet couldn't wait for birth
> Jumped into this world without a fight
> Before we knew you were ours to hold
> You were in our arms dancin'
>
> Girl, you were born with dancin' feet
> Bouncin', jumpin', leapin', Irish dancin' feet
> With the magic o' the fairy child
> You made us believe in the luck o' the green
> You were in our hearts dancin'

Girl, you were born with dancin' feet
Dancin' feet can race the diamond
Fly down the court to the tune of WNBA.
Don't let all that practice
Practice out the dance
In those dancin' feet that fly

Girl, you were born with dancin' feet
An' now that you're a woman
Those feet can talk to the shins
And those shins talk to the thighs
And the thighs to the hips that slide

Hips and shoulders and bosoms collide
Into one talkin', dancin' body
That reminds us every day
You were born with dancin' feet
An' woman – you're forever
Dancin' in our souls

Willa's artistic offering for the ceremony was a dance she choreographed. The five necklace charms she received for her celebration continue to be cherished reminders of her woman-becoming passage and the love and encouragement of her chosen elders.

Honoring the 13-year-old passage doesn't require an elaborate coming of age ceremony or birthday celebration. There are numerous ways to honor a youth's life passage at 13. Even a simple gesture of support at this age can greatly assist the emerging adult in their journey toward maturity. Consider encouraging a 13-year-old with one of the following gestures of honor and affirmation:

- Give a 13-year-old a copy of *Chicken Soup for the Teenage Soul Journal* created by Jack Canfield, Mark Victor Hansen and Kimberly Kirberger. The journal includes numerous journaling and reflection exercises to prompt a teenager to consider their inner life, the movements of their soul, their significant relationships, values, priorities, and the person they're becoming.

- Gift a 13-year-old with prayer tools to inspire explorations of the soul and spirit. On Morgan and Willa's respective thirteenth birthdays, we gifted each of them with a prayer box. Each box contains such prayer tools as an altar cloth, candles and scented matches (with safety guidelines), a blessing bowl, anointing oil, and a prayer journal. Additional prayer tools were added through the years, such as prayer beads, a small tabletop labyrinth (see page 239), a dream journal, etc. Willa and Morgan keep their prayer boxes in their bedrooms and use them to inspire quiet moments of prayer and meditation.

- Affirm a 13-year-old's growing maturity by bestowing a new right or responsibility similar to those listed on page 293. Having one's ears pierced, adding ear piercings, or getting a radical new haircut can also be a dramatic outer sign of the inner changes taking place for the 13-year-old.

- Gift a 13-year-old with poetry, stories, and artistic creations that guide them toward all that is good, hopeful, compassionate, and beautiful in the world. Such poems as "i thank you God" by e.e. cummings, "I Shall Not Live in Vain" by Emily Dickinson, or "Walkers With the Dawn" by Langston Hughes give youths inspiring messages of courage and hope for living in today's complex world.

- Assist a 13-year-old in planning a vision quest that interests them. Traditionally, such "vision quests" (based on Native American traditions) involve a journey alone into the wilderness to receive insights and visions for one's life and purpose in the world. However, a vision quest can come in many forms; it can be experienced alone or in the context of community. There are numerous wilderness survival programs and nature outings planned by professionals for groups of youth to experience together. A sweat lodge or a retreat to deepen one's spiritual connections can also be profound opportunities for a youth to deepen soulful connections. Nature challenges, such as caving, a long-distance hike, whitewater rafting, rock climbing, or camping, can include a quest for personal vision and can be entwined with more reflective moments for prayer, meditation, and visioning. I even know of one 13-year-old with a passion for flying whose family arranged for him to take his first flying lesson on his thirteenth birthday. A vision quest of a different sort, but a vision quest all the same.

- Find out what social, ecological, economic, or political issues are a concern for a 13-year-old, and assist the youth in finding ways to transform these concerns into positive action in their local community or on a larger scale. Share with them stories of youths making a difference in the world, such as the youths honored at "The Brick Awards" (www.dosomething.org) or the youths whose stories are related in the book *It's Our World, Too!* by Phillip Hoose. There's nothing like making a difference to transform a youth's feelings of hopelessness and immobility about the challenges we face in the 21st century.

- Give a 13-year-old a copy of *The Better World Shopping Guide*, by Ellis Jones. This little book grades companies on their social and environmental business practices. Using such a guide in making purchasing decisions with a youth can shed a whole new light on the larger implications of what it means to buy that *one more thing* that we can't live without. It also gives a youth a sense of empowerment that they can affect the world and humanity for good simply by "buying smart."

To be the parent or mentor of a 13-year-old today. What does it mean? It means assisting a youth in discovering hope for the present and faith for the future. It means hallowing out space in our everyday lives where a 13-year-old's soul has room to breathe.

Cultivating a New Vision of Manhood

In our culture, a man's strength is often measured by the size of his biceps or the tires on his pickup truck, among other things. We often measure a man's strength by his athletic prowess, social prestige, political power, business savvy, or monetary worth. Often men measure one another's strength by the perceived beauty of the woman on the other man's arm. Thus, males in our culture tend to place a great deal of energy and interest on navigating the physical, social, economic, and political arenas of their lives. However, these standards of male measurement leave many male youths feeling inadequate as they attempt to live up to the unbalanced, unrealistic images they're sold about what it means to be a "real man." For many boys, every step they take toward "manhood" (as it's defined by our culture) means taking a step away from their emotional, spiritual, and soulful well-being.

Youthhood is a crucial time for strengthening a male's abilities to balance the physical, soulful, and spiritual aspects of life. A youth receiving the affirmation of his most revered male elders and mentors to cultivate his emotional and spiritual life, as well as tending to the more traditionally male aspects of adulthood, can greatly affect a youth's destiny, attitudes, and choices. The following initiation ceremony is one that allows men an opportunity to bestow such an affirmation and to assist a male youth in redefining male strength and the essence of manhood.

In addition to such a ceremony, an initiation celebration for a man-becoming may involve tests of courage and physical prowess, as well as silent interludes for prayer, meditation, and artistic creations. Just as with the initiation celebration for a woman-becoming (page 174), as part of the celebration, you may want to include a blessing conferred exclusively by a young man's significant male elders. Who, more than the men a boy most reveres and admires will he look toward to reveal the path of manhood and teach him what it means to be a man?

A Man-Becoming Ceremony

> **Tools** ∾ For this ceremony, you'll need to gather the youth's significant male elders, mentors, and friends who already made the passage into manhood. Tools include smooth stones and paint pens (or craft paints and brushes) for creating "stones of strength" (see "Preparations" below); the completed stones; a drawstring bag, basket, or small box (for the collection of stones given to the youth); a hand-held instrument for the initiate to play; a blindfold; scissors or an electric razor for cutting hair; a small bowl of ashes (burned from herbs or other dried plant life); a hand drum; a bowl of water for the initiate to wash his face clean; and a towel. Candles or a fire are optional.

Preparations

Before the day of the initiation ceremony, the initiate makes a "stone of strength" for each man invited to the celebration. The stones are smooth enough for a word to be painted on them. The youth chooses the word for each participant that represents what he believes is that man's greatest personal strength, such as wisdom, persistence, love, gentleness, humor, faith, boldness, etc. He paints each word on a stone with paint pens or craft paints.

In the same way, as men arrive for the celebration, each is given an opportunity to create a "stone of strength" for the initiate. The word on the stone reflects the personal quality each man sees in the initiate as his greatest strength.

Seeking Manhood

The men sit in a circle, in silence, meditating and praying for the man-becoming. After the time of silence, the initiate begins to play a hand-held instrument from afar. The instrument can be one that the youth plays proficiently, or a simple percussion instrument like a hand drum or shaker. The initiate makes his way to the gathering of men. When he stands just outside the circle, he stops playing his instrument. The men stand and address the man-becoming in unison:

Men: Who comes seeking manhood?

Man-Becoming: It is I, *(initiate's full given name and/or his symbolic or spiritual name)*. I come seeking manhood.

Men: Look no further. Manhood awaits you here.

Man-Becoming: Where? Where does manhood await me? In this circle of elders and friends?

Men: Here, among men, manhood awaits you – in the only place manhood *can* be found – manhood awaits within you.

The initiate takes his place in the circle and everyone sits.

Claiming Manhood From Within

Story: Samson and Delilah

Before the ceremony, choose an able storyteller in the group to paraphrase the story of Samson and Delilah, as found in the Hebrew scriptures in the book of Judges (16:4-21). Ask the storyteller to commit the story to memory, even if notes are used, so the telling can come to life more easily. Below is a simple version of the story that might be used:

Storyteller:

"Once there was a man named Samson, who was an able warrior. Samson's strength was so great that he could slay whole armies single-handedly. Yet, Samson fell in love with a woman named Delilah who sold Samson out to his enemies. After much persuasion, Samson confided to Delilah the source of his strength, which lay in his hair. After luring Samson to sleep, Delilah had Samson's head shaved and delivered him to his enemies. Samson's eyes were gouged out and he was imprisoned for the rest of his days."

Father, Grandfather, or another elder says:

"To some, the story of Samson and Delilah speaks about the treachery of women and the gullibility of a man who dares to reveal his intimate secrets to the woman he loves. Consider the story in a different light. Consider the story as an allegory for a man who fears all that the feminine traditionally represents: intimacy in relationships, the emotional life, spiritual wisdom, the forces of soul. For men who build up their strength in the physical, practical, external aspects of life, Delilah represents blindness and death because Delilah proved to Samson that his physical strength is fallible and can be taken away.

"(*Name of initiate*), building true strength as a man requires a journey into the dark, unfamiliar places of the soul. It requires a man to sit with his weakness and blindness to find the strength that cannot be taken away from him."

Someone ties a blindfold on the initiate, and the youth is led by one of his elders into a room or outdoor space where his mother or another significant female elder is waiting. The initiate is guided to sit down and, in silence, the woman cuts, trims, or shaves the initiate's head (whatever the initiate has agreed to before the ceremony). Afterwards, the woman stands before the initiate to speak.

Mother, Grandmother, or another significant elder:

"*Son*, your hair is not the source of your strength, nor is any physical part of you. To believe so is to believe a lie. I send you away now, away from childhood, away from the world of women to discover the source of your strength as a man."

The male elder leads the initiate back to the circle of men, and the initiate is seated. An elder brushes the youth's face with the ashes from the bowl, then sets the bowl of water and the towel in front of the man-becoming.

Father, Grandfather or another elder says:

"All growth requires change. All change requires birth. All birth requires death. From ashes to ashes, from dust to dust; the child dies, and the man is born." (Elder removes blindfold and invites the man-becoming to wash his face clean.)

Blessing the Man-Becoming

Song: Strength, You Grow Within Me (page 206)

Strength, you grow within me,
Divine, inspired breath,
More powerful than life's defeats,
And unafraid of death.

Teach me strength in weakness,
Teach me the pow'r of love,
Teach me the might of tenderness,
Teach me what I'm made of.

Still sitting, each man holds the stone of strength he made for the man-becoming in his hand, and, one at a time, each man says:

Speaker: "(Name of initiate), I see your greatest strength as your (personal quality written on the stone)."

Each speaker, if he chooses, can share a brief anecdote about a time he witnessed in the initiate the strength he has named. Afterward, the speaker gives the stone to the initiate, who places it in the bag, basket, or box provided. Once all the stones are given to the initiate, the song of strength is sung again.

Song: Strength, You Grow Within Me (as above)

Gaining Strength for the Journey of Manhood

The initiate stands with the collection of stones he made for all participants. He makes his way around the circle one man at a time, giving each participant the stone of strength made for him.

Initiate: "(Name of man being addressed), as I make my journey into manhood, I'm strengthened by your (personal quality written on stone)."

Commitment to the Journey of Manhood

"Statement of Strength" by Kent Nerburn*

The statement of strength can be led by the initiate (as Leader 1) and an elder of the group (as Leader 2). Leader 1 invites the participants to speak the words, "We must learn to be men" with him each time the leader says, "We are born male." Leader 2 should take time with the reading so its meaning can be easily absorbed.

Leader 1: We are born male.

All: We must learn to be men.

Leader 2: Strength is not force. It is an attribute of the heart. Its opposite is not weakness and fear, but confusion, lack of clarity, and lack of sound intention. If you are able to discern the path with heart and follow it even when at the moment it seems wrong, then and only then are you strong.

Leader 1: We are born male.

All: We must learn to be men.

Leader 2: Remember the words of Tao te Ching. "The only true strength is a strength that people do not fear." Strength based in force is a strength people fear. Strength based in love is a strength people crave.

Leader 1: We are born male.

All: We must learn to be men.

You may want to end the ceremony with a song and a feast prepared by the women and children gathered to celebrate the occasion.

---

* The "Statement of Strength" is excerpted and adapted from *Letters to My Son: A Father's Wisdom on Manhood, Life, and Love* by Kent Nerburn.

Blessing the Journey Into Manhood

After weathering the passage of puberty, my nephew Rion, then fifteen, was initiated with a ceremony that articulated the support of his adult elders as he journeyed into young adulthood. The ceremony reflected Rion's earth-centered spirituality and his love for nature and the great outdoors. Several weeks before the ceremony, Rion was asked to choose an animal as his symbol of empowerment. He chose the symbol of the white wolf – the "pathfinder," "the forerunner of new ideas." He also chose recorded music to include in the ceremony, a poem that he wrote and recited, and a song he played on his recorder. Other aspects of the ceremony were planned by Rion's mom and stepdad, and a small group of family and friends gathered for the following celebration. Each participant was given a speaking part in the ceremony and asked to bring Rion a blessing and/or symbol to share with him as he journeyed into manhood.

Tools ✍ For the ceremony, as written here, the man-becoming prepares ahead of time whatever artistic offerings or spoken reflections he plans to share. You'll also need candles (including a candle to represent the initiate), matches or a candlelighter, any musical instruments used, a sage stick or incense, a small blessing bowl filled with water, a CD player (if recorded music is used), and any written blessings or symbols the participants bring to share with the man-becoming. Chairs or sitting pillows are set in a circle. A seat is placed in the center of the circle for the initiate.

Gathering

While the initiate waits in another room, participants light candles. (The initiate's candle is left unlit.) The lights are dimmed, and participants sit to center themselves. Someone beats a drum in the cadence of a heartbeat to symbolize that the ceremony is a rebirth for the boy coming into manhood. When the initiate hears the drum, he enters the sacred space and stands before those gathered.

Father/Male Mentor:

"Today *Rion* stands before us as the white wolf, the pathfinder of a new generation, a forerunner of new ideas who will return with much to teach and share."

Gratitude for the Four Elements of Being

At Rion's celebration, after he played "Chorale" by Mozart on his recorder, Rion spoke a prayer similar to the one that follows:

To the East: I give thanks for the air that I breathe, for my imagination, and new ideas that illumine my path into manhood!

Turn to the South: I give thanks for the fire and life in me, for my passion, and my will power!

Turn to the West: I give thanks for the waters of the earth, for the blood running through my veins, for my heartsong, my deep love, and my love of the deep!

Turn to the North: I give thanks for the earth that nurtures me, for the bones that carry me and the flesh that gives me form, and for the wonder and mystery of the universe!

Blessing the Circle

Everyone stands in a circle. A grandparent or other elder lights the sage stick or incense and walks counter clockwise around the group three times, while everyone sings:

Song: Circle of Life (page 207)

> I stand as one, yet not alone,
> Here on this earth I call my home,
> The circle of Life I now embrace
> And all who join this sacred space.

Blessings for the Journey Into Manhood

The parent/s lead/s the initiate to the seat of honor in the center of the circle and stand/s before him to speak the following blessing.
  (Revise as necessary.)

Parent/s:

"*Rion*, from your birth *and from our wedding*, we have been here to teach and guide you. Now as you venture into the further reaches of the spiral of Life, we acknowledge that you are increasingly becoming your own guide. We welcome and bless your ancient soul in its new awakenings. We honor you with celebration and love. We embrace you with wisdom and warmth. We watch your journey with open hearts." (The parents return to their place in the circle.)

Someone says:

"Water is a symbol of Life. We come from the waters of the womb. We are nourished and purified by the waters of the earth. Rains feed the foods we eat. Tears wash away our sorrows. The tides keep the rhythms of the earth. *Rion*, as we listen to this song, we meditate on your coming of age. We pray for the rains to sustain you, to purify you for your journey, to guide you, and to remind you of your inner rhythm. We pray for there to be a balance of rain and sun on your journey."

Song: Rain, Rain, Beautiful Rain
by Joseph Shabalala/Ladysmith Black Mambazo*

* This song is from Ladysmith Black Mambazo's *Shaka Zulu* CD.

Someone says:

> "*Rion*, your path is uniquely your own. We are in your life to support and empower you as you create that path. As kindred souls sharing your journey, we now offer you these blessings, symbols and thoughts . . ."

> Each participant, in turn, touches the initiate with water from the blessing bowl and shares with him their blessing and/or symbol.

> When the individual blessings are complete, the initiate lights the candle that represents his life and passage into manhood.

Initiate: (after lighting his candle)

> "This is my vibrant light that shines brightly from within, illuminating the world and all who know me."

The initiate stands in the center of the circle. Participants stand in a circle around him, ready to impart the "Celtic Blessing."

Mother (or other elder) says:

> "*Rion*, though you make this journey into manhood alone, know that we support all that you are and all that you are becoming. This is our blessing upon you. . ."

Celtic Blessing (words in parentheses added by Rebecca Danica)

> (Someone speaks the first line of the blessing. Then, clockwise around the circle, each participant speaks one line at a time to the end.)

> We bathe your palms in showers of wine,
> In the crook of the kindling, in the seven elements,
> In the sap of the tree, in the milk of the honey,

> We place nine pure, choice gifts in your clear beloved face:
>> The gift of form,
>> The gift of voice,
>> The gift of fortune,
>> The gift of goodness,
>> The gift of eminence,
>> The gift of service,
>> The gift of integrity,
>> The gift of true nobility,
>> The gift of apt speech.

(Distant are your travels, unknown those you will meet,
You are the white wolf, going out in courage,
Your heart within your hand, your senses alert.)

You are a shade in the heat,
You are a shelter in the cold,
You are eyes to the blind,
You are a staff to the pilgrim,
You are an island in the sea,
You are a stronghold upon land,
You are a well in the wasteland,
You are healing to the sick.

You are the luck of every joy,
You are the light of the sun's beams,
You are the door of lordly welcome,
You are the pole star of guidance,
You are the step of the roe of the height,
You are the step of the white-faced mare,
You are the grace of the (running wolf),
You are the jewel in each mystery.

(Everyone sits.)

The Initiate Speaks

Initiate's Offering

The man-becoming offers a poem, story, or some other artistic expression about his identity as a man-becoming and what the passage into manhood means for him. He may also use this time to thank those gathered for their presence and support.

Sending Forth

Song: A Young Man's Blessing (page 207)

> We bathe your palms in show'rs of wine,
> Nine pure, choice gifts within you shine,
> The young man journeys forth with grace,
> A life of beauty to embrace.

(Based on "Celtic Blessing," additional lyrics by Shea Darian)

Grandparent (or other elder) says:

"We thank the *Divine Spirit** and the ancestors who guide us. Grateful are we for the elements of earth, water, fire, and air – elements that live in this young man, that give him life and breath, imagination, form, and voice. May he, as we, go to create lives of wonder, reverence, and beauty. We walk with wonder! We walk with reverence! We walk with beauty on the earth!"

After the candles are extinguished, you may want to give the initiate his candle as a gift.

*Insert name for the Divine most meaningful to the youth and those gathered.

Reclaiming a Coming of Age Passage

There comes a time in the parenting journey – and many more than one – when we realize our efforts and sacrifices to *make it right* for our children are every bit as much about healing our own souls as they are about nurturing our children. It isn't that their lives are *about us*, but in the end, we can only impart the goodness, beauty, and wisdom upon our children that we ourselves embody and assimilate.

No matter how dedicated our parents and caregivers were in our younger years, most of us can look back on our own coming of age to find some corner of our soul aching to be healed. Coming of age is a vulnerable time that lends itself to soulful heartache; it's a time when the innocence and protection that once veiled the heart, mind, and soul of the child is irrevocably lifted. The adult-becoming is called upon to further assimilate the learnings of youthhood – to more fully embrace sorrow with joy, cruelty with compassion, death with life, alienation with companionship, and sexual longing with spiritual discovery. As adults in need of healing it isn't only the "child within" who needs our attention and nurture. The *youth and young adult within* also yearn for attention to process old sorrows, assimilate realities of death, heal wounds inflicted by cruelty (our own or that of others), transform experiences of alienation and aloneness, embrace sexuality as a sacred aspect of one's being, and generally assimilate the paradoxes and complexities of our human existence.

The youth within me almost stopped breathing when both of my daughters (who are two years apart) began their menstrual cycles almost simultaneously. Partially, my anxiety was caused by the fact that Willa was only ten when her menarche arrived (the month after her elder sister's cycle began) and came as a complete shock to all of us. Yet, my deeper anxiety came from feeling ill-prepared to lead my daughters through one of the most significant passages of womanhood they would ever experience.

When I began menstruation a month before my 12th birthday, I was delighted by the potent physical sign that I was a woman-becoming. However, there was an intense family silence around menses that suppressed my inner temptation to announce my menarche to the world. I quickly learned to dampen my enthusiasm for this passage. I also learned that the cycle of menstruation my 11-year-old self naively imagined as miraculous and empowering was diminished by the predominant cultural attitude that menses was simply one of the inconvenient bothers of being female.

Fortunately, my mother was attentive to my needs for practical information around this passage, and she seemed pleased that I was experiencing menarche with joy and enthusiasm. However, as a youth, my mom received no female mentoring about her menstrual cycle and was also wounded as a child and youth in regard to her sexuality. At the time of my menarche, my mom was striving to shield me from her ambivalence about my budding womanhood. Her support of me came in the form of being a silent gatekeeper, one who would make sure the obstacles that had barred her passage would not obstruct my own.

When I was in my mid-twenties, my mom finally revealed to me the reasons for her silence during this passage in my life. She told me the story of her own journey into womanhood. After that, instead of feeling deprived by my mother's silence and ambivalence, I was filled with gratitude that, despite her woundedness, she was able and willing to provide for me, during the menarche passage, information and affirmations (albeit, silent ones) that she never received herself.

Just like a spouse, or even a soulmate, a parent can never give us all the nurturing we need. If we're to attain soulful health as adults, at some point we must be willing to seek out the nurturing and attention of the parent within ourselves. We must be willing to take the gifts and challenges bestowed on us by our parents and transform whatever is in need of transforming. My mother did so for me; I, for my children. In so doing, we find healing for our own souls.

In guiding Willa and Morgan through their passage as women-becoming, I dug deep into the well of my own parental wisdom. At times, it was a devastating process, for I was painfully aware that I had no intimate circle of initiated matriarchs in my life to initiate *me* for this passage. Just as my mother had no such circle to initiate *her*, or my grandmother or great-grandmother before her. However, as I began the process of initiating my daughters into womanhood, I discovered that I was being called to an initiation of a different kind – an initiation not simply of the mother and the maiden within me, but of the grandmother, the wisewoman, as well. In the absence of initiated elders, I would need to stand in for my ancestors. Only in embracing the power of the elder within me could I give to my daughters what had been deprived to women in my family for generations.

As I guided Willa's and Morgan's initiations as women-becoming and helped them to gather their circle of elders to bless them, I came to view myself as a *wisewoman-becoming*. To help strengthen and encourage me during this transition, I created a rite of passage to symbolically gather *my* circle of women – women I felt I could trust to see me through this passage. In preparation, I meditated on my life and relationships from my earliest memories to the present. In my contemplations, I identified 14 women (including my mother) who had assisted me and helped guide me through at least one significant life passage. I chose women who shared with me their wisdom, compassion, awareness, and inspiration.

Since my circle of women were scattered from Davidsonville, Maryland to Spokane, Washington, I sent them all a letter of explanation about the passage of womanhood I was experiencing. I included in the letter a request for each woman to send me three items:

A STONE: Since ancient times, placing stones in a circle on the ground has been an act of creating a sacred place for prayer and worship. I ask you to choose a stone for me that represents your wisdom or what you feel is your greatest strength. The stone should be of a size you can hold comfortably in the palm of your hand; it can be store-bought or found in nature. The stone can have a symbol or word painted or etched on it, or not. Once you choose your stone, write for me a brief explanation about what the stone represents in relation to your personal wisdom or strength.

I will use these stones whenever I need to be reminded of your encouragement, love, strength, and wisdom. I will set these stones in a circle to create sacred space for family blessings and rites of passage. I will use them to inspire moments of personal prayer and meditation.

A REMNANT OF CLOTH: The remnant can be a scrap from a home-made garment or craft, or cut from a worn-out piece of clothing. I plan to make a patchwork altar cloth with the remnants.

A BLESSING: Please send me a written blessing to encourage me as I call upon the wisewoman within to help guide my daughters in their passage toward womanhood.

Of course, a man can create a similar rite of passage around male wisdom, inviting significant men in his life to give or send blessings and symbols of wisdom and encouragement, or an adult can gather a sacred circle of elders or companions that includes both men and women. Through the years, stones, remnants, and blessings can be added to the circle as new relationships are cultivated and children grow to adulthood. In fact, adding your child to your sacred circle of adult companions can be a part of their adult rite of passage at 21, or include them at some other significant adult transition. The important thing to remember is that whether or not you were fortunate enough to have a circle of elders to initiate, guide, and encourage you on the path leading toward adulthood, it is never too late to gather a circle of sacred companions to bless your journey.

Some adults choose to gather their sacred circle of elders or companions in the context of their chosen faith. Most religions and spiritual paths have their own coming of age ceremony that involves a spiritual experience, or they honor a vow of commitment (usually when a youth reaches the age of 12, 13, or 14). Although some of these rites of passage are age-related, many faith communities are open to initiating adults through ceremonies that include such rites as baptism, religious instruction and membership, blessings, or celebrating the initiation of a bar/bat mitzvah. Consider the possibilities in your own faith community, and be bold about asking spiritual and religious leaders to help you create rites of passage most meaningful for your unique spiritual journey. An extraordinary example of re-creating adult rites of passage that are relevant to one's faith perspective is Richard Rohr's work to cultivate initiation rites and vision quests for males in our contemporary culture, particularly within the context of the Christian faith community. (See his book *Adam's Return* under "On the Male Journey," page 331.)

Truly, coming of age lessons are lessons we carry with us all the days of our lives, lessons (spoken of in a Yom Kippur prayer) that move us "From offense to forgiveness, from loneliness to love. From joy to gratitude, from pain to compassion. From grief to understanding, from fear to faith." Most of the time, such learnings don't unfold in an especially neat or timely manner; fortunately, the youth and young adult we were can reach through time to remind us that we didn't quite *get it all* back then, that we need to revisit that land of opportunity.

Songs for Celebrating Coming of Age

Woman Becoming

Shea Darian

Wo - man be - com - ing, flo - wer - ing red,

Life___ pour - ing through as the child is

shed,___ Riv - er flow___ ing,

Spi - rit be - stow - ing Wis - dom we

seek_ at the source of all know - ing.

Mensi Com Ni

Words and Music by Rebecca Danica
Arranged by Shea Darian

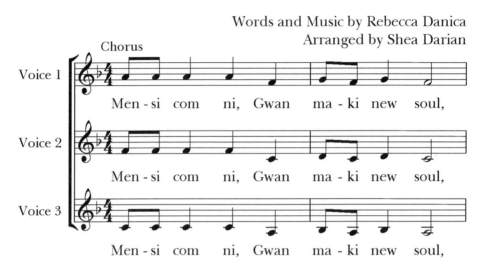

The language of "Mensi Com Ni" is based on a Ghanaian form of Pidgin English. Images for the song are based on the mythology found in the "menstrual blood" section of *The Women's Encyclopedia of Myths and Secrets* by B.G. Walker (Harper & Row, 1983).

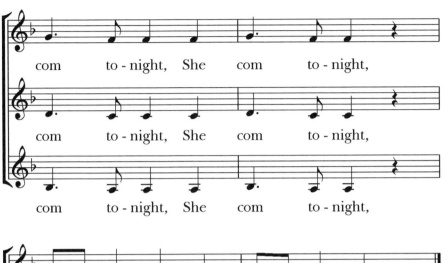

Verses: (sung freely to similar tune)

Hindu: Grat Mother com don, de moon-blood flow, (2x)
We be harmony (2x)/Grat Mother com don . . .

Ashanti: Me Ashanti girl, de mogya com (2x)*
De life, de clan; De life an clan/Me Ashanti girl . . .

Chinese: Chang-O gon to lif in de moon, shine (2x)**
De women dance, O de women dance,
Chang-O gon to lif . . .

* "mogya" means "blood."
** "Chang-o" is a moon-goddess from Chinese mythology.

Strength, You Grow Within Me

May be sung as 2-part
round or canon

Shea Darian

Strength, you grow with - in me, Di -
vine, in - spi - red breath, More po - wer - ful than
life's de - feats and un - a - fraid of death.

Teach me strength in weak - ness,
Teach me the pow'r of love,
Teach me the might of ten - der - ness,
teach me what I'm made of.

Circle of Life

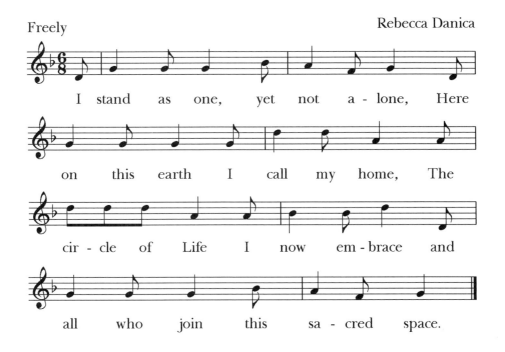

Freely

Rebecca Danica

I stand as one, yet not a - lone, Here

on this earth I call my home, The

cir - cle of Life I now em - brace and

all who join this sa - cred space.

A Young Man's Blessing
(based on "Celtic Blessing," additional lyrics by Shea Darian)

We bathe your palms in show'rs of wine,
Nine pure, choice gifts within you shine,
(The young man)* journeys forth with grace,
A life of beauty to embrace.

* Or, insert "Young woman"

5 ⤻ Fully Growin'
Rites of Passage for the Young Adult

Why stay we on the earth except to grow?

~ Robert Browning

Celebrating Young Adulthood

When I was a child and youth, I fantasized about the moment I'd finally enter the mysterious and legitimizing world of adulthood. I yearned for that moment when I would finally become a bona fide member of the human race.

Despite my youthful naivete, every adult passage that I *thought* would deem me "fully grown" only served to remind me how much I have yet to learn. Slowly, I came to grips with one of the great mysteries of adult maturity: the more an adult grows soulfully and matures inwardly, the more potential one *cultivates* to grow and mature.

From the teenage years to the present – passing my driver's test, graduating from high school, college, and graduate school, getting married, becoming a parent, raising teenagers, helping to care for my father through his death with cancer – I've been continually reminded that there is no such thing as a "fully grown human," and if there is, it's doubtful I should ever earn that honorific title. For, with each life passage that allows me to come of age in one respect or another, I'm invited as an infant into the vulnerability and awe-filled wonder at the core of such life-changing transformations. Finally, I'm learning that the best to which a human being can aspire is not to be a *grown-up*, but simply *to grow*. Perhaps, recognizing this truth is the most significant coming of age passage of all.

If parents, mentors, and elders aren't on a journey of soulful becoming, we have little to teach young adults of today. If there's one thing most young adults can't tolerate, it's elders who aren't striving to walk the talk. Walking the talk of soulful becoming can be an intimidating path because it's one on which we're sometimes forced to give up the illusion of our all-knowing adult identity.

Of all the rites of passage I encountered in my young adulthood, there was none more significant than the day my father and I had our first major conflict since I had moved away from home. I was visiting from college, and my parents and I just ordered lunch at our favorite Mexican restaurant. My dad and I were both onetime competitive athletes, and I was sharing with him the details of an article I had read in my favorite running magazine that spoke of the evolution of the female physique over time. The article asserted that as more women train as competitive athletes, the potential of the female body to build endurance will allow women to improve their distance-running results (over decades) more quickly than men. The scientific research in the article suggested that, in the not-so-distant future, women distance runners will surpass men.

My father had been an avid supporter of my athletic endeavors and did all he could to raise a strong daughter who never doubted her ability to measure up to her male peers and companions, so it was shocking for me to hear the words that came out of my father's mouth next. He looked at me and said, "Now, don't you think you're going a little too far with this *strong woman* stuff." I had no words to reply. My father was the one who inspired me to build up the inner strength that he was suddenly finding intolerable in me. Momentarily, it seemed, he was looking across the table, not at the little girl he loved or the fiery youth he admired, but at the woman who was looking dangerously like his adult equal.

I looked at my father in disbelief for several seconds. Then I got up and walked out of the restaurant without looking back. I walked around for miles, not going anywhere in particular – just allowing the gravity of my father's remark to sink in. And going through the process of deciding that very day that I would allow no man, not even my beloved father, to define how I should express my womanhood.

When I arrived home, well over an hour later, my dad was watching a game on TV, but as soon as I walked in the door, he called to me. He told me sincerely how sorry he was and that his comment was unthoughtful and unnecessary. I accepted his apology, empowered by my father's willingness to speak his mind earlier that afternoon and for the opportunity to walk away – the opportunity to walk alone as I rebirthed a part of myself. I was empowered, as well, by my father's willingness to welcome me when I returned home and for the humility expressed in his apology.

Young adulthood requires a bounty of renegotiation between parent and child. It requires parents to look long and often at our growing edges. When our children learn to drive, we're inspired to be better drivers. When they begin to date, we become more attentive to the prospect of romance in our own life. And as they clarify and articulate the adult they're becoming, they remind us to consider if the adult we are is the adult we are choosing to be.

Rites of Passage for the Young Adult

When young adults come of age in one aspect of their lives or another – when they reach dating age, earn a driver's license, reach legal status, leave home, reach drinking age, have their first intimate sexual encounter, or boldly express values and beliefs that counter our own, we parents often experience a soulful death of sorts. After years of providing protection and guidance, after years of instilling our values and priorities, we're suddenly asked to let go, to trust that all we've given, been, and done for our children is sufficient. This, as much as anything, is what makes the letting go so difficult. We have to believe, despite our foibles and shortcomings as parents and people, despite all we neglected to teach our children through the years, that what we've given them is simply enough. Period. Once we accept what has been, we can move on to parent in the present. We can accept our changing role as the parent of a young adult – a role that not only *asks* us to let go, but *demands* it, whether our children are asking for their independence or not.

Many years ago, a friend of mine died of cancer. She had been the stabilizing center and animating force of her family. Before her death, none of her children seemed to exude my friend's passion, strength or boldness for life. However, in the weeks and months following my friend's funeral, there was a remarkable metamorphosis, as each of her children gradually began to live with the passion, strength, and boldness so characteristic of their mother. This picture imprinted itself deeply upon the psyche and soul of the parent within me. It serves as a poignant reminder that effective parenting is as much about what we *don't do* and what we are *not* for our children as it is about what we do and are for them. Fortunately for these children, they internalized their mother's strengths and capabilities during her life. Her death gave them the opportunity to make them their own.

Dorothy Canfield Fisher once wrote, "A (parent) is not a person to lean on, but a person who makes leaning unnecessary." That doesn't mean a young adult won't want to crawl back into our arms from time to time or ask us to nurture the child or youth still alive and well in their soul. It simply means that we mustn't make our children so dependent upon *our* strengths that they find no need to develop strengths of their own. It also means that we must be prepared for the possibility that our children will emerge as young adults displaying strengths and capacities that *surpass* our own. After all, isn't that the hope of any great teacher?

Entering High School

No doubt the entrance into high school is a significant passage for most young people in our culture today. For some, high school offers the opportunity for achievement and competition in the realms of athletics, arts, and academics. It offers possibilities for social connections and a sense of belonging. For other students, high school is little more than an obligatory inconvenience to fulfill academic requirements placed upon them by their parents or the legal system. Unfortunately, too many high school programs fail to receive students as young adults capable of acting and thinking independently. We do our youths and young adults a great disservice when we require them to attend high school programs that are little more than a holding tank for young people until they reach legal age. In such a situation, educators, administrators, politicians, and parents create an environment for young people that fosters boredom and impotence – the breeding grounds for rites of passage common to these years: drinking, drugs, sex, and dangerous risk-taking behavior. In addition to creating more positive, life-affirming rites of passage to initiate this age group, a sure antidote to curb such behavior is to identify and create high school environments that allow young adults to articulate and assert the sense of personal freedom growing within them.

Fortunately, in addition to holistic private school alternatives, more public school systems are supporting alternative forms of education through providing homeschooling support, funding alternative and specialty schools, and allowing for open enrollment. When Morgan and Willa entered high school, Andrew and I felt it was crucial for them to select their school of choice from the alternatives available, rather than making the choice for them. At one point, Morgan chose to attend a high school that required a thirty minute commute, even though the local public high school was only five minutes away from our home. Later, when Willa and Morgan were in ninth and eleventh grades, they both chose to attend a performing arts charter school for a year. After her freshman year, Willa chose to combine homeschooling courses with courses taken at the local community college, allowing her to finish high school early. For her senior year, Morgan was accepted into an acting program for high school students at North Carolina School of the Arts. Although these educational plans required flexibility and a willingness to think outside the box, they allowed Morgan and Willa to take greater responsibility to make their high school education what they desired it to be.

High School Mentors

The summer before Willa and Morgan each began high school, Andrew and I asked them to identify older adults in their lives who could serve as mentors during their high school years. They each considered adults with whom they were intimate at the time, friends and relatives they thought had something to teach them. Willa chose two mentors with whom she had been intimate most of her life, another who shared her passion for athletics, and one who shared her interest in music. Morgan chose an uncle and aunt as long-distant mentors. She also chose the parents of a dear friend who lived only a few minutes away from our home. These mentors took Morgan on family outings and gifted her with thoughtful reminders of their loving support and presence. Some of Morgan's and Willa's mentoring relationships deepened and continue to thrive, others provided them with occasional moments of insight and encouragement. Most importantly, these relationships fostered intimate friendships and bonds of genuine community across generations.

When Morgan and Willa each chose their potential high school mentors, Andrew and I sent a letter similar to the one that follows:

Dear (*Name of potential mentor/s*),

They say it takes a village to raise a child. We're fortunate to have many friends and relatives who have helped to love and guide our children through the years. As Willa begins high school this fall and steps boldly into the years of young adulthood, we know it's important for her to have other adults she can count on when she needs a voice of reason, a sounding board, or a shoulder to lean on.

Recently, we asked Willa to choose a few other adults in her life to ask to be her mentors during her high school years – adults who can, along with us, help provide her with the love and encouragement she needs. We asked her to choose people she feels are supportive and interested in her life, adults she admires and respects, and from whom she feels she has something to learn. Willa has included you in this small circle of potential mentors. Enclosed is Willa's invitation to you. We ask that you thoughtfully consider her request, and please do not feel obligated if this feels like a burden in any way. Willa will know you still love her.

If you decide to accept this mission, we ask, as your first act of mentorship, that you write out some words of wisdom for Willa about what you think is important for her to contemplate as she enters high school. (You need not write much. A paragraph or two will suffice. Simply speak from your heart.)

We plan to celebrate a blessing ceremony for Willa a day or two before school begins. Mentors who can attend will share their words of wisdom with Willa at the ceremony. Others can send their words to be read to her.

Thank you for considering Willa's request, and for the love and encouragement you impart on Willa's life.

With appreciation, Shea and Andrew

The evening of the blessing ceremony, Andrew and I hosted a dinner at home. After we ate, we moved into the living room, lit a candle, and sang a song of blessing. The ceremony included the written blessings shared by mentors, and the new high school student gave thanks for the guidance the mentors provided and would provide in the future. At Morgan's ceremony, she gave each mentor a stone heart as a symbol of her love and gratitude. We concluded the ceremony by gathering around the new high school student in a circle, touching her gently, and speaking the following blessing in unison:

> May the blessing of God go before you.
> May her grace and peace abound.
> May her Spirit live within you.
> May her love wrap you 'round.
> May her blessing remain with you always.
> May you walk on holy ground.
>
> by Miriam Therese Winter

Adult Risk-Taking

Young adulthood is notorious for risk-taking behavior: fast cars, drinking parties, mailbox bashing, graffiti art, hazings, sex, and (one of my brother's favorites) blowing up chemicals in the basement. We do well as a culture to focus more enthusiastically on risk-taking opportunities for young people that don't involve illegal or questionable behavior. An ability and willingness to take risks isn't just for the deviant or hormone-affected. Taking risks is an essential aspect of a healthy, satisfying adulthood. We parents and mentors do well to affirm and encourage risks that call forth new life-giving capacities in a young adult. We do well to promote risks that are genuinely life-transforming, risks that serve as a catalyst for an intrapersonal death and rebirth. Some young adult passages involve a great degree of inherent risk; for example, a young adult learning to drive or leaving home for the first time. The significance of other young adult passages, such as reaching a particular age related to adulthood or completing a program of study, may be experienced more profoundly by the young adult if the life passage is celebrated in relation to a well-selected personal challenge to overcome.

Physical Risks

Beyond the thrill factor, transformative *physical* risks, in which we place ourselves in situations of real or imagined physical peril, can inspire a humbling recognition of one's mortality and inspire a person not to grasp so tightly to life. Additionally, meeting individual physical challenges successfully brings a sense of heightened independence and freedom. I recently read a newspaper article about a young woman whose rite of passage on her 14th birthday was taking her first solo flight in a Schweizer 232 glider plane. 7,000 feet high, the young paraglider held the control stick between her knees, put her hands behind her head, and belted out Tom Petty's song, "Free Falling," as her parents kept a watchful eye from below. This young woman spoke of being exhilarated by the freedom of the flight and felt empowered by her new independence to fly alone.

Paragliding may not be for everyone, but it's an example of one of the many risk-taking activities that might bring deeper meaning to a young adult rite of passage. Depending on the temperament, personality type, needs, and interests of a young adult, s/he may find one of the following physical risks compelling:

- Participate in a physically and/or emotionally demanding recreational sport, such as parasailing, canoeing, caving/spelunking, hang gliding, rapelling, long-distance hiking or biking, parachuting, rock climbing, zip lining, or whitewater rafting. The sport may require training, preparation, and/or professional supervision. Some of these sports also have age requirements.

- Participate in a demanding individual sport, like track and field or swimming, in which an athlete can compete against their own personal best times and distances. High school track and field programs typically turn no one away, and athletes of all skill levels can usually participate in competitions.

- Participate in a demanding physical activity, like yoga or tai chi, that requires mental focus and connects the body, soul, and spirit.

- A tough challenge in our fast food culture is to transform one's relationship to food by learning about healthy nutrition and creating a healthy eating plan. A young adult might begin by purging their diet of all fried or fast food and/or all soft drinks. When a person makes one change at a time, it's easier to believe that a transformation in diet is possible.

- Commit to a new job or internship, and learn to work with money and care for personal finances.

- Transform a longtime physical fear, such as learning to dance or swim, or learn to enjoy rides at the amusement park that previously brought up only feelings of panic.

In addition to meeting the above challenges solo, taking physical risks with others can be intensely bonding for a group of young adults experiencing a collective rite of passage. Also consider these group challenges:

- Participate in a service project that requires intensive physical labor, like helping to build a house with Habitat for Humanity, sorting food at a food pantry, or working to help rebuild a community recovering from an environmental emergency.

- Participate in advanced cooperative games or a ropes course challenge (with skilled leadership), or participate in a wilderness survival program or vision quest for young adults.

- Imagine the possibilities. . .

Intellectual Risks

When we take *intellectual risks* to question our own long-held beliefs about the world, expand our perceptions, challenge the authorities, or formulate new solutions to social, economic, spiritual, political, or scientific problems, we must die to our fear of being made a fool. Young adults thrive on pushing the intellectual envelope. That's why the most successful academic programs for high school and college students are not based on rote memorization of facts, but are those that encourage young adults to foster an attitude of inquiry and expansive thinking.

Isaac Asimov once said, "The most exciting phrase to hear in science, the one that heralds new discoveries, is not 'Eureka' but 'That's funny. . .'" Whenever a young adult is motivated to explore a particular subject or aspect of life, we do well to tune into the young person's curiosity, doubt, speculation, concern, and sense of awe and wonder because these particular responses are the most effective hooks to pull a young adult into intellectual exploration and risk-taking.

One of the most potent tools to inspire such intellectual exploration is to expose young adults to great risk-takers who made a difference in relation to the subject at hand. Consider the biographies of people who questioned what is, in order to formulate new theories and realities: Galileo, daring to develop the first telescope that changed the way people see the universe, or Sojourner Truth, who devised a foolproof system for returning to the South again and again to rescue thousands of people from slavery. In music, think of Mozart, who popularized the piano concerto. In dance, consider the startling contemporary innovations of choreographer Martha Graham. In the world of athletics, think of Dick Fosbury, who, in the 1968 Olympics won a gold medal in the high jump, utilizing a new jumping technique he developed that remains the dominant technique used in high jumping today. All new ideas, inventions, and artistic styles are created by people who are willing to think outside the box, to see what others do not see, to hear what others do not hear, to use the imagination as well as the intellect. In some ways, the great intellectual thinkers are the ones who are able to see some aspect of the world with the eyes of a child, as if everything is new. Albert Einstein explains:

> I sometimes ask myself how it came about that I was the one
> to develop the theory of relativity. The reason, I think, is
> that a normal adult never stops to think about problems of

space and time. These are things which (the adult) has thought about as a child. But my intellectual development was retarded, as a result of which I began to wonder about space and time only when I had already grown up.

Yes, Einstein was grown up, but also growing. He was willing to stretch his imagination and intellect to draw a circle around himself and find the hundreds of things right in that circle that he had never seen before. Many times, that ability is the most distinguishing quality of those we call genius.

A young adult need not develop the theory of relativity to be an able intellectual risk-taker. Intellectual risks may lead a young adult to discover a personal technique or method that allows them to improve performance in their chosen sport or art, or grasp a deeper understanding of an academic subject. Taking intellectual risks may even give a young adult a connection to an aspect of life they never imagined would be a priority until they were prompted to face the confines of a problem obstructing their path. Consider Norvelle Smith, a young woman highlighted in the book *It's Our World, Too!* by Phillip Hoose. When faced with the pressure of joining a gang that controlled her Southside Chicago neighborhood, Norvelle was prompted not only to take a stand against gangs as a speaker in the Chicago school system, but also to organize a team of youths in grade school through high school to speak to other students about the advantages of a gang-free life. Norvelle used her mind and imagination to meet the problem in a new way, and her willingness to think outside the box has positively affected the lives of thousands. Affecting positive change can be a profound rite of passage for a young person.

As parents, teachers, and mentors we're called to help young adults utilize their imaginations in addressing the unique problems they face in their immediate environments, whether these problems are social, economic, political, scientific, artistic, creative, or spiritual. We're not called to be authorities that impart information upon young adults today. We're called to inspire them to boldly express their curiosity, doubt, concern, speculation, and sense of awe and wonder about any aspect of life they find especially compelling to consider. We're called to remove the intellectual straight jackets too often given to our young adults when they enter the doors of our formalized education system and to give them, instead, our blessing to discover what we ourselves do not know to teach them.

Emotional & Social Risks

When we take *emotional risks* to share our feelings and take responsibility to create mutual, caring relationships, we die to the idea that each of us is an island, fully self-sufficient and alone. When we take *social risks* to reveal our individual uniqueness or speak as a minority voice, we learn to die to our fears of rejection and alienation. When parents, teachers, and mentors take time to cultivate healthy communication and share emotions in an environment of compassion and safety, young adults are encouraged to gather the tools they need to navigate their emotional and social landscapes.

Erin Gruwell, the Long Beach, California high school teacher depicted in the 2007 film *The Freedom Writers* is a model of emotional and social risk-taking. As a 23-year-old novice, Erin challenged her "unteachable," "at risk," ethnically-diverse high school students to take emotional risks on a daily basis. She challenged her students' own racist attitudes. She gave them an opportunity to reveal their prejudices, yearnings, and life experiences in a personal writing journal she provided for them. In classroom conversations, Erin encouraged the students to express their emotions about racism and articulate the injustices they were experiencing in their daily lives. Simultaneously, she prompted her students to wrap their minds around the racism and injustice of the Holocaust, a historical event of which most of the students were previously unaware. A field trip was planned to the Museum of Tolerance in Los Angeles. Erin planned a dinner for the students to meet and speak with Holocaust survivors. The students raised money to fund a visit by Miep Gies, the woman who helped to hide Anne Frank and her family during World War II. What a profound young adult rite of passage for this teacher and her students – students who were previously not expected to finish high school! Yet, because of the sense of community these students and their teacher were able and willing to build together, many of the students were encouraged not only to finish high school, but to go on to college and careers they never imagined for themselves – until they met Erin Gruwell. This classroom biography demonstrates what can happen when young adults are empowered to create a safe community where they can take emotional risks, challenge the status quo, commit to personal visions of growth and change, and create caring relationships that transform prejudice and intolerance.

Most young adults, regardless of background or life circumstances, crave authentic community beyond their own family circle in which they feel accepted, valued, and can freely process their emotional lives. At the suburban high school Morgan attended in ninth and tenth grades, a group of courageous students began a support network for gays, lesbians, and bisexuals. Some of the most dedicated advocates of the group were heterosexual students taking a stand for their peers – to heighten awareness and sensitivity and advocate for the acceptance of homosexuals and bisexuals as respected members of their high school community.

Everyone needs a place to belong, a place where a person doesn't have to justify their identity and being. Parents, teachers, and mentors do well to support young adults in their quest to build an authentic community in which diversity is not only tolerated, but encouraged. Participating in such a community is the foundation for learning the art of deep listening and cultivating an ability to articulate the movements of one's own heart, mind, and soul.

The list of emotional and social risks (on pages 222-225) is far from complete. Allow these ideas to be catalysts for imagining activities and exercises most appropriate for the young adults with whom you live and work. Remember, young adults who aren't used to disclosing emotional information or sharing their inner life with others may need to be encouraged gently. That's why Erin Gruwell's original tactics with the Freedom Writers were, simply, ingenious. Erin began the process of disclosure by having the students write in a private journal that they were not required to allow her to read. Sometimes, just the process of articulating our thoughts and feelings to *ourselves* (in words we can see and read) prepares us to share our inner lives with others more freely. Similarly, a "line game" Erin played with the students required nothing more from them than stepping onto a line taped across the classroom floor. She began with low-risk statements, such as "Step on the line if you have the CD by. . . ," and worked up to more risky statements, such as "Step on the line if you've lost a friend or relative to gang violence." The game was a first step in building intimate community and recognizing that, despite their ethnic diversity, the students were not so different from one another after all.

The Examen: The "examen" is a practice clearly described in the book, *Sleeping With Bread*, by Dennis, Sheila, and Matthew Linn. Examen means "to examine one's conscience" or "to bring out into the open one's inner reflections." This simple practice involves lighting a candle and reflecting on two questions: For what moment today am I most grateful, and for what moment today am I least grateful? Feel free to adapt these questions, perhaps phrasing the first question as "what is the greatest joy in my life," "where do I feel the greatest sense of belonging," or "when did I give and receive the most love today?" The second question might be phrased as "what is my greatest struggle" or "what causes me to feel sad, helpless, lonely, or angry?" The examen can be used to reflect on the day, week, or year. It can also be used as a onetime reflection to consider the gifts and challenges of a particular experience: upon returning from a trip, reflecting on a collective group experience, at the end of a program of study, or reflecting on one's entire life journey. In large groups, when time allows, everyone can be given a few minutes to share with the entire group, or the group can break into dyads or trios for sharing when time is short.

Ins & Outs: In my work with young adults, the following self-disclosure exercise is a favorite. Each participant is given a large brown paper bag, old magazines, scissors, and gluesticks. Participants are asked to reflect on the similarities and contrasts of their inner and outer lives. On the outside of their paper bag, each participant glues pictures, words, and phrases from the magazines to create a collage of the ways they appear to others on the outside (in their public life). On the inside of the bag, the young adults place pictures, words, and phrases that reflect who they are on the inside – the aspects of their lives they keep hidden or, generally, choose not to share with others. Participants can share reflections about their creation within the family circle, in dyads, or in a large group setting.

Jump-start: To inspire journal entries and/or focus a conversation, offer a prompt in the form of a question: What is my greatest fear? Who am I? What do others think of me? What do I think of myself? What causes me to be embarrassed or ashamed? What brings me the greatest joy? What is my greatest (scariest, most embarrassing, saddest, or worst) memory? Who is the person I most admire and why? Who is the person who has inflicted the greatest harm on my life? Who is the person I know I can always count on? What do I envision for my future? What beliefs, if any, do I hold sacred? What makes it easy for me to hate someone? Why do people hurt those they love? Why is it so hard to forgive? What is it like to be dead? What gives me the greatest sense of purpose in my life? With whom or where do I feel the greatest sense of belonging? What do I worry about most? How will my life make a difference? Pose any question that arises out of a young adult's life experience or ask a group of young adults to brainstorm the question "What are my biggest questions about life?" Make a composite list, cut up the questions, and draw one from a hat.

Listening 101: The art of listening is a much needed skill in our families and communities. Parents, grandparents, teachers, and mentors do well to practice artful listening with young adults. Such a practice gives a young adult the message that we're interested in their life and reflections and allows a young adult to internalize a model of communication that leads to genuine conversation. One simple listening exercise involves participants reflecting on a question about themselves, then breaking into dyads. One member of the dyad shares about themselves while the other listens attentively without interrupting. After the speaker finishes, the listener reflects back what they heard, to see if what they heard is what the speaker intended to communicate. Another way to focus as a listener is to listen to the speaker without saying a word. Then, when the speaker finishes talking, write down two or three questions that come to mind to clarify what the speaker was attempting to share. In conversation, many of us have a tendency to be thinking of what we'll say next rather than focusing on the person who's speaking. This is especially true in conflict situations, so these basic listening exercises are indispensable in resolving conflicts. When there's a conflict at our house, everyone involved has an opportunity to tell their side of the story, uninterrupted. When each person is finished speaking, other family members reflect back what they heard and ask questions of clarification. Sometimes, being heard is all one needs to see a situation more clearly and have more grace while listening to the perspective and reflections of the other person.

Talking Stick: This Native American tradition can be used to foster attentive listening and valuing the spoken words and wisdom of each family member or group participant. A stick (or any small object) is passed around the circle. Whoever holds the object is the only one allowed to speak. Others give the holder of the object their undivided attention.

Circle Prayer: In my work in spiritual settings, I've been awed by the intimacy and compassion that results from one simple practice at the beginning or end of a group meeting or performing arts rehearsal. The practice is simply to stand in a circle and ask people to share any concerns or joys they have that they want to ask the group to hold with them in prayer. Afterward, one person in the circle begins a "circle prayer," speaking a few sentences. When the speaker is finished, s/he gently squeezes the hand of the person on their right or left. If that person wishes to pray aloud, they do so. Those who don't wish to pray aloud squeeze the person's hand next to them, and the prayer continues around the circle. In a secular setting, participants can share concerns and joys aloud, then honor a moment of silence for people to pray or reflect in their own way.

The following affirmation games, "Love Notes" and "Imagine," work best after a group has time and opportunity to build up intimacy and trust.

Love Notes: Tape a sheet of paper to each person's back. Ask each family or group member to write a sentence or two on each person's sheet of paper, revealing what they most love or admire about the person. When everyone is finished, participants can read their affirmations silently or aloud.

Imagine: This affirmation game is one I learned in my high school Interpersonal Communications class. The game is played by sitting in a circle and asking participants to reflect on the personal strengths of each of the other group members. Before group sharing, each person fills out a sheet that includes such prompts as:

- If I were stranded on a desert island, I would want to be stranded with (*group member's name*).

- If I had a secret I wanted to entrust with someone, I would tell (*group member's name*).

- If I had a conflict to solve, I would ask for (*group member's name*) to help me think it through.

For the above section, participants use each group member's name only once. The second section of the written responses includes such prompts as:

- Ten years from now, (*group member's name*) will be working as a. . .

- If (*group member's name*) was a place (movie, book, car, color, or whatever), s/he would be. . ."

In the large group, participants share their responses and what thinking, feelings, or perceptions went into each choice. This affirmation exercise gives each participant a clear sense of the personal qualities and strengths that others perceive in them.

Whenever sharing intimate reflections and personal information, make it clear that each participant need only share what they feel comfortable sharing. Also, create a verbal or written covenant with one another to clarify that "what is spoken in the group stays in the group." Some of the visioning and self-knowledge exercises in the "Soulful and Spiritual Risks" section on the following pages can also be shared in a community setting.

Soulful & Spiritual Risks

When we take *soulful* risks to explore the relationship between physical and spiritual realities, create art, cultivate intuition, and explore the terrain of our inner selves, we die to the notion that what is real can only be seen with the eye and understood with the mind. Young adulthood can be a significant time for a young person to acquire tools for seeking vision and soulful guidance. Activities that nourish and refresh the body, soul, and spirit can be key for reducing stress and finding balance as young adults meet the intellectual, social, emotional, and physical demands of their lives. The soulful refreshment most meaningful to a young adult will depend upon their spiritual perspective and religious beliefs, as well as their temperament, personality type, and ways of being and relating to others and their environment. The possibilities are plentiful:

- learning a form of meditation or centering prayer; setting up a personal prayer/meditation altar, or identifying a sanctuary, chapel, synagogue, or place in nature to pray, meditate, and contemplate

- creating a personal creed: "Ten Rules to Live By"

- writing out a vision for one's future, writing in the present tense as if the vision has already been actualized (page 262-265)

- taking a class in yoga or tai chi

- creating a dream journal

- creating art that reflects one's identity, desires, visions, and longings

- creating a list of "100 things to do before I die" and committing to do one or two of these in the coming year

- attending a silent Quaker meeting or a Taize prayer service (which also honors periods of silent meditation), or participating in a weekend retreat that focuses on solitude and silence

- walking a labyrinth – an ancient walking prayer/meditation form; indoor and outdoor labyrinths are becoming more popular. (Check the internet to find a labyrinth in your area.)

- learning to knit, sculpt pottery, paint, or engage in some other relaxing craft or art form

- participating in a sweat lodge

- dedicating at least 10 minutes a day to sit quietly and do nothing more than stargaze, cloudgaze, moonbathe, or lie on the ground and look up through the branches of a tree

- making or purchasing a greeting card with an inspired message or picture on the front and writing in it words of wisdom to oneself – whatever wisdom is most needed at the time; the envelope is addressed to the writer and given to a friend or relative who mails the card on a random date between three to eight weeks later

- scheduling a monthly meeting with a spiritual director or life coach

- going on a long-distance journey by oneself for the first time, which, of course, involves physical, emotional, social, intellectual, and soulful challenges – a total risk-taking adventure. . .

Each of us has our own unique appetite and tolerance for taking particular kinds of risks, which may or may not correlate with our public persona. The big, tough football player may be an awesome emotional risk-taker, while the sensitive poet may be the first to volunteer for bungee jumping. It's helpful to identify the risks we're most comfortable taking; our areas of greatest comfort may be a good place to start challenging ourselves to take more daring risks. However, committing to occasional risks in areas of our greatest *discomfort* can be especially life-transforming. Parents, teachers, and mentors do well to encourage young adults to challenge themselves to take risks in areas where growth is most needed. Those who are not enthusiastic risk-takers in a particular area may do well to begin with an activity they consider a mild-to-medium risk. More seasoned risk-takers can choose an activity that gets the adrenaline going. *For all activities that require professional supervision or expertise, make sure to do your homework. A qualified, knowledgeable leader is essential for ensuring the success of a risk-taking experience.*

Dating & Romance

In North American culture, the Hispanic Quinceanera celebration for 15-year-old females and the Sweet Sixteen ceremony have traditionally been the more formal rites of passage to announce a young person's readiness for dating. Although the Quinceanera celebration continues to thrive, most Sweet Sixteen celebrations are less about one's readiness for romantic relationships and more about earning one's driver's license. This may be due to more parents allowing young people to date before their 16th birthday. Dating is an adult status symbol that many parents want for their offspring. In my work with young people, I often witness parents becoming overly invested in the idea that a young person's life is not complete unless they have a romantic friend. One parent I know started setting up one-on-one, unchaperoned "dates" for her daughter at the age of twelve. Granted, the dates were always at public places like the bowling alley or skating rink, but I puzzled over what benefit these dates served for the youth or her mother.

For youths to grow into young adults who are clear-thinking romantic partners, it's helpful for them to receive clear guidance through the years. Setting clear, age-appropriate boundaries for youths gives them a foundation for creating boundaries for themselves as they mature into adulthood. Parents do well to create a clear plan for dating expectations early on. When Willa and Morgan began middle school, we allowed them to meet their friends at school dances and other public social events. We also allowed them to invite "boyfriends" to share family time in which we interacted with them and could get to know the boys they brought home.

In seventh and eighth grades, Willa attended a middle school where she was originally taken in by a group of friends who were considered to be the *popular* crowd. Many of these middle schoolers hosted parties and mixers at their homes with little adult supervision. After it became clear that Willa wasn't allowed to attend these social gatherings and had parents who were invested in knowing Willa's friends and what they were up to in their spare time, many of Willa's friendships, including her romantic interests, went cold. No doubt, it was a difficult time of discernment, and Willa sometimes struggled in her quest for friendship and camaraderie. For awhile, she had to pull her self-esteem up by the bootstraps. However, because Willa also had the invested interest and support of her family, this passage gave her the opportunity to develop an ability to be herself and choose wisely in the face of peer pressure and misguided expectations. During eighth grade, Willa's principal told me that Willa was one of the most humbly confident and self-assured middle schoolers she had ever known. I have little doubt that the social trials Willa survived during these years strengthened her social gesture as a compassionate, clear-thinking, down-to-earth, "what you see is what you get" young adult.

In ninth grade, Morgan and Willa were allowed to go on group dates with friends – to the movie, bowling alley, dinner, school dances, etc. Of course, parents or some other trusted driver served as taxi. We allowed Morgan and Willa to go on individual dates at 16, and were poised to throw a festive Sweet Sixteen party to honor the occasion. Interestingly, by the time their respective 16th birthdays arrived, dating was low on each of their priority lists. Although they each had "romantic interests" throughout middle school and Willa had an extended romantic relationship as a freshman, by the time they each reached dating age, they chose to cultivate platonic friendships for the duration of high school so they could more easily focus their time and energy on the artistic passions they desired to pursue – acting, singing, and dance. Ultimately, Willa and Morgan chose not to celebrate their sixteenth birthdays with a party. They each valued our family birthday celebration and considered that to be celebration enough. So, we found other ways to honor their clarity and personal choices about romance and dating as young adults.

A cherished 16th birthday tradition that Andrew and I borrowed from my eldest brother's family was giving Willa and Morgan a "promise ring" as a birthday gift. The ring represents a promise the young adult makes to themselves to stay true to their values and beliefs in creating healthy romantic relationships; it reminds them to set clear boundaries and expectations with romantic partners. For this rite of passage, you may want to invite the young adult on a shopping excursion to choose just the right ring for themselves, or enlist an artisan who makes jewelry to create a special ring for the occasion and allow the young adult to help design it.

As an aspiring actor, Morgan clarified early on that romance comes second to pursuing her passions in the world. For a time, Morgan's unusual clarity about refraining from participating in the dating scene as a high school student caused her to feel like a fish out of water, such a different breed from her high school friends. As a gesture of support, when Morgan was 16, I wrote her the following poem on Valentine's Day:

> Put love away for another day, I say,
> Too much to be, too much to do.
>
> No man can keep me from my dreams,
> It's true, I'm so much more than
> A date to the prom.
>
> See that ring on my hand?
> A simple band, but no less than
> A promise to myself.
>
> No one told me it would be this hard.
> Commitments always are.
>
> It's not about keeping *him*
> from stealing my dreams.
> It's about me loving me.
>
> Just the way I am.

Of course, now as Morgan enters her twenties, she's striving to reconcile her artistic passions with her desire to cultivate romantic friendships. For Andrew and me, as parents, this cycle requires us to be vigilant in a different capacity. We continue to make it a habit to know the young men spending time with our daughters. Though we trust Morgan and Willa to make healthy choices and set clear boundaries with the young men they date, we continue to dialogue with them (from the perspective of our own hard-learned wisdom) about what it means to cultivate compassionate romantic partnerships. The promise ring they each wear is a reminder to be true to themselves. Moreover, they have parents who consistently remind them to seek clarity about their own sexual boundaries and expectations so they can clearly communicate them to the young men they date.

Initiating the New Driver

What rite of passage do most young adults anticipate more eagerly than earning a driver's license? Earning the right to drive at 16 may well be the most significant cultural rite of passage bestowed in the years of young adulthood. Given the potency of this passage and the freedom and risk factors involved, it's a passage that requires intention and thoughtfulness. Young adults and their parents do well to consider ideal timing for a young person to acquire their driver's permit, receive quality driving instruction, and earn that coveted card that gives them the right to join the great community of motor vehicle operators.

One young person I know was only given the privilege of earning a driver's license by his parents after he became more responsible with other expectations they had for him, like completing his homework on time, fulfilling household chores on a daily basis, and making enough income to pay for gas and partial insurance payments on the family car. His mother told me she didn't care when he earned his driver's license, but she did care about her son earning the right *as a privilege* bestowed in relation to his growing maturity. Just because a young person is *legally* able to earn a driver's license at 16 doesn't mean that parents and teenagers have to abide by the cultural norm. Discerning when a young person is ready for this rite of passage can be a collaborative effort between the young person and their parent/s.

Because we lived in one of the accident capitals of the U.S. (Phoenix, Arizona) when Willa was learning to drive, she chose to postpone earning her driver's license for an extra six months. Andrew and I offered to pay for Willa to attend a driver's training course run by off-duty police officers. The course was excellent and allowed Willa to learn to drive in a much more relaxed atmosphere than Andrew or I tended to create for her with our well-meaning but overzealous, instructive banter. Willa passed her driving test with a perfect score and is now probably the best driver in the family.

To honor Willa's accomplishment and initiate her for this transformative adult passage, we enjoyed a family dinner and celebrated the following ceremony for the new driver:

> **Tools** ⤜ For this ceremony, you'll need the initiate's driver's license, a copy of the "Driver's Oath" to sign (page 234), a pen, and symbolic and practical gifts to be given to the new driver. For our ceremony, the gifts we chose were a car key and key chain; a mini copy of the driving oath to place in the car as a visual reminder; a laminated map, erasable pen, and car compass; a visor clip; a card printed with the "Meditation for the Driver" (page 235); and a scenic picture and map to a surprise destination.

Acknowledging the Accomplishment

Song: Be Like A Bird words by Victor Hugo (revised)*

> Be like a bird, who, halting in *her* flight,
> On a limb too slight, feels it give way beneath *her*,
> Yet, sings, sings, knowing *she* has wings,
> Yet, sings, sings, knowing *she* has wings.

Reflections on Earning A Driver's License

The following spoken reflections can be divided among speakers, as written below, or spoken by one person. With multiple speakers, each one holds the driver's license and passes it around the circle to the next speaker. *As always, rewrite the following words for the young adult being initiated.*

A parent or grandparent reflects on the initiate's journey:

"Willa, not so long ago, you burst into our lives – even before the midwife could arrive. Soon, we were steadying you to walk for the first time, then protecting you from all the objects that got in the way of your speedy path, because before we could blink an eye, you had already learned to run! Then, it was mile-high tire swings by the age of 18 months, roller coasters at four, and "The Big Drop" at ten. (Even though you were throwing up from the teacup ride, you insisted on going — twice!) Since the day you were born, you've been our tiny, fiery adventurer. Tiny in stature, massive in spirit."

*The music for "Be Like a Bird" is available in the songbook and CD, *Fire Within*, by the women's world music ensemble, Libana (www.libana.com).

Someone says:

"Willa, that's why we're so impressed with the way you've chosen to come to this significant passage. You've been clear and intentional about choosing the time to earn your driver's license. You didn't pursue it until you knew you were ready. You've been fully committed to learning what you needed to know to make this passage possible. And now, finally, after months of reflection and learning, you've done it!"

Someone says:

"It's only a piece of paper and plastic, but it bears your name and image, a part of your identity. More than paper and plastic, it's a symbol of maturity, a symbol of freedom and independence, a symbol of responsibility and privilege, and yes, a symbol of adventure."

Commitment to Responsible Driving

Words of Commitment & Support

Elder: (*Name of initiate*), as you receive this driver's license, do you accept the responsibility of driving as a privilege not to be taken for granted?

Initiate: Yes, I do.

Elder: As you receive this driver's license, do you acknowledge your readiness to be an independent driver?

Initiate: Yes, I do.

Elder: (*Name of initiate*), we support your decision to accept the responsibility and freedom of driving. We celebrate with you in this new adventure.

The initiate is given the new driver's license and invited to share the driver's oath.

Driver's Oath

Initiate: As I, *(initiate's full name)*, accept the privilege and
responsibility of driving:

- I promise to get behind the wheel only when my mind is clear and my feelings are composed.

- I promise to uphold, to the best of my ability, all safety guidelines for myself, my passengers, and other co-travelers.

- I promise not to talk on my cell phone while I'm driving.

- I promise to maintain the vehicle I drive by learning basic car care (including changing a tire), keeping the vehicle clean inside and out, and always making sure my insurance coverage is sufficient and up-to-date.

- When appropriate and safe, I promise to practice random acts of kindness toward my co-travelers and yield to pedestrians, bikers, cyclists, and animals safely and courteously.

- I promise to keep my feelings "in check" when other drivers make rude or unsafe choices; I will choose not to retaliate, but will compensate for their behavior to the best of my ability.

- I promise to know directions to my destination before I begin my travels and to leave with plenty of time to spare. When I'm running late, I'll sacrifice timeliness for the sake of safety, and, whenever possible, I'll call to let others know I'll be late.

- I promise to ride as a passenger only with conscientious and responsible drivers. I will voice my concerns about any unsafe driving choices a driver is making. If my concerns are ignored or dismissed and I feel unsafe as a passenger in the vehicle, I will call to get an alternate ride from a trusted family member or friend.

- Finally, I promise to celebrate driving as a rite of passage that affirms my growing independence and freedom as an adult member of this family and the larger world community.

(Willa signs and dates her copy, and witnesses sign.)

Blessing the New Driver

Meditation for the Driver

The new driver is given the following meditation on a card which can later be clipped to the car visor. Participants are invited to close their eyes, take a relaxing breath, and envision the initiate being filled with the qualities named in the verse. The initiate speaks one line of the verse at a time, followed by moments of silent contemplation:

> My mind is filled with Peace,
> My seeing is filled with Clarity,
> My heart is filled with Compassion,
> My whole body, my hands, my feet
> are filled with Right Action.

After the final silent interlude, the new driver repeats the verse in its entirety (without the pauses).

Five Gifts for the New Driver

Speaker: "(*Name of initiate*), to bless your driving journeys, we give you five gifts:"

Gift-giver: "We bless you with the gift of *adventure and freedom.*"

The new driver is given a car key and key chain. (At our ceremony, we gave Willa a key to one of the family cars she was allowed to drive, with the understanding that driving times would need to be negotiated with other family members.)

Gift-giver: "We bless you with the gift of *clarity and wisdom.*"

The new driver is given a miniature copy of the driving oath to keep in the car as a visual reminder of her/his commitment.

Gift-giver: "We bless you with the gift of *purpose and direction.*"

The new driver is given a laminated map, erasable pen, and compass.

Gift-giver: "We bless you with the gift of *Divine protection.*"

The new driver is given a visor clip of an angel or other symbol of protection.

Gift-giver: "We bless you with the gift of *beauty and delight*."

The new driver is given a picture of a scenic destination planned for a surprise family road trip and a map to plan the route. The destination can be local or long distance (depending on family travel plans), and the new driver can do some or all of the driving.

Song: Safe Travels (page 266)

Great blessings we impart on body, mind, and heart,
We bless you with great patience when the road is slow,
We bless you with compassion, safe travels and good journeys,
We bless you with great wisdom wherever you go.

Final Blessing

(Give out speaker numbers for the final blessing before the ceremony or rotate speakers around the circle.)

All: (*Full name of initiate*),
may the *Divine Protector** bless your journey with:

Speaker 1: adventure,

Speaker 2: freedom,

Speaker 3: purpose,

Speaker 4: direction,

Speaker 5: clarity,

Speaker 6: and wisdom.

All: May the *Divine Protector** bless your journey
with beauty and love.

*Insert the name for the Divine most meaningful to the young adult being honored.

Is There Life After High School?

Having been through the high school years with both of my children, I have a new appreciation for the stress and challenges the last few years of high school conjure up for young adults today. The montage of stresses include deciding whether one will attend college and, if so, sifting through myriad options to choose the *right* college or university; working to save money for college or living on one's own; identifying a career path; taking and retaking the ultimate in standardized tests – the SAT and ACT; filling out college applications and writing college entrance essays; applying for grants and financial aid; differentiating one's own preferences and passions from the expectations of family members, friends, teachers, and mentors; stretching time between academics, work, social relationships, family, and extracurricular activities, as well as squeezing in time for eating and sleeping. . . It's enough to push a young adult into an abyss of stress, depression, or immobilizing confusion! Perhaps the best we can do at this time in a young adult's life is to give them *a lot* of elbow room and some tools of discernment:

- Help a young adult to identify a trusted counselor, mentor, or spiritual director (other than a parent or close relative or friend) who can help the young adult sort through their own feelings and thoughts about their decisions concerning *life after high school.*

- Give the young adult a journal to record their thoughts and feelings about life after high school. Encourage them to write about various options (and the pros and cons of each), pressures they feel, what brings them the most joy in life, their ideal vision of life as an adult person, what they want to say to those who may be disappointed or angry if they make a choice that isn't *acceptable,* or whatever feelings or reflections arise.

- Help a young adult to identify choices that may not be immediately apparent, such as taking a year off after high school to work close to home, utilizing the time to clarify visions and desires and means to achieve them. Recognize together that there are numerous people who are happy and successful who *did* or *did not* attend college. If it's appropriate, given a young adult's desires, encourage them to look into short-term training programs, apprenticeships, internships, or hands-on opportunities in their field of interest.

- Help a young adult to identify ways to reduce stress. Encourage an overly responsible young adult to make *play* the rule rather than the exception. Assist a forgetful young adult to learn to organize the details of life that require time and attention (so they don't have to depend on Dad or Mom, or stay up nights thinking about what they're forgetting to remember. Take time together to reassess a young adult's commitments and help them consider letting go of activities that don't contribute to their quality of life or well-being. Cultivate leisure time to trade massages, play catch, or read a funny story together. While some of the risk-taking activities on pages 216-227 may cause added stress for a young adult, everyone is likely to identify risk-taking activities that can serve as major stress reducers and allow a young adult to blow off steam.

- Watch a movie together that deals with issues common to this period of life or that deals with specific issues a young adult is experiencing: *Dead Poet's Society* (1989), *Little Women* (1994), *Perfect Score* (2004), *Finding Forrester* (2000), *That Thing You Do* (1996), *Rudy* (1993), *The Breakfast Club* (1985), *Freedom Writers* (2007), *Stand and Deliver* (1988), *School Ties* (1992), *Coach Carter* (2005), *Fame* (1980), *What's Eating Gilbert Grape?* (1993), and *October Sky* (1999). Two movies rich in comedic insight about the pressures and conflicts of suddenly being thrown into the "real world" of adulthood are *Big* (1988) and *13 Going on 30* (2004). After viewing a film, set aside some time for conversation.

- If a young adult is considering several college options or is unsure about the best college/university program for them, encourage them to begin looking at colleges early. This way, financial plans can be well thought-out and college visits can be worked into family travels or planned periodically to avoid the mad rush before a decision has to be made.

- Celebrate the little steps along the way. Instead of nervously waiting for SAT scores, make the *process* the significant part of the journey. When a student begins to prepare for the exam, get them a copy of the funny and informative SAT preparation book, *Up Your Score* (www.workman.com). The day they complete the exam, take them out for a celebratory dinner or cook a special meal. When a young adult sends in the commitment deposit to attend a college program or attends the first day of work at a new job, offer a symbolic gift or a letter of encouragement.

Graduation

Whether a student is graduating from a traditional high school or college that celebrates a community graduation ceremony or not, this pivotal time of change calls for a more intimate graduation ceremony, as well. Make an effort to gather family and friends to bless the graduate with expressions of congratulations and encouragement. Sometimes a graduating senior needs to be reminded that, although they may have to step out into their future alone, they have a strong foothold of support. As well, a graduate needs to be reminded that the learning in life continues.

> **Tools** ✧ For this ceremony, you'll need a candle or oil lamp to use as the "lamp of knowledge," a small table top labyrinth (described below), powdered myrrh or other symbolic incense, matches or a candlelighter, and the blessings or gifts that participants have prepared for the graduate ahead of time.

Tabletop Labyrinth

The labyrinth is an ancient prayer and meditation tool, usually constructed on the ground with stones or painted on a floor or large canvas, as a walking path. Its imagery combines the circle and the spiral to create a meandering and intentional journey. A labyrinth has only one path; the way in is the way out. The journey of the labyrinth leads you to the center of the path and out again. One version of a tabletop labyrinth is "The Sand Labyrinth" by Lauren Artress, which is in a 10 inch square wooden frame. The labyrinth path is indented and covered with fine, white sand; it is meant to be traced with one's fingertip. I create tabletop labyrinths simply by using a drawing of a labyrinth that I have copied onto foam board at a copy shop. A stylus (small pointed stick) or fingertip can be used to trace this version of the labyrinth as well. (To explore the various designs, do a search of labyrinth stories and images on the internet, or check out a book on labyrinths, such as *Labyrinths From the Outside In: Walking to Spiritual Insight, A Beginner's Guide* by Donna Schaper and Carole Ann Camp.)

Lighting the Lamp of Knowledge

Opening Verse: I Light This Lamp

Graduate: I light this lamp –

Everyone: the lamp of knowledge.

Graduate: True knowledge

Everyone: illumines the darkest corners of the human soul.

Graduate: True knowledge

Everyone: reveals the mysterious nuances of the human heart.

Graduate: True knowledge

Everyone: sheds light on the greatest questions of the mind.

Graduate: I light this lamp –

Everyone: the lamp of knowledge. (Graduate ignites the lamp.)

Someone says: (speaking at an easy pace, thoughtfully)

"What is knowledge. . . ? Some say knowledge has to do with gaining facts and information; yet, we can bury ourselves in information and lose all sight of knowledge. Philosophers have been debating the definition of knowledge for centuries, and there's still no commonly accepted definition. Plato said knowledge is 'justified, true belief.' Robert Nozick said that knowledge 'tracks the truth.' Some Christian traditions assert that knowledge is a gift of the Holy Spirit, while the Hindu scriptures identify two types of knowledge – knowledge obtained through books and hearsay and knowledge discovered for oneself, born of one's own experience. Perhaps the most challenging definition is one that can be pulled from the subtle nuances of the history and etymology of the word itself. In Old Icelandic, the root word 'know' meant 'I can,' and in English, at one point, the suffix, 'ledge,' was equated with 'ness.' Knowledge: 'I can-ness.' Brilliant! For, true knowledge, born of inquiry and experience empowers a person with an inner gesture of 'I can-ness.' Francis Bacon alluded to knowledge as 'I can-ness' when he said that 'knowledge is power.' Likewise, Proverbs 24:5 tells us that 'a wise person has great power, and a person of knowledge increases strength.' (*Name of graduate*), may the knowledge you gained in your studies empower you with a sense of your own 'I can-ness,' and may your *continuing* experience of knowledge increase your strength."

Song: Rise Up, O Flame (page 274)

> Rise up, O flame, by thy light glowing,
> Show to us beauty, vision and joy.

Reflecting on the Journey

Labyrinth Journey

The graduate traces the labyrinth inward, reflecting on the effort, joys, and challenges of their journey to graduation. When they reach the center, the graduate pauses and contemplates the single word that best describes their journey. The graduate speaks the word aloud and, if they choose, can share reflections on the most difficult challenges encountered along the way, as well as the most cherished memories and learnings. Then, the graduate quietly contemplates their feelings and thoughts about their ongoing journey from this day forward. The graduate chooses a single word to describe their feelings and thoughts about the future and, again, shares reflections. After the graduate speaks, they trace the labyrinth from the center outward. (If you don't have access to a tabletop labyrinth, this portion of the ceremony could be replaced with a spoken reflection from the graduate, which might include thanking those in attendance for their support and love.)

Blessing the Graduate

Someone says: (taking a pinch of powdered myrrh and sprinkling it over the flame of the "lamp of knowledge.")

"(*Name of graduate*), we place in this flame powdered myrrh. Since ancient times, myrrh incense has been a symbol for prayers rising to heaven. Today, these are our blessings and prayers for you:"

Each participant, one at a time, speaks a prayer or blessing for the graduate and sprinkles a pinch of myrrh over the flame. These blessings can be spontaneous or prepared ahead of time. (If you desire to include in this portion of the ceremony the blessings of loved ones who have passed over, consider utilizing appropriate excerpts of letters or cards they wrote to the graduate for previous occasions. You might also prayerfully ask a loved one who has passed to impart words upon your heart and mind that you can share with the graduate on their behalf.)

When all participants have offered their prayer or blessing, everyone stands for the remainder of the ceremony. . .

Someone says:

"'Graduation is only a concept. In real life, every day you graduate. Graduation is a process that goes on until the last day of your life. If you can grasp that, you'll make a difference.'* So, 'wherever you go, go with all your heart.' "**

Song: Shine Your Light by Willa & Shea Darian (page 268)

Walk on the path of truth, Walk on the path of joy,
Shine forth the light of your soul's desire,
Shine your light a little bit stronger,
Shine your light a little bit longer,
Shine your light until there's a turning
of the way we see the world.

Final Blessing   (Traditional Native American)

All: (in unison, or as a call-and-response pattern, in which a leader speaks one line at a time and everyone repeats it)

Go gently,
Be pure,
Be brave,
Be as humble as the earth,
And as radiant as the sun.

*Quote by Arie Pencovici
**Quote by Confucius

Leaving Home

For many parents, a child leaving home for the first time to live on their own ranks right up there with the day of their birth in terms of its world-shifting capacities. When Morgan decided to attend North Carolina School of the Arts for her senior year of high school, the rest of the family was delighted for her. However, the fact that she'd be living 2,100 miles away from home was a hefty reality for the whole family to digest. We knew a meaningful rite of passage was needed not only to initiate Morgan, but to prepare the entire family for birthing our new long-distance relationships. Morgan certainly made the passage easier by preparing a thoughtful gift of departure for each family member. My gift was the following poem she wrote and recited for me with all the strength and love she could muster. Receiving the poem provided my rite of passage as a parent sending forth my eldest child.

The Journey...

A new born babe looked up at her mother-spirit. . . and cried.
So the mother-spirit gathered the babe into the core of her very heart. . .
   and the babe felt safe.

The mother-spirit wondered if she was doing all she could
   to ensure the young one's safety and well-being. . . and the babe grew.

A toddler stumbled into the arms of her mother-spirit. . . and giggled.
And as the spirit caught the toddler, she swung the little one into the air
   and shouted words of joy and play. . . and the child felt love.

The mother-spirit wondered what this miracle of flesh and bone
   would do in the world. . . and the little girl grew.

A young girl of seven reached up to touch her mother's face. . .
   and pondered.
The lines of laughter and tears told the girl stories of the spirit's past. . .
   and the girl felt wise.

The mother-spirit wondered what part of her teachings the girl would
carry in her heart forever. . . and the girl grew.

A preteen watched her mother's hands. . . and learned.
The girl treasured the art of helping and giving. . .
   and the girl felt needed by the world.

The mother-spirit wondered if her daughter-spirit would know
   how to make the right decisions for herself. . .
   and the teenage girl grew.

A young adult held hands with her mother-spirit. . . and smiled.
She was ready to make new lines on her own face. . .
   and the young woman felt scared.

The mother-spirit spoke:
   "Daughter-spirit. . . Do not be scared.
   When you feel lonely, all you need do is call.
   When you feel lost, all you need do is remember.
   When you feel frightened, all you need do is believe. . .
   I will always be with you."

The young woman felt the love that was constantly pouring out of her
mother-spirit. . . and cried.

The mother-spirit gathered all her teachings, wise words,
   love and memories, and placed them in her daughter-spirit's heart. . .
   and the young woman felt ready.

The mother-spirit wondered if she had done all she could
   to ensure the young woman's future. . .
   and the young woman smiled and said:
     "Dear mother-spirit. You gave like no other spirit has sacrificed.
     You taught like no other wise woman has taught.
     You loved like no other mother-spirit has loved.
     You healed like no other being has healed.
     You have persevered beyond your call as a mother-spirit.
     You are and always will be a part of your daughter-spirit.
     And for that I will always be indebted to you."

The two spirits felt the connection they had as mother-spirit
   and daughter-spirit. . . and laughed.
They knew their connection was too strong to ever be severed.
   so the two beings parted for the first time. . . and their spirits felt closer.

A Ceremony of Sending Forth

Tools ❧ For this ceremony, as it's written here, you'll need to begin indoors and have access to an outdoor space. Prepare tools and space for a relaxing massage (if a massage is given). Gather lots of candles. You will need a candle to represent each family member or friend present and one for each intimate family member or friend who can't be physically present, or who has passed over (tea lights will do). You will also need a special candle to symbolize the honored one's life, several floating candles, and a candlelighter. Other tools include slips of paper and pens, colored pencils or crayons for participants to write affirmations for the initiate; "The Blessing Book" (if one has been made) and "Gifts of the Heart" (see page 247); a tub or basin of water, towel, and chair for the footwashing; two baskets (one for the written affirmations and one for the floating candles). Secretly create a path for the initiate to walk with two rows of luminaries (small paper bags with a few inches of sand in the bottom to hold a tea light). For the ceremony, as it's written here, the luminary path needs to begin behind a closed door. It can lead through an indoor space and continue outside an exterior door, or the path can begin directly outside the exterior door. Outside, you'll need a pool of water for the floating candles (a simple, "kiddie pool" will work). Luminaries are set around the pool of water at intervals. You also need an outdoor firepit or small portable grill and materials to build a fire.

Note: This celebration can be simplified by deleting the floating candle portion of the ceremony. If the floating candles are deleted, participants can share affirmations before the initiate builds the fire. (See "An Act of Commitment" on page 249.)

Movements of Change: A Preparation

At Morgan's ceremony, Andrew, Willa, and I lit candles, warmed some massage oil, and offered Morgan a massage (reminiscent of the massage she received the day of her woman-becoming ceremony five years before). The massage began with a recording of soft instrumental music. As the music played, we spoke the following words. (These words can be revised for the one being honored):

Speaker 1: "Morgan, tonight is a celebration of *Light*. It's a celebration of Morgan DeShea Darian: the "Great Brightness," the "Great Light" who has shone in our lives for over 17 years. Now, it's time to allow this light to shine forth in the larger world."

Speaker 2: "Morgan, tonight is a celebration of *Change*, a celebration of the earth shifting beneath your feet as life guides you East to a new place of learning, a new place of being. And because you live within the heart of our hearts, tonight represents Change for all of us."

Speaker 3: "Five years ago, you were prepared for your first coming of age ceremony with the gift of massage. Through that massage, every atom in you was welcomed to celebrate the change of a girl's body hinting at womanhood. Today, you are fully a young woman, a young woman ready to journey forth from the family of your birth."

Everyone: "Morgan, we welcome every atom in you to celebrate this change."

If more than one person offers the honored one the massage, decide beforehand how you'll proceed. You may decide for one person to massage the back, another the legs and feet, another the arms and hands, etc., or you may rotate positions. For tips on giving a satisfying massage, check out *The Massage Book* by George Downing. After the massage, allow the honored one to relax and dress in solitude. At Morgan's celebration, we took her out for a special dinner before gathering for her ceremony of sending forth.

Gathering the Larger Community

You may want to light the luminary path before the ceremony begins or before the section: "Journeying Out Into the World."

Calling forth the Spirits of Loved Ones

On a table or altar cloth, in the center of the circle gathered, the honored one's life candle is set with the candles of other family members and friends around it. To begin, the initiate lights the candle representing their life, and one by one, the others present light one of the other candles.

> Speaker: "(*Name of initiate*), we aren't the only ones who support you in this time of change. There are many who've been inspired, touched, and warmed by your light. In Spirit, they are here with us, too. The candles we light represent them all." (Other candles are lit for the absent and departed.)

> Everyone: "Be with us tonight, (*Name of initiate*)'s true family, (*Name of initiate*)'s true friends – those who live on earth and those who live in Spirit."

Blessing Book & Gifts of the Heart

For Morgan's ceremony, we put together an album of pictures and blessings from Morgan's friends and family who were scattered throughout the United States and beyond. Since our celebration was an intimate one, we took time to read through the album together. Afterward, those present each gave Morgan a handmade or symbolic gift as a blessing for her journey.

Reflecting the Initiate's Light

During a few moments of quiet or with music playing softly, participants are asked to reflect on ways they see the initiate shining forth as a light in the world. Participants are given slips of paper and writing instruments; they are asked to write one affirmation for the initiate on each slip of paper given. (If there's a large group gathered, one slip of paper for each participant will do. If an intimate group is gathered give each person several slips of paper to write on.) *Each affirmation states how the initiate, in profound or subtle ways, shines as a light for those around them.*

Journeying Into the World

Everyone gathers with the initiate at the closed door behind which the luminary path begins. The luminaries have already been lit. The tub of water, towel, and chair are set nearby.

Speaker: "(*Name of initiate*), through this door is a passage – a symbolic passage leading out into the world. Before you walk this path, we invite you to take off your shoes and bathe your feet. Wash them with the boldness of your dreams, the strength of your bones, and the love of your heart." (The initiate sits to bathe their own feet and dry them.)

Speaker: "(*Name of initiate*), carry this basket with you – to receive the blessings this path has to offer. . ."

The door is opened and the initiate is invited to lead the way on the path. Someone carries a basket filled with floating candles and a candlelighter. Before the initiate continues on the path that leads around the pool of water, the group pauses and someone says. . .

Speaker: "(*Name of initiate*), the lighted path around the pool represents your life's path as a young adult journeying into the world. It's a path that leads you away and a path that can lead you home again."

The initiate is invited to walk around the pool, pausing at each luminary, so affirmations can be shared by others. After a participant speaks an affirmation to the initiate, naming one way they see the initiate shining as a light in the world, the person places the slip of paper in the initiate's basket and lights a floating candle. The candle is handed to the initiate to set on the water.

Song: Shine Your Light (page 268)

Walk on the path of truth, Walk on the path of joy,
Shine forth the light of your soul's desire,
Shine your light a little bit stronger,
Shine your light a little bit longer,
Shine your light until there's a turning
of the way we see the world.

An Act of Commitment

Everyone gathers by the firepit/grill for a final blessing.

> Speaker: "(*Name of initiate*), there are many kinds of fires:
> hearth fires, sun fires, volcanic fires, forest fires,
> and wildfires on the prairie.
> There are fires used to harm and fires used to heal;
> fires used to destroy and fires used to create.
> There are fires used to communicate
> and fires to keep away the cold."

> Speaker: "(*Name of initiate*),
> let your fire be superlative,
> a sacred altar fire. . .
> a fire that speaks of your life and your gifts
> as fuel and light for the world."

The honored one is invited to build a fire with the materials provided and to place the slips of paper with the kindling or in the fire after it's blazing. While the fire is being built, participants may want to sing "Shine Your Light" (page 268) or "Rise Up, O Flame" (page 274). *Be sure to be attentive to fire safety and extinguish the fire before returning inside.*

Final Blessing

Everyone: (speaking to the initiate in unison)

> "(*Name of initiate*), you shine with radiant light.
> In this circle of earthly existence, you shine so finely
> it surpasses understanding.
> God hugs you.
> You are encircled in the arms of the mystery of God.
> (*Name of initiate*), go forth! Be a light in the world!"

> ~ By Hildegard of Bingen (last line added)

Blessing For Departing On a Significant Journey

The following ceremony was created for Morgan before she departed to begin her freshman year as a musical theater major at the Boston Conservatory. Morgan was already initiated into dorm life as a high school senior, yet after spending the summer together again, this was another huge transition for the whole family. The ceremony we created to bless Morgan's departure includes humor about her ongoing shoe fetish. As always, revise the ceremony as necessary for the one being honored.

Setup ✥ For this ceremony, as it's written here, you'll need to take the initiate shopping for a new pair of shoes or boots, and put the purchase away for the day of the ceremony. To prepare for the section, "A Journey of Reflection," the initiate is given a printed copy of the questions several days in advance and asked to contemplate them. If s/he chooses, written notes can be used during the ceremony. You'll also need blessing water or oil and seven stepping stones. The stepping stones in our ceremony were earthen tiles left over from some remodeling that had been done on our house. Stepping stones cut from heavy cardboard could work as well. The seven stepping stones are set in a symbolic path, spiraling outward in a clockwise motion. The first six stones, beginning on the inside of the spiral, are inscribed with a single word in the following order: where, why, when, who, what, and how. The seventh stone is painted with a red heart. At the beginning of the path, set the new pair of shoes.

Envisioning the Journey

Song: One Step At a Time (page 270)

One step at a time, I'll take this journey,
One step at a time, I'll see it through,
One step at a time, I'll live into the visions
and dreams that I'm set to pursue.
One step at a time, I'll see this journey through.

The Sole of Shoes

Speaker: It has been said that we need to learn to walk in someone else's shoes. And that's a good and right thing to do. But *daughter*, one day. . . someday. . . for you this very day. . . we each must learn to walk in shoes of our own. We gotta learn to walk in shoes of our own.

Speaker: We've seen you grow through so many shoes. So *many* shoes! And when your feet stopped growin', the shoes just kept comin'. Sometimes they filled up your closet; sometimes they filled up your drawer; sometimes they filled whole suitcases and roomy bins underneath dorm room beds. Oh, so many shoes!

Speaker: It's been said there's nothin' like an old shoe. And the old shoes have been good ones for you:

(the following lines are spoken by individual family members)

saddle shoes

hopscotch shoes,

bouncin' Irish dancin' shoes,

flip-flop shoes,

high-heeled shoes,

smoke-the-competition runnin' shoes,

jazz shoes,

tap shoes,

even secondhand bowling shoes.

Speaker: No doubt, the old shoes have been good ones for you.
But, *sister*, I've walked beside you since the beginning,
and I know you. . .
I know you love nothin' better than a just-bought,
waitin'-to-be-broken-in, brand new shoe.
For you, it's like puttin' on a new adventure.
Steppin' into a journey just waitin' to happen.

Speaker: So, go ahead. Step into these shoes. Shoes of your own.

Speaker: 'Cause you'll never stop growin'.

Speaker: You'll never stop goin' on adventures.

Speaker: Go, ahead. Step into these shoes.
They're an adventure just waitin' to happen.

New Shoes for the Journey

The initiate is invited to stand at the beginning of the spiral path of stepping stones and to put on their new shoes. In the "Journey of Reflection" below, the initiate will walk the spiral path one step at a time.

Journey of Reflection

Speaker: When a person decides to go on a journey, many questions are asked of the traveler along the way. Tonight, in preparation of your travels, we ask you these questions:

All: (*Name of initiate*), take one step, one step at a time, (s/he does) Holding this question in your heart and mind:

Speaker: Where are you going? (Initiate answers)

All: (*Name of initiate*), take one step, one step at a time, (s/he does) Holding this question in your heart and mind:

Speaker: Why have you chosen this destination? (Initiate answers)

All: (*Name of initiate*), take one step, one step at a time, (s/he does) Holding this question in your heart and mind:

Speaker: When will you depart? (Initiate answers)

All: (*Name of initiate*), take one step, one step at a time, (s/he does) Holding this question in your heart and mind:

Speaker: Who are you going to see or find there? (Initiate answers)

All: (*Name of initiate*), take one step, one step at a time, (s/he does) Holding this question in your heart and mind:

Speaker: What do you hope to accomplish there? (Initiate answers)

All: (*Name of initiate*), take one step, one step at a time, (s/he does) Holding this question in your heart and mind:

Speaker: How will you know you're successful? (Initiate answers)

All: (*Name of initiate*), take one step, one step at a time, (s/he does) Holding our love in your heart and mind. . .

Blessing

One at a time, each participant comes to stand before the initiate and bestows a blessing. After each blessing, the initiate can be anointed with oil or water and offered an embrace.

Song: One Step at a Time (page 270)

You may want to conclude the ceremony with a meal or dessert feast.

Returning Home Again

As difficult as it can be to send a young adult on a journey away from home, even in the best situations, it can be equally challenging to welcome them home again. Each time a young person lives away from the family nest, they come back markedly changed by their experiences. In the young adult's absence, the relational dynamics between family members at home can change markedly as well, as more time and focus is freed up for one another. Upon a family member's return home for a short-term break, summer vacation, or a more permanent stay, it can be helpful to welcome the sojourner back into the fold. A tangible rite of passage can assist family members to make room for one another in their hearts, minds, and souls, and help family members to cultivate grace for each other as relational dynamics shift again.

Tools ⚜ For this ceremony, as it's written here, you'll need a plastic tub, large bowl, or basin for the foot and hand washing; a pitcher of water; rose petals or another scent to add to the water; a towel; sunflower seeds; and planting cups with soil. Each participant chooses a symbolic oil, lotion, scented water, or other ointment or liquid to bless the initiate's hands after the handwashing (see "The Anointing" on page 256). Also, have participants memorize the two-line blessing of welcome on page 255.

Gathering the Circle

Welcome Song: Welcome Home*

> Welcome, welcome, welcome home again,
> We missed you, we love you,
> Our hearts have so much room for you – welcome!

Family Chant

Long ago, I wrote a chant with the meaning of our family name in mind. "Darian" is a combination of two Hebrew names, meaning: "heart of wisdom, compassion, and grace." Since our children were young, we have used the chant in many family celebrations. As we speak the words together, we walk in a counterclockwise circle – a symbolic way of asking time to stand still, so we can be with one another in the present moment. Consider writing a family chant or song to reflect the meaning of your family name and identity.

Washing the Dust from Your Feet

A family member says:

> *"(Name of the one returning),* your journey of *(name the time the loved one has been away or the purpose of their journey)* is complete. At journey's end, we invite you to wash the dust from your feet and be welcomed home."

In silence, someone pours water from the pitcher into the bowl, places the returning family member's feet in the tub of water, and washes them. Afterwards, the following words are spoken:

> *"(Name of the one returning),* we wash the dust from your feet.
> You can only wander for so long
> before you find every path you take leading you home.
> Back to the heart of your existence,
> back to the roots that ground you."

Another family member washes the loved one's feet; afterwards, the following words are spoken:

> *"(Name of the one returning),* we wash the dust from your feet
> and bid you to set your journey
> in that honored place of remembrance."

*The music for the song "Welcome Home" can be found in *Sanctuaries of Childhood: Nurturing a Child's Spiritual Life* by Shea Darian (www.gileadpress.net).

Another family member washes the loved one's feet; afterwards, the following words are spoken:

"(Name of the one returning), we wash the dust from your feet
and invite you to lay down any burdens
you've carried during your journey."

The loved one is invited to reflect, silently and aloud, on any aspects of the journey that s/he is relieved to let go of or be done with. . .

When the loved one finishes speaking, another family member gently dries their feet.

Blessing of Welcome

Everyone stands in a circle, holding hands (right palm down in a gesture of giving and left palm up in a gesture of receiving).

Participants speak in unison from memory:

"(Name of the one returning), stand with us here
and be rooted again in this circle of family."

Song: Roots (page 271)

Roots that bring me back into the core of my existence,
Roots that bring me back into the heart of love's embrace,
Reaching ever deeper to the Source of Resurrection,
Ground of my Being, I rest here in your grace.

(Everyone sits again)

Embracing the Gifts Of the Journey

Handwashing

A family member says:

"(Name of the one returning), we've washed the dust from your feet to signify the end of your journey. Now, we invite you to wash your hands. As you do, consider the gifts you received on your journey that you desire to carry with you into the future." (The one returning washes their own hands in silence, shares their reflections aloud, and dries their hands.)

The Anointing

One at a time, each participant anoints the loved one's hands with the particular ointment (oil, water, lotion, etc.) they chose before the ceremony for its symbolic meaning.

Each blessing-giver anoints the loved one's hands with their ointment and says:

"(*Name of the one returning*), I bless you with (*ointment chosen*).
It's a symbol of (*share the meaning of the ointment chosen*).
As you return home from your journey, my blessing for you is. . ."

Planting Seeds in the Present

A family member says:

"(*Name of the one returning*),
now, with your feet washed clean, releasing the old,
with your hands washed clean, embracing the new,
you're fully prepared for the present moment. . .
a time of pause, rest, and rejuvenation.
Within the stillness of this present moment, within you,
lies the power of transformation."

A family member says:

"The seed rests in the earth,
Is nourished with water, sun, soil, and air;
Day-by-day, invisibly, it grows,
At long last, revealing its utter beauty
with such boldness, it cannot be overlooked."

A family member says:

"One by one, plant these seeds.
Let each represent a vision, goal, hope, or desire
for this season of your life.
As you return to the ground of your being,
as you return to the roots of family,
plant these seeds and name your visions and hopes. . ."

The loved one is invited to plant sunflower seeds one at a time. With each seed planted, they name a vision, goal, hope, or desire for their time at home. When the planting is finished, everyone stands in a circle for the final blessing song.

Blessing Song: God Stir the Soil (page 272)
Words by Singapore Church Missionary Society

> God, stir the soil,
> Run the plowshare deep,
> Cut the furrows 'round and 'round,
> Overturn the hard, dry ground,
> Spare no strength nor toil,
> Even though I weep.
> In the loose, fresh, mangled earth,
> Sow new seed.
> Free of withered vine and weed,
> Bring fair flowers to birth.

Twenty-One

As removed as we may be from the seven-year cycles of human development first fleshed out by the Greeks, our culture retains subtle and not-so-subtle ties to these seven-year cycles. The Greeks identified young childhood from birth to 7, older childhood beginning at 7, youthhood at 14, and young adulthood at 21. Today these seven-year cycles are vaguely associated with our educational rites of passage. In a child's seventh year (at six years old), they usually begin grade school; at 14, a student usually finishes their final year of middle school; and traditionally, for many at 21, they begin their final year of a four-year college or university program. But what of the more common cultural passage for 21-year-olds (in the United States) when a young adult is given the legal right to purchase alcoholic beverages? Such an odd passage of young adulthood! Especially considering that before the 21st year, a young adult has already been granted the right to drive, buy a gun, have sex, fight in wars, participate in political elections, live independently of their parents, get married, get a credit card, and be tried as an adult in our courts of law. By reserving public alcohol consumption as the final adult rite of passage conferred by our legal system, we've managed to identify *drinking alcohol* as the *ultimate* adult status symbol.

Through the years, I've heard parents and young adults grieve the fact that going out with friends and getting plastered on the 21st birthday is an *expected* rite of passage for young adults in our culture. Fortunately, it's a rite of passage that many young adults resist, but it's also a rite of passage many young people don't know how to transform. I recently read a blog on the internet inspired by a 20-year-old asking for advice about how to get out of the usual drinking scene with friends on her 21st birthday. A few responses included encouraging the 20-year-old to be bold about not wanting to engage in this unwanted celebration, but other responses ranged from suggesting feigned sickness to claiming to be on medication that doesn't mix with alcohol. I doubt this is what this 20-year-old had in mind when the question was asked (that is, spending the evening lying to friends and acting sick). But these well-meaning responses reveal how trapped many young adults feel by the expectations placed upon them by our laws and cultural practices (or *lack* of them when it comes to celebrating meaningful rites of passage).

Our role as parents and mentors initiating the 21-year-old is less about us creating a rite of passage *for* the young adult and more about fueling a young adult's imagination about what's possible in celebrating this significant life passage. This, I believe, is what the 20-year-old internet blogger was really asking – for someone to fuel her imagination about how to articulate and celebrate this important life event. After all, isn't self-determination what this passage of adulthood is all about?

As parents and mentors, if we hope to assist young adults in honoring effective rites of passage at 21 (or any age associated with adult status), we need to help young adults clarify what it means to be an "adult." What does adulthood ask of a young person? What does it offer them? How does it require them to change? These questions can't be answered easily, especially if one is insightful enough to look past adult expectations imposed by our culture, family members, friends, and acquaintances. Whatever else a genuine passage into adulthood may be, it's a passage that requires a young adult to answer the above questions for themselves.

In considering alternatives to the midnight rush to the bar on the 21st birthday, a young adult may find one of the following suggestions for a meaningful rite of passage more compelling:

- Ask a few friends or family members to help you plan a party that doesn't focus on drinking alcohol. Have a dance with a deejay or plan a picnic at the lake. If alcohol is served, include it as a special toast during which friends and family members share their birthday blessings.

- Ask a mentor, parent, or friend to help you create a rite of passage along the lines of the adult-becoming ceremonies on page 174 and 188. Incorporate symbolism, rituals, songs, and spoken passages that are meaningful to you. Decide who to invite to the ceremony, whether it's a few good friends or a large gathering of loved ones.

- Plan a road trip for your 21st birthday (or during a break or vacation time during your new year of life). The journey might be taken solo or with friends to a destination you long to visit. It could also include a journey into your past, taking in destinations that include your birth place and other communities in which you've lived, or to the homes of important people in your life. Reflect on how geographical landscape affects the way you experience yourself and how geography shapes your daily experiences and relationships. Before you depart on your trip, consider asking your intimates to bestow the blessing (on page 250) for departing on a significant journey and/or receiving you back home with a footwashing ceremony similar to the one on page 253.

- Ask a mentor, parent, spiritual teacher, or elder to teach you a specialized skill or commit to an ongoing conversation on a subject of interest.

- Write your own definition of adulthood. Include personal qualities and ways of being that you desire to actualize as an adult. Ask yourself what you expect from yourself as an adult.

- Prior to a celebration with family and friends, create a time of solitude for yourself – a solo trip into nature or time spent at a retreat center or some other quiet sanctuary. During this time, clarify personal identity and visions. You may even want to choose a spiritual name for yourself that reflects who you are becoming as an adult.

- On your birthday eve, create a late night ceremony with someone you love to bestow a prayerful birthday blessing and pour a glass of wine at midnight to toast your new year of life.

- Create a work of art that, for you, is a symbol of adulthood, or write serious and/or humorous reflections on life as a young adult. Your creation can be shared with those gathered at your rite of passage or birthday celebration.

- If you're an artist or performer, plan an art showing, concert, or performance for your birthday. It doesn't have to be at a gallery or concert hall. Some of my favorite artistic experiences have been in-home concerts and performances where things are up close and personal. Make sure you have plenty of family members and friends on board to make the event a success.

- Ask all your family members and friends over 21 to write you a letter or select a symbolic gift for you that reflects the greatest wisdom they have learned as an adult.

- On your birthday, share a special meal at a restaurant with family and friends, and order a drink or request a bottle of wine to share with those 21 and older so you can get carded, or go to the liquor store and purchase a bottle of wine or ingredients for a specialty drink to serve with a home-cooked birthday meal.

- Design or choose a small, tasteful tattoo as a symbol of adulthood, and seek out a reputable tattoo artist to inflict the pain.

- Create an artistic or written reflection of your first 21 years of life, and include the life situations, events, people, decisions, challenges, and joys that you feel contributed to you becoming the person you are today.

- Become a mentor for someone younger. Consider a friend or relative who may need your guidance, or volunteer at a Boy's or Girl's Club, Big Sister/Big Brother program, school or church-related program, or children's hospital.

- In the months or weeks leading up to your 21st birthday, reflect on the visioning exercise on pages 262-265. On your birthday, share the results with someone you love.

Reclaiming a Passage of Young Adulthood

Paula Poundstone once said that "adults are always asking little kids what they want to be when they grow up because they're looking for ideas." I hope Paula Poundstone is right. I hope that's the motivation because when adults lose the imagination to dream ourselves anew, it's a sorry state we've gotten ourselves into. Many of us, as we leave the years of young adulthood behind, need to retune our inner ears to that soulful whisper so familiar to the young adult, that soulful whisper that announces to our senses and sensibilities that "any good thing is possible."

I know a middle-aged woman who decided her life required what she called her "Leap of Faith." At the time, she felt her life was intensely limited by fears she had carried with her into adulthood – a fear of heights, the unknown, death, disappointing others, not being in control. This woman, who appeared to others as brave and courageous – an able pediatrician and mother – inwardly felt like an imposter. As long as she was the decision-maker in charge, all was well, but whenever the unexpected occurred, she lost all trust in herself. The woman recalls her pediatric residency when she was in charge of the emergency room at night. She would walk by the children's rooms mentally rehearsing the worst possible scenario that could happen to each one, so she would be prepared to respond in advance. She was constantly living in the future and left little time for the present. Ultimately, the woman felt her intuition and her spirit being silenced by her obsessive, controlling behavior.

However, the events of a September Sunday (just a few weeks after the terrorist attacks of 9-11) changed all that. This can't-bear-to-be-out-of-control woman checked her control at the door and jumped out of an airplane. That's right. She went skydiving. She flew through the air and for the first time in her life, felt no fear. Her fear vanished because she was jumping into the present moment where fear has no room to reside. She was flying through the air, smiling, and has a photograph to prove it.

Each one of us needs to take a leap of faith now and then. Each one of us needs to retune our ears to the soulful whisper that allows us to imagine that any good thing is possible for us. One way we learn to do that is by envisioning a future we can trust and being courageous enough to jump into it. The visioning exercise on the following pages may help you to do just that.

Bringing Your Personal Vision to Life

This visioning exercise is one I learned from a friend many years ago; it's inspired by an exercise presented in *The Fifth Discipline Fieldbook*.* I've used it a handful of times when I needed to gain clarity about my life and identity as an evolving human being. A unique aspect of the exercise is to eventually write out your life vision in the present tense, as if the vision is already being actualized. This visioning process will take time, thoughtful meditation, and effort, but it will be worth it! Remember – our visions call for the use of our hands to work and our legs to walk about, lest our hearts and minds become heavy with the weight of our imaginings. Clarity is the unrippled pool upon which we see our future. Yet, we mustn't stand gazing too long, for we have a journey to make – a journey to that crossroads where our present and our future meet.

Intention One: Engaging Desire

Seek out a quiet place of solitude and sanctuary. Breathe deeply, relax, empty your mind, and allow yourself to be filled with peace and well-being. When you're ready, open your entire being to something you deeply desire. Perhaps you desire more quality time alone, or with a child or spouse. Perhaps you desire to begin a new home business, work for a more ethical company, or start a new career. Perhaps you desire to transform your home into a sanctuary for soulful deepening and nourishment. Whatever desire lives strongly in you, clearly imagine it and ignore any negative messages about why you can't have it. Remove all obstacles from your view and simply allow one, singular desire to fully live within your heart, mind, and imagination without reservation. When the desire is clear to you, journal about it, brainstorm about it in words and pictures, or sketch a diagram of it. Most importantly, describe this one desire in the *present tense*, as a *present* reality. Flesh it out in detail.

Intention Two: Contemplating Your Desire

Now reflect on the desire you articulated in the first step. Is it something you are genuinely compelled to manifest in your life? Sometimes it's difficult to discover our deepest visions and desires because we have to dig underneath our long-held fears and limitations in our thinking. As we imagine our future, many of us are experts at sabotaging our greatest personal visions. In your reflections, strive for the following. . .

* *The Fifth Discipline Fieldbook* by Peter Senge, Art Kleiner, Charlotte Roberts, Rick Ross, and Bryan Smith. (NY:Doubleday, 1994)

- **Let go of your doubt, fear, and negativity.**
  Living into a deep desire can be frightening because we fear that we might be disappointed, or we imagine that following a deeply-held desire will mean losing an important relationship or our job. We allow fears and negativity to talk us out of our visions of what's possible. In this exercise, you'll need to suspend all negativity that comes flying at you when you dare to express your true desires. Write your vision trusting that life is large enough to hold it.

- **Concentrate on what YOU desire.**
  Some of us are so focused on fulfilling others' expectations of us that we lose sight of who we desire to be. In this moment, set aside what you think your parent, child, mentor, boss, spouse, counselor, spiritual director, partner, or friend wants for you. Tune into your deepest desires for yourself apart from what others want.

- **Don't belittle your visions.**
  In the midst of adult responsibilities, we often set aside the desires most significant to us because we don't have time or energy to put into them. Life's demands and significant relationships sometimes suck the marrow out of the bones of our visions. Don't belittle the significance of your visions and desires. Imagine results and rewards as if you count – because you do!

- **Don't assume you have your visions all worked out.**
  As you allow yourself to vision anew, you may be surprised to see your visions transforming before your mind's eye. A personal vision is a living entity. It continues to evolve as you interact with it. Allow your vision to continue to grow and change.

- **Trust the process of change.**
  Some of us have a high tolerance for change and accept it as part of our life's journey. Others are afraid that any sort of change means losing control. This is *your* vision. It can't run your life because it only has a life in relation to you. Trust yourself and trust your vision to serve you.

- **Believe that there IS a great vision inside you.**
  Cultivating vision means cultivating hope. Some of us live with a subtle despair that may be barely detectable in our daily lives but that keeps us from believing that we're worthy of a great life vision. It may be helpful to think back on another time of life when vision and hope lived more boldly in you. What was your vision then? Simply allow your vision to breathe in the light of day.

Intention Three: Articulating Your Life Vision

Journal on one or all of the following areas of your life, or identify other areas of focus to consider. *Write about your vision in the present tense as if your vision is manifesting now.* Stay with this intention for days or weeks if necessary, until you create a living imagination of the life you desire. See it, feel it, walk around in it.

- ◆ **You:** Imagine the person you desire to be.

- ◆ **Physical Body:** Imagine your ideals for health, diet, fitness, physical activities, physical nurture, and expressing your sexuality. How do you choose to relate to your body and physique? How do you choose to nurture a healthy body image?

- ◆ **Home:** Envision the living space that best provides shelter and sanctuary for your body and soul.

- ◆ **Intimate Relationships:** Imagine your relationships with family members and friends. What relationships are most significant to you? How do you desire to be in relationship with others?

- ◆ **Relationship with the Natural World:** Imagine your relationship with the earth and nature. How do you choose to relate to creation?

- ◆ **Possessions:** Imagine the material items you choose to own and how you relate to these possessions.

- ◆ **Work:** Imagine the work that brings you the most delight and greatest sense of satisfaction. What are the intended results of your work? How does your work affect others?

- ◆ **Learning:** How do you desire to learn about the world? Imagine your ideal learning environments, books you desire to read, areas of life and experience you choose to explore, and places you desire to travel.

- ◆ **Your Larger Communities:** Envision your ideals of community and the collective qualities and practices of the culture in which you live.

- ◆ **Spirituality:** Imagine your spiritual life and relationships being fully nurtured and expressed.

- ◆ **Core Purpose:** Identify the gesture and intention – the core purpose – of your life. Articulate it. How do you express this intention and purpose in your actions, being, and relationships?

- ◆ **Ask Yourself:** What else do I envision?

Intention Four: Expanding & Clarifying Your Vision

As you clarify your visions and desires, you may recognize that some are self-focused while others are more altruistic. We all need a balance of giving and receiving in our lives. Don't feel guilty because you desire to take an exotic vacation or construct a home theater. Simply accept each vision and contemplate each one singularly, asking yourself, "How will my life be different if I attain this desire?"

Keep striving to understand what's important to you. With each aspect of your life, consider the underlying motivations of your visions and desires? What's the ultimate goal you're striving to achieve? If family intimacy is important to you, what choices will help you to foster it? Why do you want to pursue a new career, express your spirituality in a new way, or change your eating habits? Do your answers lead you closer or take you further away from the core purpose of your life?

Intention Five: Make Your Vision Uniquely Your Own

After you complete steps one through four, rewrite your vision more concisely in a form that's meaningful for you. Consider sharing your vision with another. This is a wonderful exercise for marriage partners or other family members to do together. A group of friends and colleagues may find it an exceptional group-building exercise. In addition to the written portion, feel free to add sketches or express your vision in a creative or artistic form – a painting, song, poem, quilt, dance, sculpture, collage, or whatever is relevant to your personal vision that can serve as an additional symbol of commitment.

Some people enjoy doing this exercise in a weekend; others may take weeks or months to complete it. If you do it over a period of time, you may want to set aside the same block of time each week to focus on it, or commit to the exercise with another person so you can hold one another accountable when the going gets rough. Revisit your vision often and rewrite it every few years, or use the exercise to celebrate each new seven-year cycle of your life. The "seven-year itch" will take on an entirely new meaning.

Songs for Celebrating Young Adulthood

Safe Travels

Shea Darian

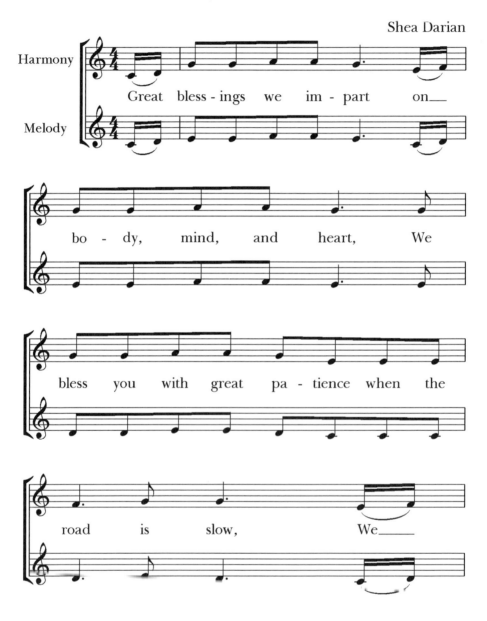

Harmony / Melody

Great bless-ings we im-part on__ bo - dy, mind, and heart, We bless you with great pa - tience when the road is slow, We__

Shine Your Light

Shea Darian & Willa Darian

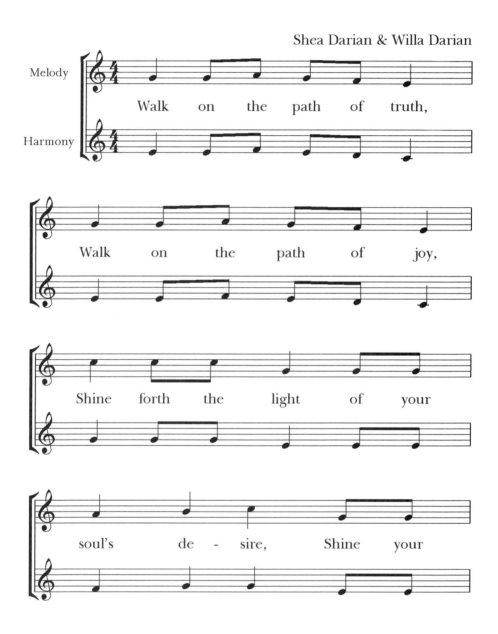

Living Passages for the Whole Family

light a lit - tle bit strong - er, Shine your light

a lit - tle bit long - er, Shine your light

un - til there's a turn - ing____

____ of the way we____ see the world.

One Step at a Time

Shea Darian

One step at a time, I'll take this jour-ney, One
step at a time, I'll see it through, One
step at a time, I'll live in-to the vi-sions and
dreams that I'm set to pur-sue.____ One
step at a time, One step at a time, One
step at a time, One step at a time, One
step at a time, I'll see this jour-ney through.

Roots

Shea Darian

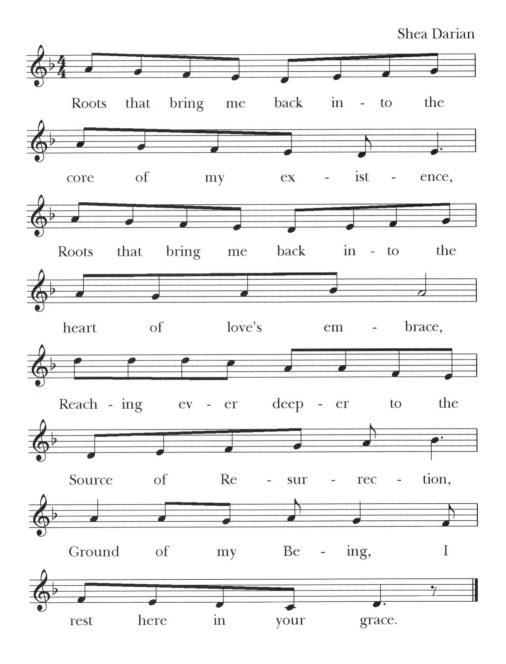

Roots that bring me back in - to the
core of my ex - ist - ence,
Roots that bring me back in - to the
heart of love's em - brace,
Reach - ing ev - er deep - er to the
Source of Re - sur - rec - tion,
Ground of my Be - ing, I
rest here in your grace.

God, Stir the Soil

Singapore Church
Missionary Society

Music & Arrangement
by Shea Darian

Rise Up, O Flame

From "Rise Up Singing"*

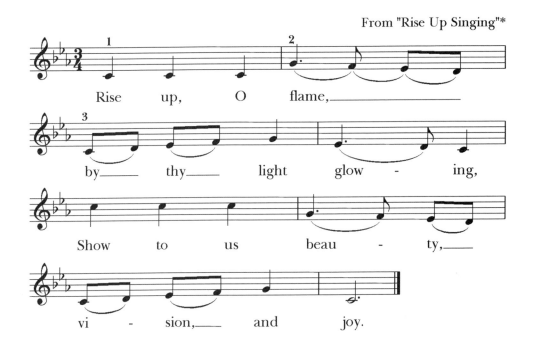

Rise up, O flame, by thy light glow - ing,
Show to us beau - ty, vi - sion, and joy.

Lyrics for "Rise Up, O Knight"
(For knighting ceremony, page 130)

Rise up, O noble knight, the
Fire of your life glowing,
Shine forth with deeds of courage,
Shine with wisdom and love.

*The original version of "Rise Up, O Flame" is included in the *Rise Up Singing* Songbook, edited by Peter Blood-Patterson, (A Sing Out Publication, 1988).

6 ᔛ Knowing the Miracle By Heart
Celebrating Birthdays

Soon as the evening shades prevail,
The moon takes up the wondrous tale,
and nightly to the listening earth
Repeats the story of her birth;
While all the stars that round her burn,
And all the planets in their turn,
Confirm the tidings as they roll,
And spread the truth from pole to pole;
Forever singing as they shine,
"The Hand that made us is divine."

~ Joseph Addison

Celebrating Birthdays

Several years ago, a friend confided to me the details of her seventh birthday. The day before, my friend had done something that angered her mother. She couldn't remember her transgression, but the response it elicited is indelibly impressed on her memory. My friend awoke on her birthday morning, anticipating the big day. She wasn't often the center of attention with her mother and older siblings, but a birthday could change all that. My friend was hopeful.

When she woke, she pulled on a favorite dress and hurried to the kitchen for breakfast. The conversation was unusually quiet. No one offered birthday greetings. No one even noted the significance of the day. When her mother went into town later that morning, my friend stood on the porch, eager for her return, imagining the trip was inspired by a special cake from the bakery or a surprise gift. But when my friend's mother returned, she was empty-handed; she walked past that eager seven-year-old without so much as a word. Suddenly, the little girl's heart sank as the gravity of her mother's punishment began to dawn on her: her mother meant to take away her birthday.

My friend went to bed that night without a single recognition that she had grown a year older. She woke up the next morning and the morning after that, wondering if anyone would ever admit to the conspiracy, wondering if someone would let her in on the big joke. No one ever did.

When I heard this story, I listened open-mouthed in disbelief. Having been graced with a mother who was the queen of birthday celebrations when I was young, my mind couldn't wrap around the parental cruelty that prompted such a punishment. However else we may be ailing from uncelebrated rites of passage, birthdays tend to be the passage ceremonies we can most depend upon in our culture. Granted, too often birthdays become excuses for overindulgence; yet, ideally, birthdays can be sacred portals through which we remember the soulful significance of our lives and relationships.

My own childhood birthday memories aren't filled with a bounty of *presents*, though my family members were thoughtful gift-givers. My memories are filled with *presence* – the presence of a family, animated with gladness that I was a growing sprig on their family tree.

My early birthday memories are filled with vivid images of my mother bustling about in the kitchen – decorating, baking, and cooking up a birthday to remember. I recall being asked to choose the menu for the birthday feast (which for me always included chicken and dumplings). I remember how the dinner conversation quieted down, and my parents and older siblings suddenly focused on all the topics of conversation that interested *me*! I recall deliciously decorated homemade cakes, the magical flickering of candlelight, and being sung to by a chorus of voices brimming with affection.

What I remember most is the feeling of my life being honored, knowing my family was truly grateful I was a part of their lives. As ordinary days cycled on, I didn't often see this gratitude as poignantly expressed. Yet, I could always carry this annual memory inside me.

Having been taught by the best, I've been inspired with Andrew to create a number of birthday traditions for our children and, consequently, ourselves. As we've shared these birthday traditions with extended family members and friends, I've realized it's a grand omission to reserve special birthday celebrations for the young. As we age, birthdays may continue to be touchstones upon which we affirm our deepening human capacities. After celebrating nigh five decades of birthdays, my own continue to thrill me with their potential for gratitude expressed, growth acknowledged, and visions ignited. What greater commentary can I give my children about the potential of the second half of the human life cycle?

Honoring each year of our lives, whether we're 7, 47, or 107, reminds us and our children that all of life is sacred, that it's good to grow old, and that celebrating the growth and learning of each passing year doesn't end with childhood. In fact, to the amusement of my family, I'm known to whoop with delight, as I stand in front of the bathroom mirror, detecting a new sprinkling of silver in my hair. For me, it's the fairy dust of age and wisdom. It holds a magic all its own. And I imagine, from the knowing smiles of my children, they understand. For me, every year is an adventure. Its something I learned at my family birthday celebrations when I was young. I pray that my children have learned it as well. I pray that with each passing year, they can throw back their heads and sing out with the poet Walt Whitman: "I ask not for great fortune, I am great fortune!"

Birthday Traditions

Family birthday traditions rise up out of the unique personality and soul of a family. Whether family birthday traditions exude with reverence, revelry, practicality, magic, heartfelt gestures, or roaring laughter, they can foster unity and camaraderie among family members. They can also provide encouragement and affirmation to the one whose life is celebrated. Whether you desire to begin new family birthday traditions or build on the ones you already celebrate, consider the following birthday rites. . .

Light of Life

In our culture, few moments of a birthday celebration are as teeming with magic as the moment a birthday honoree pauses in the glow of candle-light atop the cake – the reflection of visions, dreams, and wishes dancing in their eyes, an entirely new year of possibilities before them. In myriad countries and religions, the candle flame has long been associated with life and spirit. The candles on the cake represent each year lived, and some-times an extra candle is added – for good luck in the coming year. To further grace a birthday celebration with light, consider these birthday candle traditions:

From Dawn to Dusk: In some cultures, a birthday *begins* with candles. Long-lasting candles are lit at dawn and burn all day long until, in the evening, the one whose life is being celebrated is sung a birthday song and invited to make a wish or inwardly speak a silent prayer before blowing out the candles. The smoke that trails skyward is said to carry the person's prayers and wishes to heaven.

Life Candle: Choose a special candle to give to a birthday honoree as their "life candle." The candle can be lit throughout the year – for daily prayers, when the person needs prayers and support from other family members, or when the person has cause for celebration. If a life candle is given each year, a person's old life candle (from the year past) can be lit on the eve of their birthday. Family members can recall memories from the past year and offer prayers of gratitude. With young children, you may want to conclude remembrances with the "Birthday Eve Lullaby" on page 310; then invite the child to blow out or snuff the candle. On the birthday, when the new life candle is lit, the birthday person can hold the candle, or it can be passed around the circle as each family member or friend offers a birthday prayer, compliment, or expression of gratitude to the birthday person. Ask everyone to complete a sentiment, such as "Something I love about you is. . . ," "I'm so grateful you're in my life because. . . ," or "My wish for you in the coming year is. . ."

Story Light: When our children were young, our birthday traditions included an evening candlelighting ceremony. As we lit a candle for each year of the birthday child's life, we told a story or two about them during that year. We used the candlelighting ceremony for Andrew's and my birthday, as well, telling only a few sporadic stories from our biography as we lit the candles representing all the years of our lives. Of course, as we cycled into our thirties, the candlelighting became a bit more humorous with its bonfire-like quality. It was a relief when we discovered the magic of using a "penny box" for our storytelling tradition (pages 280, 298).

Remember Fire Safety ❧ When using candles for the celebration, safety is crucial. If candles are lit in the morning to burn all day long, put them in a safe place and use a candle snuffer to extinguish them when you need to leave the house; then reignite them upon returning home. When candles other than cake candles are used, make sure they're in safe, sturdy containers or candleholders. Scorched hair and burns have added unneeded excitement to many a birthday celebration. Keep matches in a safe place, teach children fire safety tips, and, of course, as Smokey the Bear says, "never leave a fire unattended." A telling instruction, since a person's birthday candles represent the fire of one's life.

The Penny Box

My sister, Rebecca, acquired my mom's ability to transform a birthday into a soulful rejoicing. On my 33rd birthday, Rebecca sent me the children's book, *The Penny Box*, by Sharon Bell Mathis. In the book, a boy's great-great aunt is dying. The aunt lives with the boy's family, and he has the opportunity to get to know her through a "penny box" given to the aunt years before by her spouse. In the box, pennies are kept – one penny minted in each year of the aunt's life. The boy is repeatedly drawn to the penny box, inspiring his aunt to relay a bounty of stories about her life.

In addition to the book, my sister sent me a decorative box, filled with 34 pennies, dated from 1959–1992. She had also collected a story from each of my childhood family members about an event they remembered from a particular year of my life. My father wrote about the day I was born. My eldest brother, Jim, wrote about my father's joy on the day I was born and how my birth represented a new beginning for our family. My brother Roger wrote about the excitement and pride he felt watching me win the 200 meter dash at the state track meet in high school.

Although none of my childhood family members were physically present for that birthday celebration (as we were scattered from east to west), their presence was as real that day as it had been at birthday celebrations when I was a child. Through laughter and tears, I read their stories to my spouse and children. Through laughter and tears, they listened, gleaning the memories of those who were intimate witnesses of my life in days gone by.

When Andrew's birthday rolled around the following year, I presented him with a penny box. To their delight, Morgan and Willa received their penny boxes on their 10th birthdays. Although we continue to enjoy a candlelighting ceremony atop a birthday cake or pie, the penny box has replaced the bonfire of candles that once lit up our birthday storytelling circles. A penny is added to the collection each year, pennies that have become the soulful measures of our lives; for, as my sister inscribed to me in the front pages of *The Penny Box* book she gave me:

> "There are many ways to measure time. . .
> I measure our friendship in memories,
> for memories are changes of the heart
> which last a lifetime and beyond."

Birthday Trials & Tribulations

A slew of questionable birthday traditions revolve around the birthday honoree enduring a physical trial to prove themselves worthy of their new age – birthday spankings, arm punches, earlobe pulls, and being turned upside down to have one's head thumped on the floor. Of course, the honoree receives one spank, punch, pull, or thump for each year (and sometimes one to grow on). Another age-old trial involves ambushing the celebrated one to grease their nose with butter – to make the birthday person too slippery for bad luck to catch them.

I'm not a big advocate of such trials since they can get out of hand, especially in an unsupervised young peer group, but tests of courage, skill, and perseverance can be a strengthening experience to prepare for the growth a new year of life asks of us. Of course, life often provides naturally occurring challenges, and a birthday can be a time for simply acknowledging the birthday honoree's success in meeting and overcoming such trials. At other times, an age-appropriate trial can be a means for a person to gain confidence in one's growing ability to meet life with courage and ingenuity. Depending on the age of the birthday honoree and their desire to partake in such a tradition, a birthday trial might include:

Uplifted: After a birthday song, the birthday person is lifted up and down in a chair by a strong and able group of well-wishers. The years of life are counted out with each lift of the chair.

Hugs & Kisses: A game of hide-and-seek in which the birthday boy or girl, upon being found, receives hugs or kisses equal to their age.

Skill-building: The birthday person is given a new task that requires skills appropriate for their age. Consider such tasks as cooking a dish for the birthday meal or making the birthday cake; being given a gift that requires a physical feat that the birthday person is ready to tackle – a first bicycle, roller blades, a snow board, an archery set, hiking gear, or some other gift that tests physical prowess; or reclaiming the opportunity to learn a skill that might have been learned at an earlier age. (See my brother Jim's story on pages 103-104 of "Reclaiming a Passage of Childhood.")

Trust Walk: One is blindfolded and led on a walk (perhaps to a birthday surprise) by a trustworthy family member or friend.

Natural Challenges: An older child, youth, or adult may desire to take on the trial of enduring a challenge of nature – an arduous hike, a caving expedition, rock climbing or rappelling, a canoe trip, a whitewater rapids adventure, a long-distance bicycle trip, etc. (Of course, it's crucial to prepare for such a challenge with appropriate training, planning, leadership, and safety considerations.)

A birthday trial should be an age-appropriate challenge that the birthday person is willing and enthused to accept. Coercing the birthday person to participate in a birthday trial can be disastrous and opposed to the intentions of such a feat. So when planning, keep in mind the birthday person's stage of development, interests, and abilities. Younger children will be especially drawn to birthday trials they've witnessed others celebrating successfully and those with elements of familiar fun, such as the suggested hide-and-seek game.

Royalty for the Day

It's thought that, at one time, only royalty celebrated their birthdays with a feast or party, thus the birthday tradition of crowning the birthday child and decorating their chair as if it were their throne. Being queen or king for a day is the antithesis of having to endure trials and tribulations on one's birthday, and it can be a welcome gesture when one's life has been filled with naturally occurring trials. Being treated like royalty might also be the reward for enduring a birthday trial successfully. Young children will delight in wearing a birthday crown, tiara or flower garland, and a silken cape. Older children and adults can be fortified with a more subtle approach to the "royal treatment." Such treatment might include breakfast in bed; minstrels serenading the "royal one;" no chores; no work or school; a relaxing massage; a bath prepared with soothing scents and music; choosing the menu for the birthday meals; and choosing activities for the day. We all deserve to have our way at least one day a year because somewhere, deep in the crevices of our imaginations and the corners of our souls, we are, each one of us, royalty.

Birthday Greetings

The tradition of sending birthday cards was begun in England as a way to apologize to the recipient for not being able to celebrate their birthday with them in person. Today, birthday cards are given more often and generously. However, there are ways to diverge from the usual store-bought cards to offer bolder expressions of affection. Consider these wilder and more adventurous birthday greetings:

First Things First: A birthday greeting placed strategically in the birthday person's bedroom can be a heartwarming surprise upon waking. Consider a flower bouquet (one flower for each year of life); a collage of biographical photographs; a giant homemade birthday card; paper streamers or beaded strands (one for each year of life) hung in the bedroom doorway (as a symbol of passing through the door into a new year); or a golden or rainbow-colored ribbon tied to a bedpost or doorknob of the bedroom to lead the birthday person on a journey to a morning birthday surprise (perhaps a gift or a festively decorated breakfast table).

A Feast for the Eyes: One longtime family birthday tradition at the Darian house includes a "birthday elf" decorating the common space of our house surreptitiously on the birthday eve after everyone goes to bed. The birthday person arises in the morning with an immediate acknowledgment of joy expressed in their honor. Easily done in secret when our children were young; now that we have four adults in the house (albeit, two young ones), we often have a good chuckle about the birthday decorating that can be heard *magically* materializing in the wee hours of the night. Birthday decorations needn't be extravagant or pricey. Even a simple visual display can add beauty, artistry, or a sense of revelry to a birthday. Years ago, a friend gave me some reusable party decorations she made by cutting out triangular flags from colorful fabric remnants. The festive little flags are strung on white string, and the length can reach several times across a room. Ever since I received them, they have graced every family birthday and a few other raucous occasions.

Sidewalk Talk: Draw a giant birthday card with chalk on the sidewalk, driveway, or patio. A cement fence, garage floor, or basement with a drain for cleanup can work just as well.

Dramatic Expressions: Rollicking birthday greetings can come in the form of a silly or touching birthday skit, practiced surreptitiously. Dramatic scripts for such occasions can be gleaned from poetry, songs, stories, or created from your own imaginations.

Museful Meanderings: In lieu of birthday cards, ask everyone to write or select a poem for the birthday person. A few years back, my family created an audio birthday card for a friend with failing eyesight. Each of us chose a poem that reflected our prayers for our friend in the coming year of her life. We recorded the poems for her so she could enjoy them at her leisure.

Singing Telegrams: When loved ones are long distance on their birthday, be bold enough to gather around the phone to call and bless the birthday person with a song of celebration. The traditional birthday song is not the only option. Consider the brief, heartfelt birthday songs on pages 308-317, or write one of your own.

Leaves of Gold: Family members can write a cooperative letter or individual letters to the birthday person on each birthday to express gratitude, affirm admirable personal qualities, and recall significant memories, learnings, and events of the year past. The letters can be kept in a treasure box, notebook, or journal, and an annual birthday photograph can be kept with the letters.

No doubt, birthday greetings can come in many forms. Imagine the possibilities and allow your creativity to be your "hallmark."

Truly Gifted

When I recall gifts I received in my nigh five decades of life, few are more precious than the one I received on my sixteenth birthday. My father came through the door after a hard day's work, his face beaming, and handed me a bouquet of 16 perfectly pink roses. Those shimmering roses were, for me, more than a birthday gift from my father. They were his way of saying that he noticed I had become a woman and that he would be the first man in my life to gift me with such a radiant bouquet of his affection. The truest gifts we receive are those that communicate to us that we are known and loved by the giver.

Today, material gifts are often the focus of a birthday gathering; however, in times past, gifts were a peripheral part of the celebration. Birthday parties began out of the belief that a person was especially vulnerable to evil spirits and negative forces on their birthday. To protect a person from such negativity, friends and family gathered to create a happy occasion filled with love, joy, and laughter. In lieu of gifts, family and friends showered the birthday person with their wishes, blessings, and affection.

With children and adults alike, one well thought-out gift can be more meaningful and memorable than a heaping pile of birthday loot. As one part of a meaningful rite of passage, gifts take on a different quality as they are given in the context of a celebration that emphasizes relationships, gratitude, growth, and learning. The most significant material gifts are those that reflect these deeper elements of the birthday celebration.

In our consumerist culture, we do well to put gift-giving in its proper place. With young children, it's especially important to keep gift-giving simple. If more than one or two gifts are given, spreading the opening of gifts over the course of a day or week can help the child receive the gifts in an attitude of interest and gratitude. For larger gatherings for which gifts are an expectation, don't be afraid to come up with an alternative plan. I once heard of a family that asked those celebrating their child's birthday with them each year not to buy material gifts for the child but, if they chose, to contribute to the child's college fund. I wish I had thought of that when *my* children were young! Such a fund not only keeps the celebration from being about "stuff," it also creates an invaluable resource for the child, which can be set up in a tax-advantaged account.

Consider ways you can reconstruct gift-giving so that material gifts don't become the focus of the celebration. Depending on the birthday person's age, you may want to use one of the following gift-giving ideas (or the birthday party gifts mentioned on pages 304-305) to inspire fun, heighten the relationship aspects of the gathering, and reflect the deeper meaning of the passage at hand:

Working For It: Create a treasure hunt with clues that the birthday person can unravel or participants can solve together. Make the treasure a special birthday gift for the honored one or simple gifts for everyone. If you don't have time to plan a treasure hunt, simply hide gifts (in Easter egg fashion) and as the birthday person searches, sing a birthday song or ring a chime or bell. When the seeker comes near a gift, sing or play more loudly; when they are distant, sing or play more softly. As each gift is found, take time to enjoy it before continuing the search.

Gifts of the Heart: Sometimes, the most meaningful gift can be an original song, poem, performance, work of art, or an item crafted by your own hands.

Gifts in Action: A coveted gift at our house is being given coupons and personal gift cards. Coupons might include doing the person's regular household chores for a day or a week; massages; cooking a special meal, favorite dish, or dessert; taxi or delivery service; offering handy-person services or lawncare; a donation of time or expertise; childcare; a mystery date; a road trip adventure; organizing a closet or neglected storage space; or whatever you can imagine.

Lovingly Adorned: In some cultures, a person celebrating a birthday or new year of life takes a cleansing bath to prepare soulfully for this annual rebirth. Afterward, the person dresses in new clothes. Consider gifting the birthday person with a new outfit, garment, or piece of jewelry to wear, or cutting or adorning their hair.

Another Year Wiser: Play a gift-opening game in which the birthday person must relate one new learning or insight from the past year before they're allowed to open each present.

Affirmation Cards: For her spouse's surprise 50th birthday party, a friend of mine asked all those invited to submit a word that described her spouse and a brief quotation or proverb to accompany it. The submissions could be serious or humorous. My friend and her children created "affirmation cards" by typesetting the words and quotes, cutting them into small cards, and laminating them. The name of each friend who submitted a word and quote was included on the affirmation card.

Sweet Dreams: Give the gift of a dream pillow for each birthday or on a significant birthday. A dream pillow is a small pillow filled with sweet-smelling lavender and other herbs to inspire sleep and relaxation at bedtime or quiet time. A dream pillow is easy to make and there are myriad instructions on the internet by searching "how to make a dream pillow." For an older child, youth, or adult, include with the gift a note of explanation:

> "This is your dream pillow. At bedtime, enjoy its relaxing scents to inspire restful sleep and pleasant dreams. Any time of day, breathe in its aroma to quiet your mind, body, and soul and remember your life dreams – the ones you may actualize with your eyes wide open."

A dream pillow can make a meaningful gift for a young adult away at college or anyone away from family and friends on their birthday. The gift might prompt a youth or adult to dream and vision about their new year of life. A brief list of prompts for the birthday person to consider can be included:

> As I dream of my new year of life –
> ~ a top priority is. . .
> ~ I will worry less about. . .
> ~ I will accomplish. . .
> ~ I will learn. . .
> ~ I will enjoy life more by. . .

(Include whatever prompts seem appropriate for the person receiving the dream pillow.) A book on dream symbols or a journal for recording one's dreams might also be given with the dream pillow.

Gift Reversal: Expressing gratitude for one's life and growth is a significant aspect of celebrating one's birthday. I once read of a family who adopted the tradition of each child giving their mother a gift on their own birthday as a way of saying "thank you for birthing me into this world." Another way of balancing giving and receiving energy on a birthday is for the birthday person to prepare small gifts for their family or party guests as a way to say "thank you for your love and support." Expressions of gratitude to the Divine can also remind us not to take the gift of life for granted. On one's birthday, gratitude can be expressed prayerfully through a compassionate action, such as planting a tree, assisting someone who needs help, or contributing time or money to a food pantry or homeless shelter and committing oneself to the project for the coming year. In some families, the birthday honoree chooses a charity and asks family members and friends to make a donation to the charity in lieu of birthday gifts. Birthdays are a significant time to be reminded of the positive impact our lives can have on others.

A New Privilege: Granting a child an age-appropriate privilege on each birthday can be a poignant affirmation of a child's growth. On Willa's and Morgan's seventh birthdays, Andrew and I granted each of them the right to ring the crystal singing bowl (pages 297, 299) that we use for our family birthday celebrations. A simple gesture, but one they had each looked forward to with great anticipation. At the age of nine, we gave them each their first big birthday party and the right to have individual sleepovers with their friends. At 13, they were each given their own CD player to use respectfully. Reserving a new right or privilege to grant a child in their new year of life – whether it's on or near their birthday, on their half birthday, or when a new grade in school begins or ends – can give a child confidence and encourage the child to celebrate and savor each new stage of their development. (See the following pages on "Granting Rights and Responsibilities.")

Granting Rights and Responsibilities

Setting boundaries for children and intentionally granting them age-appropriate rights and responsibilities is one of the toughest jobs involved in parenting. Doing so effectively requires us to share quality time with our children so we can clearly see and understand their age and stage of growth. It requires us to learn about human development and age-appropriate expectations and behaviors. It requires us to be firm with a young person when we set a boundary and to be strong when they push against it. It also requires us to trust a young person to boldly meet the joys and challenges that come with each new right and responsibility being granted.

When our children were young, Andrew and I realized that many of the birthday gifts Willa and Morgan appreciated most were the ones associated with a new right or privilege. So, when they were six and eight, we sketched out a plan for giving them certain rights and responsibilities at each new age and stage of their growth. We used the sketch as a guide to help us consider new rights we could grant Morgan and Willa with each passing year. We tweaked the sketch as we responded to the questions and issues that arose along the way. Many times a new right was granted on or near a child's birthday; always a new right or responsibility was granted only when we witnessed each child's readiness to take it on.

Our main motivation in granting our children new rights from year to year was to make them more aware of the gradual unfolding of their maturity. Likewise, we wanted them to recognize that with each right granted, a subsequent responsibility is attached. We found through the years that as we intentionally chose to trust our children with new rights and responsibilities, they simultaneously developed a deep sense of trust in our parenting abilities. By the time the teenage years hit, our children already knew they could depend on us to set limits and grant privileges that were fair and based on the realities of their development and maturity. They knew we were willing not only to challenge them with appropriate boundaries and responsibilities, they also knew we were willing to challenge ourselves to rethink appropriate rights and privileges according to the human beings we saw maturing right before our eyes. Such a process forces us to face our own insecurities as parents as we gradually release our parental hold of protection. It means not only trusting our children, but trusting life to hold our children in ways that we, as parents, cannot.

The examples of rights and responsibilities on the following pages are merely food for thought. They aren't meant to be prescriptive. I've included some examples from my own family's journey. Many reflect our Darian family traditions and the unique interests and requests of our children. These rights and responsibilities were not always given on a birthday; sometimes, we correlated a new right with a new grade in school or a half birthday. Sometimes Willa or Morgan received a privilege at a younger or older age than the other, depending on their growth and development and our family situation at the time. For example, there were some rights and responsibilities associated with puberty that Willa was granted earlier because she met that passage at an earlier age; conversely, due to our family moving to a city with a high accident rate, Willa earned her driver's license when she was six months older than Morgan had been.

One area in which Andrew and I could have been more intentional with our children through their younger years was in the area of personal finances. We had a lot of catching up to do as Morgan and Willa became young adults. Therefore, along with examples of rights and responsibilities we've granted our children concerning money, I've added and embellished suggestions to deepen a child's interest and expertise in the area of personal finance. Because most educational systems aspire to teach students algebra, calculus, and trigonometry, but often fail to teach them the basics of everyday finances, children often depend on parents and grandparents to teach them these valuable lessons. (See the books on personal finance on page 332.)

As you consider rights and responsibilities to grant your child through the years, sketch out possibilities based on your own beliefs, values, views on human development, and the temperament, personality, and interests of your child. Of course, it's important for parenting partners to converse and agree on rights and responsibilities to grant a child through the years. It's equally important to rethink the plan as a child's life unfolds. In situations of divorce, granting appropriate rights and responsibilities can be problematic due to contrasting values and beliefs of two households and due to children in blended families having input from stepparents. Ideally, divorced parents can work together to come to some agreement about consistent rights and responsibilities for their child; realistically, it's sometimes difficult for divorced parenting partners to see eye-to-eye. Do the best you can. Clarity and consistency in one household is better than none.

One important aspect to consider in granting new rights to children in a gradual manner are the rights that are often granted unintentionally. In the absence of clear parental guidance, children are apt to take hold of certain rights before they have the maturity or capacity to take on the corresponding responsibilities. Don't overlook such rights as answering the telephone; using the phone for social calls; using the computer; watching TV during leisure time; having electronic equipment (such as a cell phone, ipod/MP3 player, or stereo) in a child's bedroom or for their personal use; having sleepovers with friends (aside from childcare situations); playing team sports; or taking dance or music lessons. Such rights, when given according to a child's development, can be experienced as significant milestones in a child's life. These anticipated milestones can foster confidence and a healthy sense of responsibility. Additionally, well thought-out rights and responsibilities allow the parent to clearly set rules and guidelines that foster healthy family relationships. Remember – in facing the challenges of parenting, there are no easy answers, but there are ample possibilities to discover the answers!

Examples of Rights and Corresponding Responsibilities

Choose rights and responsibilities for your child based on your own beliefs, values, views on human development, and the temperament, personality, and interests of your child.

Age 7: Rights	Corresponding Responsibilities
• Granted an allowance	Begin savings account with parental support; take on a new household chore; donate a portion of allowance to charity; with parent, research the organization to which the child desires to donate and learn how the donated money will be utilized; reassess charitable donations/commitments on an annual basis
• May begin Irish dance lessons	Practice dance (outside class) twice a week
• May ring singing bowl at birthday celebration (pages 297, 299)	Given more responsibility preparing for and hosting family celebrations

Age 8: Rights	Corresponding Responsibilities
• Receives a raise in allowance with each birthday (to age 12)	Learn to read bank statements and fill out deposit slips; given new household chore each birthday

• May answer home phone	Learn telephone etiquette for answering phone, how to take messages, and how to deal with strangers and telemarketers

Age 9: Rights · Corresponding Responsibilities

Age 9: Rights	Corresponding Responsibilities
• May have individual sleepovers	Carry family guides & rules into independent experiences
• May play rec league softball	Learn league rules, practice twice a week, display sporting behavior on & off the field
• Receives a watch (w/analog face) on their birthday	Learn to tell time the traditional way
• May do odd jobs for family members and friends for cash	Keep a ledger of all money earned, saved, invested, or spent
• May invest a portion of money	With strong parental support: learn basic ideas of investment and return on money saved and earned; choose a solid, world-friendly investment and reassess it twice a year; learn about ethical banking and investment practices through such resources as *The Better World Shopping Guide* by Ellis Jones; start or become a steward of college fund

Age 10: Rights · Corresponding Responsibilities

Age 10: Rights	Corresponding Responsibilities
• Receives a penny box on birthday (page 280)	Learn to record important autobiographical events (in journal and/or photo album)
• May use home phone for brief, purposeful calls	Learn proper phone etiquette for placing calls, use of telephone book, & placing calls to directory assistance
• May begin music lessons	Practice three times a week outside lesson

Age 11: Rights · Corresponding Responsibilities

Age 11: Rights	Corresponding Responsibilities
• May use phone for brief social calls	Be able to keep time limits & make calls when it doesn't detract from family life
• May play rec league basketball and run on school track team	Learn rules, practice three times a week, display sporting behavior
• May join mom and dad for late night New Year's Eve Celebration	Prepare for self-reflection/visioning portion of celebration

Age 12: Rights

- May host first slumber party

- Girls may use makeup sparingly

- May use family computer for brief, purposeful tasks

Corresponding Responsibilities

Help to create invitations and plan activities

After applying, get mom or dad's okay

Learn how to use computer, basic computer care, keyboarding, how to avoid viruses and other computer problems; be able to keep time limits; use when homework and chores are completed and when it doesn't detract from family life

Age 13: Rights

- May have CD player in bedroom

- May invite "boyfriend" or "girlfriend" to share family time

- May begin email account

- May take on such jobs as baby-sitting or lawncare for cash

Corresponding Responsibilities

Use when it doesn't detract from other activities/family relationships; use headphones at other family members' request

Converse with parent/s about setting appropriate boundaries in romantic relationships and boundaries set in current relationship

Choose two days a week to use briefly after homework/chores are done and when it doesn't detract from family life

Take CPR and baby-sitting course to baby-sit or learn skills to complete chosen job well; create a personal budget and keep ledger; review banking and investment options and charitable donations with parent as earnings increase; learn about income limits for tax purposes; may take out loan from parent/s (with interest) to invest in public relations or buy needed tools (loan agreement is written up and interest paid)

Age 14: Rights

- May own a cell phone

Corresponding Responsibilities

Use for purposeful and long distance calls when it doesn't detract from family life or other activities; respect time limit given; review cell phone bill each month with parent; contribute portion of payment and pay own overage charges

• May go on group "dates" to a public place: restaurant, movie, bowling, etc.	Unknown friends meet parent/s; enlist parent driver; honor set curfew/call if late; learn to tip service people appropriately

Age 15: Rights   **Corresponding Responsibilities**

• May earn driver's permit	Check on state legalities and age requirements; go to insurance agent with parent/s to talk about how coverage works for student driver and ways to receive driver discounts; learn to wash car and change flat tire
• May seek employment	Research minimum age for job sought; research possibilities for employment, compensation, treatment of employees and benefits; learn how to calculate and report income tax; converse with parents about acceptable number of work hours and schedule
• May participate in "Face Book," "My Space," or similar website	Converse with parent/s about privacy issues; appropriate material on site; choose two or three days a week to use for brief periods when it doesn't detract from family life or other activities; share site with parent/s occasionally
• May make own fashion choices on hair, clothes, makeup without parental input	Know dress codes for school, work or other larger community settings; converse with parent/s or other mentors about any questionable choices that arise

Age 16: Rights   **Corresponding Responsibilities**

• May go on individual dates	Invite unknown date over to meet parent/s; make sure driver is responsible; honor set curfew, call if late; let parent/s know where you will be and call if location changes; converse openly with parent/s about appropriate sexual choices and boundaries
• May earn driver's license	Contribute resources to care for family car (cleaning car inside and out, buying gas, partial insurance payment, oil change, arranging maintenance checkup, etc.), negotiate car use with parent/s
• May receive one body-piercing (top of ear, belly button, etc.)	Research cautions and dangers of body piercing, research quality standards of piercing establishments

- May drink one glass of wine with family at home on special occasions *only**

Converse with parent/s about responsible use of alcoholic beverages; no drinking in any other settings or when other minors outside immediate family are present

- May begin to make choices about future work and/or college plans after high school

Plan for college and/or work after high school; for work – find mentor and training program in field of interest; for college – research programs and financial resources (college fund, scholarship, grant sources, parental assistance, work-study, etc.), apply for programs, visit potential schools, process needed paperwork with parental support

Age 17: Rights

Corresponding Responsibilities

- May live away from home for extended periods in settings with limited adult supervision (summer training programs, international exchange programs or work trips, specialty boarding schools, etc.)

Carry family guides and rules into new setting; inform parents of plans and activities beyond scope of program; create own budget and adhere to it; and, as E.T. says, "phone home"

- May receive one small tattoo

Research cautions and dangers of tattooing; research quality standards of tattoo parlor; design/location of tattoo OK'd by parent/s

- May purchase own car

With parental support, consider: advantages and disadvantages of sharing family car, using public transportation, or riding a bicycle or scooter; budget for cost of car, gas, insurance, and maintenance; best options for buying (used or new) or leasing; ins and outs of a commercial loan; safety, quality, and consumer ratings; negotiating price of car; ecological issues associated with gas usage and emission levels; check out ethical standards of auto dealer if buying new

*Of course, granting a young adult a right such as drinking a glass of wine on special occasions will depend upon the laws in your state, your religious beliefs, your family's history (and a young adult's personal history) with alcohol, and the maturity of the young adult being granted the privilege. Since Andrew and I both have extended family members who had problems with excessive drinking in the past, we chose to grant our children this limited privilege at an age when we still had considerable influence to guide them toward responsible drinking. Willa and Morgan both attribute being given this right at 16 as a key to their lack of desire or need as young adults to drink socially with their friends.

Age 18: Rights	Corresponding Responsibilities
• May legally vote/sign petitions	Be informed on local, national, and world news and politics; receive a personal copy of *The Better World Shopping Guide* by Ellis Jones as a way of encouraging the young adult to "vote" through their purchasing decisions
• May make own choices on body piercing, tattooing, etc.	Continue to research and converse with parents or other mentors about cautions and dangers; consider personal image, permanence of tattoos, and how such choices may affect future employment and career goals, etc.

Age 18-21: Rights	Corresponding Responsibilities
• While living at parent's home, or attending college this is a period of receiving full adult rights and being treated as a capable and responsible adult who can make decisions for oneself	Be familiar with laws and college rules (if applicable) that affect age group; agree on collective household expectations with other family members, and consider creative solutions to differing expectations; share responsibilities for household chores; be collectively responsible for family needs and decision making; be involved in creating/maintaining family budget, paying bills, etc.; learn about the pros and cons of using credit, securing loans, and life insurance
• At 21, can legally drink alcoholic beverages in public and purchase alcohol	Be familiar with alcohol limits for driving and institutional rules for work and/or school; drink in moderation; be familiar with health issues; choose a designated driver when drinking and volunteer to be one when not drinking; be aware of "date rape" drugs; never serve alcohol to or purchase alcohol for a minor; never use alcohol as an initiation or competition; don't feel obligated to drink with friends; be boldly yourself and have fun without the stuff

The above list is not prescriptive and hardly exhaustive. My hope is that these examples may inspire you to identify rights and responsibilities that are appropriate for your own child. Rest assured, the time and effort you invest in this exercise will more than pay for itself along the way. Such reflections not only allow parents to be more confident about setting boundaries and granting privileges as a child matures, they allow us the freedom to fully celebrate and enjoy a child's growing independence. Moreover, our efforts allow a child to absorb a bit of J.D. Rockefeller, Jr.'s wisdom that "every right implies a responsibility; every opportunity, an obligation; every possession, a duty."

The Family Celebration

The highlight of a Darian family birthday is an evening rite of passage ceremony. After a festive, leisurely, and (usually) collectively homemade dinner, we gather in the living room where the coffee table has been transformed into the stuff of which memories and dreams are made.

Tools ❧ On the coffee table is a crystal singing bowl (an instrument thought to evolve from a Tibetan tradition, used as a tool to promote inner harmony and soulful cleansing); two life candles – one burnt down in the past year and a new life candle for the year to come; matches and a candle snuffer; a small bowl or vial of blessing water, fairy dust (fine, sparkling glitter), or anointing oil; and the birthday person's special "penny box" (described on page 280). The penny box is open and the pennies are laid out on the table in some sort of chronological design; a newly minted penny is laid out to add to the collection. (Those born near the beginning of the year may need to receive a penny from the past year.) The table and its contents are covered with a beautiful, lightweight cloth. Nearby are some large, sturdy feathers and a few simple instruments – a hand drum, chime, shaker, etc. The birthday person is invited to sit in a chair placed in the center of the room, facing the coffee table.

Releasing the Past

Family members stand behind the birthday honoree who is seated. One holds the bundle of feathers, others hold a percussion instrument. After a few moments of silence, the feathers are fanned in strong, definite strokes to create an air current, felt by the birthday person as a symbol for the years of the past "taking wing." One stroke is made for each year of life, and with each stroke of the feathers, the percussion instruments are played for one beat. (An alternative is to nix the instruments and have each family member hold a large feather, fanning the feathers in unison.)

Embracing Significant Memories and Learnings

Song: Joyous Birthday (page 317)

Joyous birthday to you,
Joyous birthday to you,
Now may all your wishes be
Filled with love and destiny,
Now may all your dreams come true,
May they become you,
And may all your visions fly
Free across each new sky.
Joyous birthday to you,
Joyous birthday to you.

During the birthday song, two family members stand at opposite ends of the coffee table and grasp the corners of the covering cloth. Everyone sings, and on the word "filled," the cloth is lifted upward with a brisk motion so that it floats magically over the contents of the table. As the song continues, the cloth is lifted up two or three more times. Then on the phrase, "Now, may all your visions fly," the cloth is lifted up and back behind the coffee table to be laid gently on the floor.

The Birth Story

The birthday person's life candle from the year past is lit, and someone speaks of the day of the honored one's birth:

"On *November 5th, 1989, at 5:55 p.m., Willa Andi Darian* was born."

The birth story is told. It can be a full or abbreviated version of the birth events, well thought-out or spontaneous, symbolic or biographical. (See the "Create a Birth Story" section on page 70.)

Story Circle

One at a time and in chronological order, beginning with the birth year, the birthday person picks up a penny, calls out the year, and drops the penny in their penny box. For young children, a family member tells at least one brief story for each year of the child's life. With older children and adults, each family member plans to tell one or two special stories, each from a particular year, so when that year is called out, the story is shared. When the final penny is added to the penny box, everyone shares at least one memory of the birthday person's life, learnings, accomplishments, humorous moments, or important events from the year past.

Envisioning the Future

Lighting the New Life Candle

The birthday person is invited to light their new life candle from the old one and to blow out or snuff the old life candle.

Blessing the New Year

Family members stand in a circle around the birthday person with the blessing bowl of fairy dust ready. One at a time, each person shares their wishes, prayers, or visions for the birthday person's coming year. Then the blessing giver sprinkles the birthday person with a bit of fairy dust. (If you prefer, you can bless the birthday person with water or anointing oil.) After family members share their blessings, the birthday person may choose to share prayers, wishes, or reflections about their new year of life.

Song: One More Year (see page 314)

One more year our hearts have held you,
One more year you've gladdened our lives,
One more year we want to say:
"We honor you on this mem'rable day."
Happy birthday, happy birthday,
Happy birthday to you.

Ringing in the New Year

After the final birthday song, everyone stands in a circle around the coffee table. The birthday person strikes the inner lip of the crystal singing bowl with its suede-covered mallet (one stroke for each year of life), then circles the outer top edge of the bowl with the edge of the mallet to ring in their new year. (Of course, a resonant chime or another instrument may be used for this part of the ceremony, as well.) The awesome, resonant tone of the singing bowl seems to go on forever. We remain silent until its music finally fades and then burst into congratulatory revelry!

Although establishing a birthday rite of passage takes a bit of planning, it can make birthday preparations easier because, with each family birthday, family members come to anticipate what's needed and can do their part to make the celebration possible. Such a meaningful tradition often inspires enthusiastic cooperation because the outcome provides such a heartwarming opportunity to bask in one another's affection, laughter, and spirited conversation.

A few months before Willa's 16th birthday, our family moved to Phoenix to help care for my father who was dying of cancer. Although my dad was just a few months away from death, he was fully able to contribute to Willa's birthday rite. The festive evening included recalling together heartfelt and hilarious memories of Willa's life, and my dad had the opportunity (along with the rest of the family) to verbally bless Willa before he passed. Because my father participated enthusiastically and lovingly, that birthday celebration is one of Willa's most heartwarming memories of her grandfather.

If you have yet to establish a birthday rite of passage in your family, don't pressure yourself to create it all at once. Choose one new tradition to establish with each birthday until you've created the celebration you desire. You may want to begin with a penny box story circle (pages 280, 298), by learning a new birthday song (pages 308-317), or whatever new birthday tradition would be meaningful to you and your family. Remember, the Darian family birthday celebration evolved over a handful of years. The life candle (page 278) was one of our first family birthday traditions. "Fairy dust" (see "Blessing the New Year," page 299) was added at Morgan's request on her seventh birthday. The penny box came into play when Andrew and I were in our thirties, and for Morgan and Willa when they were ten. So, don't feel you have to do it all at once. Establishing birthday traditions is an evolving family experience. Let it unfold with an unrushed sense of adventure.

The Birthday Party

When birthdays are honored with intentional, loving, family celebrations, the significance of birthday parties sometimes pales in comparison. The first time my parents hosted a birthday party for me, I was in middle school. As exciting as that all-girl slumber party was, it didn't replace the richness of a family gathered to express joy and thanks for one of its cherished members. Nothing can replace that.

Having learned that lesson early in life, as a parent I've never felt an obligation to throw annual birthday parties for my children (or any of my intimates). Before agreeing to the idea of a birthday party for myself or a family member, the question I ask is: "Will a party add meaning and a greater sense of celebration to the occasion?" If I imagined a birthday party had to be the usual sweetfest and gift orgy so popular in our culture, my answer would, undoubtedly, always be "no." However, over the past two decades, in cultivating meaningful rites of passage, I've realized what a potent initiation a birthday party can be.

During the years of Morgan's and Willa's youth, in addition to our more intimate family celebrations, Andrew and I chose two particular milestones to celebrate with a birthday party. For their ninth birthday passages, a knighting ceremony was planned (page 124). The knighting seemed to us a vibrant gesture to acknowledge the change that occurs around the age of nine, when a child comes to see themselves as an individual standing alone in the world. It's a time of recognizing one's personal power, as well as one's vulnerability and mortality. For their twelfth birthday passages, the party included group-building trials and a friendship celebration (page 145) to acknowledge the growing importance and complexity of peer relationships at that age. These birthday parties inspired an obvious deepening of confidence in both our children as they gained clarity about themselves as individuals and in relationship to others.

Unfortunately, the best birthday parties in our culture tend to focus on the young, and we often miss opportunities to initiate adults as we grow and change. This may be due to our fuzziness as a culture about when significant adult passages take place. While youths and young adults celebrate major cultural transitions at 13, 16, 18 and 21, older adults have few set age transitions to depend upon. No one really knows when middle age begins and, in differing situations, senior status is conferred at 50, 55, 60 or 65.

The ancient Greeks offered a model of the human life cycle, identifying early childhood from birth to age 7, and older childhood from 7-14. In the ancient Grecian model, the evolving human becomes a youth at age 14, a young adult at 21, an adult at 28, an elder at 49, and enters old age at 56. Although most ancient Greeks didn't reach these elder passages, the natural end of life was thought to come at 70. More recent theorists, including Rudolf Steiner (the inspiration behind Waldorf education), have presented seven-year cycles of human development as applicable for people of more recent eras.

In addition to the picture of human development based on seven-year cycles, there are many other age-related models to consider. Perhaps the best known model for human development in our culture is the model of psychosocial development proposed by Erik Erikson. In Erikson's model, he identifies four stages of childhood from birth to age twelve, including infancy from birth to 18 months, early childhood from 18 months to 3 years, play age from ages 3 to 5, and school age from 6 to 12. In Erikson's model, adolescence is identified from 12-18, young adulthood from 18-40, middle adulthood from 40-65, and mature adulthood at 65.

Whatever age-related model of human development one embraces, it's important to remember that there are unique aspects of development based on gender, and that human beings don't always fit neatly into such ordered pictures of human growth. In Gail Sheehy's work, she has identified unique passages that have evolved for adults given contemporary cultural changes. If age-related models of the past are to assist us in meeting life passages today, we must consider such variables. We also must consider that our human development doesn't happen in a linear way. Though such labels as "child," "youth," "adolescent," "adult," and "elder" may help us organize our thinking, they don't necessarily reflect the gradual unfolding that takes place as a human being grows and matures.

However, even with the shortcomings such age-related models of human development may present, each model suggests life passages to observe and consider. Each points us toward a truth often mislaid in our contemporary culture – that one's development doesn't end with entrance into adulthood. Social, emotional, psychological, and spiritual growth continue long after our physical development is complete. The potential joys of middle age and elderhood are no less great than those of our youth. Birthday parties to acknowledge the progressive stages of adulthood remind us and our children of our continuing capacities for soulful development. They affirm that the wisdom available to us in middle age and elderhood should, indeed, be revered and celebrated.

To plan birthday parties that focus on honoring life and relationships, you may find the following ideas helpful:

1. Identify milestone birthdays for your family.

Milestone birthdays can be defined by a particular view of human development that identifies age-related transitions, religious rites of passage (e.g. a bar/bat mitzvah celebration), culturally defined passages (e.g. earning a driver's license at 16), or may be related to a transitional life event or circumstance (e.g. a change in career or retiring from a longtime profession). Today, the decade birthdays are considered milestone birthdays for adults and are often celebrated with a greater sense of revelry beginning with the 30th birthday. After 50, the five-year birthdays gain new meaning, often identifying 55, 65, and 75 as years commonly associated with entrance into the senior years, retirement, and honoring one's elder status.

Milestone birthdays can also be associated with life situations and biographical events: a family member healing from an illness or overcoming some other trial in the year past, a family member returning home from an extended trip or military service overseas, a young adult moving away from the family home to establish their own residence, a woman cycling through menopause, or an elder retiring. Birthdays can be an opportunity to acknowledge such life-changing shifts in consciousness and can bring deeper meaning to a birthday celebration. Also, because birthdays are commonly celebrated in our culture, honoring a significant rite of passage with a birthday party can inspire enthusiastic participation from those unfamiliar with celebrating other rites of passage.

2. Consider the number of guests and age-groups to be invited.

The number of guests and their ages can greatly affect the atmosphere and focus of a birthday party. Since young children easily become overwhelmed and overstimulated by large group gatherings (especially the birthday child who is the center of attention), it may be best to keep the number of guests for children's parties relatively small. Several families I know invite the number of guests that correlates with a child's age; for example, a four-year-old may invite four guests, a seven-year-old, seven.

A fun alternative to a children's party is an intergenerational party. My sister and brother-in-law recently started a new birthday tradition of hosting a birthday brunch for their young children on the weekend preceding or following the child's birthdate. A few close family friends are invited and guests are greeted early in the day while the children are refreshed from a good night's sleep.

Of course, some birthday passages warrant a larger gathering despite their more demanding preparations. A few months before my father died of cancer, my siblings and I, along with our stepmother, hosted my dad's 75th birthday party, which was the birthday extravaganza of his life. Over a hundred friends and family members gathered to honor, pray for, and celebrate my dad. For many of my father's intimates, this party was a key to our acceptance and healing before his death. No doubt, a well-placed and well-planned birthday party has the potential to change lives and outlooks.

3. Consider creative and meaningful alternatives to gift-giving.

For children, receiving a shower of gifts can be the highlight of a party; it can also be overstimulating and detract from the meaning of the celebration. I've attended adult surprise parties during which the guest of honor either managed to put off the gift-opening until most of the guests were gone, or visibly begrudged opening the overwhelming shower of gifts placed before them. Sometimes it's difficult to know how best to shower a birthday person with joy, affection, and support without succumbing to our consumerist tendency to express affection and good wishes with material gifts.

In a variety of birthday party situations, my family and friends have asked those invited to refrain from bringing the usual birthday loot. Sometimes guests have been asked to bring the birthday person a written blessing, an artistic expression (a poem, story, song, etc.), one of the birthday person's favorite foods, a story from the birthday person's life, a symbolic gift from nature (a rock, shell, crystal, flower, etc.), or simply for the participants to consider their presence at the gathering as "present" enough. (For more ideas, see pages 285-288.)

Before they were nine, Willa and Morgan had never received the common shower of birthday gifts. However, for their ninth birthday knighting celebration (page 124), Andrew and I decided not to discourage those invited from bringing the usual gift offerings. We strategically interlaced the gift-giving with the medieval feast we planned. At spontaneous moments during the meal, Andrew (who was playing the part of King Arthur) called one of the gift-givers forward to bestow their gift on the youth of honor. In this way, the gift-opening happened gradually, and the birthday person had time to absorb and express thanks for each gift.

At my dad's 75th birthday celebration, a simple gift of prayer was created before the party began. In the foyer of the church, where the celebration was held, guests were greeted and asked to write a word of prayer on a small, flat rock – just a single word that represented the giver's greatest prayer for my dad as he celebrated his 75th birthday. (Fast-drying silver and gold paint pens were used.) Guests kept their rock until a prayerful moment during the celebration when all the rocks were gathered in a basket and given to my dad. After the party, my stepmom placed the basket of rocks where she and my dad could see them every day and be reminded of the support, affection, and prayers of friends and family as they faced together the transition of my father's death and rebirth.

4. Consider how the planning, preparation, hosting, and cleanup for the party can be shared.

Whether you're throwing an intimate, simple celebration or the birthday party of someone's life, consider how friends and family members can work together to make the birthday party a success, avoid stress, and save time. Party preparations and cleanup can be less labor intensive by having an able group gather before the party to decorate or stay after for cleanup. Expense and time for food preparation can be avoided by asking each person or family invited to bring a special dish to share.

When our family hosts a large birthday gathering, we think through the logistics a month or two in advance. Then, a day or two before the gathering, we all work together to prepare all the needed elements. Interestingly, some of our best and funniest memories of these events have taken place during our collaborative preparations.

Reclaiming a Birthday Passage

There may be numerous reasons to revisit and reclaim the significance of a birthday event: a family may be apart for the big day, or a personal, family, or community crisis may require attention. Unfortunately, like my friend whose mother ignored her seventh birthday, some of us continue to harbor birthday memories associated with past pain and woundedness. However a particular birthday may have been overlooked or uncelebrated, it isn't necessary to allow it to remain so. To reclaim or transform the significance of a birthday passage, consider the following ideas:

- **Un-birthdays:** Although one's birthdate can be a potent time to celebrate one's journey of growth and change, occasionally the stuff of life makes a genuine celebration on the birthdate difficult. Some families routinely plan birthday celebrations on the weekend following a family member's actual birthdate, so the celebration can happen more leisurely. When my family chooses this alternative, the actual birthdate is acknowledged in a few simple ways and the main birthday event is saved for the weekend with its potential for dallying in one another's presence. When an unexpected crisis arises or a family situation requires the birthday celebration to be put off further into the future, you may want to have a bit of fun with the idea of a half birthday or un-birthday celebration. Now that Willa and Morgan are grown, and sometimes away from home on family birthdays, we often plan family birthday celebrations around a holiday when we can all be together. As you consider the possibilities, remember that most any day will do as long as a family comes to it with a sense of intentionality and gratitude. As Lewis Carroll reminds us, "There are three hundred and sixty-four days when you might get un-birthday presents, and only one for birthday presents, you know." Think of the possibilities.

- **New Year of Life:** One Chinese tradition involves a person becoming a year older at the New Year. New Year's Eve (or the first few days of the new year) may be a potent time to celebrate a person's new year of life – when attention is focused on self-reflection and new beginnings. Consider making the alternative birthday event a two-part celebration or midnight vigil. On New Year's Eve focus on remembrance, gratitude for the past, and shedding the old. On New Year's Day focus on visions for the new year and expressing gratitude and joy for the present.

❧ **Celebration of Healing:** For adults who are holding on to painful memories surrounding a particular birthday due to life circumstances or a caregiver's insensitivity or negligence, it can be helpful to reclaim that painful birthday memory and transform it into something positive. For your own healing and growth, you may want to reflect on the challenges and joys you experienced at that particular age. Gather photos and mementos, and ask those who knew you intimately during that time in your life to share memories. Consider what your ideal birthday celebration would have included, then ask a few close family members or friends to help you create a birthday celebration that affirms who you were then. Contemplate how that "younger you" can bring healing and insight to your life now. It's never too late to celebrate and reinterpret the significance of the past.

❧ **Birthday Circle:** When I was 32, some friends and I decided to form a birthday circle for the year. Some of the folks in the group hadn't experienced a heightened sense of their life being celebrated by others since they were children, if then. We were mostly in our thirties and forties. Some of us were raising young children. Some were married, others divorced or single. Our intention was to create nurturing birthday celebrations for one another (in an all-adult setting) that reflected the deeper meaning of the life passages we each were experiencing at the time. One or two group members planned the birthday celebration (with input from the person being celebrated). An invitation was written to clarify the deeper meaning of the celebration and what participants needed to prepare or bring to the event: a gift from the heart, a brief reflection, a symbol, or a dish to share. Enriched with music, acts of nurturing, affirmations of rebirth, and artistic gifts created for the birthday person, each party powerfully reflected the unique passage being experienced. Each honoree felt genuinely blessed and prepared to walk into a new year of life. Of course, the birthday circle celebration for me didn't replace the delight of the family celebration Andrew and my children (who were three and five at the time) planned for me. However, being celebrated by a group of adults, who genuinely knew how to impart meaningful gifts of support, remains one of the most profound rites of passage I've experienced in a community other than my immediate family.

Songs for Celebrating Birthdays

Open Wide the Door

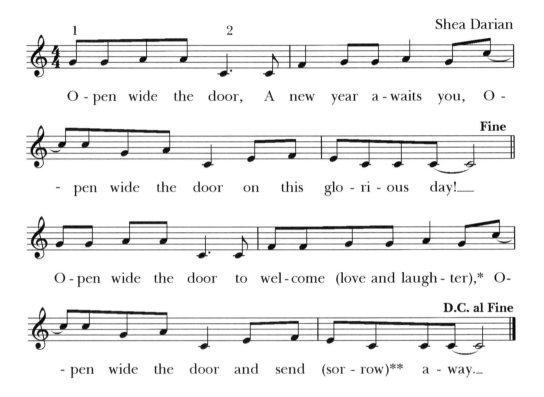

Shea Darian

O - pen wide the door, A new year a - waits you, O - pen wide the door on this glo - ri - ous day!

O - pen wide the door to wel - come (love and laugh - ter),* O - pen wide the door and send (sor - row)** a - way.

The old tradition of clapping for the birthday honoree was thought to dispel evil spirits and negativity, and can be done before and/or after this birthday song. Clap in unison, once for each year, and add one extra clap for good luck in the new year.

*alternative lyrics: growth and wisdom, peace and healing, hope and vision, etc.
**alternative lyrics: mischief, pain, worry, etc.

Wishing

Shea Darian

Wish - ing on the birth - day lights, Each
one a prayer so wise,_____
Blow them out, we'll give a shout, And
bless your wi - shes as they rise.
Wish - ing on the birth - day lights, Each
one a prayer so dear,_____
Blow them out, we'll give a shout to
bless your com - ing year!_____

Birthday Eve Lullaby

Shea Darian

To - night when I close___ my eyes, When I lay to rest___ my head_____ I'll be (three)* years old and a mea - sure of days, To - night when I'm tucked in - to bed._____ To -

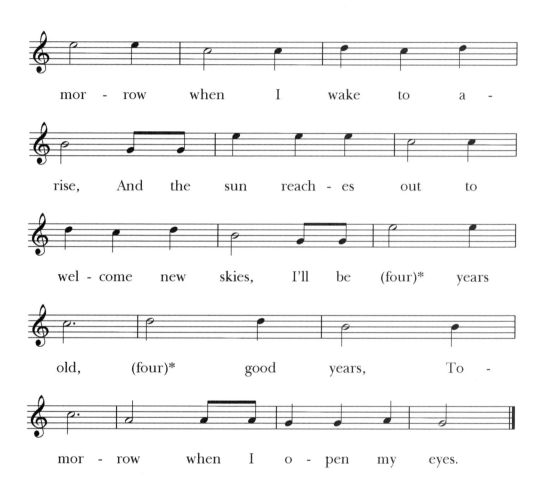

mor - row   when   I   wake   to   a -

rise,   And   the   sun   reach - es   out   to

wel - come   new   skies,   I'll   be   (four)*   years

old,   (four)*   good   years,   To -

mor - row   when   I   o - pen   my   eyes.

*Insert appropriate ages of birthday child.

You Shall Arise

Shea Darian

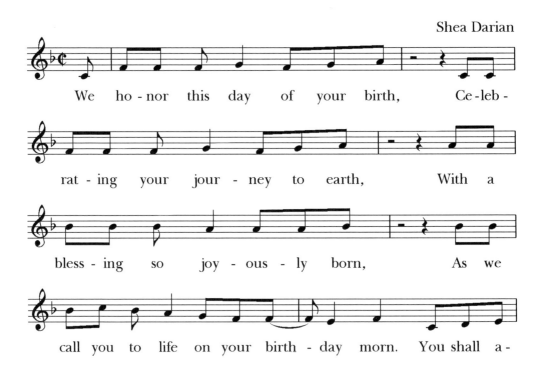

We ho - nor this day of your birth, Ce -leb -

rat - ing your jour - ney to earth, With a

bless - ing so joy - ous - ly born, As we

call you to life on your birth - day morn. You shall a -

> Use this morning song to wake the birthday person or as a birthday blessing at the breakfast table.

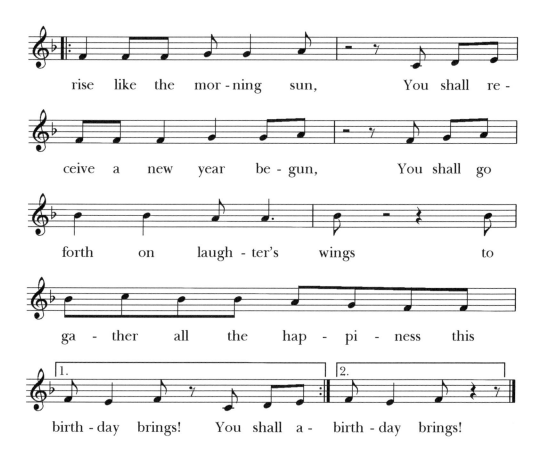

rise like the mor - ning sun, You shall re -

ceive a new year be - gun, You shall go

forth on laugh - ter's wings to

ga - ther all the hap - pi - ness this

1.
birth - day brings! You shall a -

2.
birth - day brings!

One More Year

Shea Darian

1. One more year our hearts have held you,
2. One more year our hearts have held you,

One more year you've glad-dened our lives.
One more year you've glad-dened our lives.

One more year you've grown so (tall,)*
One more year we want to say:

One more year (we gath-er to call:)*
"We ho-nor you on this mem'-ra-ble day!"

Hap-py birth-day, Hap-py birth day,

Hap-py birth-day to you!

* Alternate lyrics: replace "tall" with "wise," and replace
"we gather to call" with "our blessings arise."

Verse 1: (1) One more year our hearts have held you,
         (2) One more year you've gladdened our lives.
         (3) One more year you've grown so tall,
         (4) One more year we gather to call:
         (5) Happy birthday, happy birthday,
           Happy birthday to you!

Verse 2: (1) One more year our hearts have held you,
         (2) One more year you've gladdened our lives.
         (6) One more year we want to say:
         (7) "We honor you on this mem'rable day!"
         (5) Happy birthday, happy birthday,
           Happy birthday to you!

Movement ଈ Everyone stands in a circle facing the birthday person who is seated in the center of the circle. Beginning with hands at sides, the following motions accompany the singing (refer to number guides above).

1. Gathering motion: move hands up and out to sides, then together and in, palms coming to rest over heart.

2. Move hands out away from chest and arms open up in a gesture suggesting a bounty of gifts.

3. Beginning with hands at sides, face palms up and move hands above head.

4. Everyone takes hands with those beside them.

5. Walk in a clockwise circle around the birthday person, gazing at them with a sense of joy and blessing.

6. Everyone takes hands with those beside them.

7. Everyone curtsies or bows to the birthday person.

On the Day You Were Born

Shea Darian

Joyous Birthday

Shea Darian

Joy - ous birth - day to you,

Joy - ous birth - day to you.

Now may all___ your wi - shes be

filled with love___ and des - ti - ny,

Now may all your dreams come true,

May___ they be - come you,

And may all your vi - sions fly

Free a - cross each new sky.

Joy - ous birth - day to you,

Joy - ous birth - day to you.

Conclusion ﹋
Fostering Faith in the Future

The future enters into us,
in order to transform itself in us,
long before it happens.

~ Rainer Maria Rilke

Inspiring our children to grow into mature, confident human beings, who live fully into each cycle of their lives, is no small endeavor. We live in a society in which the majority *expects* today's busy schedules to deprive us of time for soulful contemplation or dallying in one another's presence. We live in a society in which the majority *expects* family dysfunction, marital strife, and the eternal battle between generations. But this is not who we are as a people. This is not who we aspire to become.

In the book, *Sleeping With Bread*, by Dennis, Sheila and Matthew Linn, the authors relate the story of children who were left homeless and hungry during the bombing raids of World War II. These children were taken into refugee camps where they received food and care. However, due to the losses and trauma they suffered, many children feared going to sleep at night. They worried that if they went to sleep the security they had been provided – caregivers, a bed to sleep in, and food to eat – would be gone when they opened their eyes in the morning. Many of the children were inconsolable until one of their caregivers came up with the idea of giving each child a portion of bread to hold in their hand as they slept. Bread in hand, the children were reminded that their needs were provided for today and would be provided for again tomorrow. The reality of bread in hand allowed the children to sleep believing the gifts of a new day would be sufficient to hold them. Living fully in the present requires faith in the future. Sometimes all it takes is a piece of bread – a symbol of life and sustenance.

Meaningful rites of passage are like bread in the hand. They remind us that we are surrounded by a caring community that upholds and sustains us. They remind us to offer our gratitude for what has been, and what will be tomorrow. They remind us that, no matter what trials we have endured, we can have faith in our future.

Creating meaningful rites of passage is a soulful revolution. A revolution to build community, express gratitude, celebrate and heal the past, envision the future. A revolution to create soulful pauses in our lives to honor the sacred essence of a soul, a family, a community. It doesn't take an army to begin. It only takes one person believing that it's possible. It only takes one family inspired by the bold confidence that meaningful rites of passage foster. It only takes one celebration community daring enough to propose a more vibrant, contemplative way of life.

Many years ago, when I decided to marry and help nurture a family, I was bowled over at times by the words of caution I received. When Andrew and I were married, someone told us that the first year would be the most difficult. After a year of married bliss, someone told us that it was too bad the honeymoon couldn't last. When I was pregnant, parents of babies and parents of teenagers warned me of sleepless nights I would suffer at the hands of my children. But, in the midst of those foreboding prophecies, there was an angel that appeared one day in Bellingham, Washington at the polling place where Andrew and I went to vote.

I was waiting for Andrew to finish voting, playing with ten-month-old Morgan, when I noticed a grey-haired man standing a few feet away. His face opened into a magnificent smile as he observed the love and joy between parent and child. He leaned toward me as if he had a coveted secret to tell and whispered loudly, "It only gets *better*, and *better*, and *better*." I wanted to hug that old man. I wanted to engrave his face upon the eyes of my intuition, record his words in the echo chambers of my soul. The simplicity of his gift to me was wrapped with a divine confidence by which every young parent deserves to be blessed. The old man didn't tell me the secret of *how* to make it better, he just inspired me with the wisdom that it was possible. That's all I needed to hear, all I needed to be blessed with as a new parent: faith in the future.

For me, this is one of the most profound outcomes of celebrating meaningful rites of passage – *cultivating faith in the future*. Rites of passage allow us to believe in what comes next, to affirm to ourselves and the loving community that holds us that we are equal to the task of life at hand. In the absence of such a rite of passage when Andrew and I were new parents, an old man sharing with me his "coveted secret" became just the rite of passage I needed at the time. This old man's message was my bread in hand.

So, as you dare to cultivate meaningful rites of passage, begin where you are and fuel your mind and imagination with a good measure of faith! As you grow familiar with such celebrations, they only get *better*, and *better*, and *better*. What we can imagine, we can believe, and what we believe becomes the seedbed from which our visions may sprout to life. There is nothing like a little faith to grow our dreams on.

Appendix ≼

Resources for the Journey

Every end is a beginning.

~ Ralph Waldo Emerson

Planning a Rite of Passage

Planning a rite of passage can be an act of prayer. It can be a ritual that throws a shaft of light on the soulful meaning of the life passage at hand. Whether a rite of passage is simple or elaborate, rises up spontaneously or is well-planned out, is a newly created rite or a tradition that has stood the test of time, it's more likely to be effective if it's prepared thoughtfully and lovingly with intention. Consider the following suggestions:

Reflect on the significance of the life passage at hand. Journal or write notes to yourself as you consider the significance of the life passage you desire to acknowledge and celebrate. Ask such questions as

- What is the significance of this life passage – spiritually, physically, socially, emotionally, legally, intellectually, mentally, and/or soulfully?

- What has changed or will change because of this life passage?

- Who is most directly affected by the passage? Is it an individual, multilayered, or collective passage?

- In the context of the individual's or family's biography, how significant is the life passage? What time and resources are available to honor it?

- How will each person most directly affected by the life passage be involved in planning and/or honoring it?

Although young children thrive on living into rites of passage created *for* them, as a youth matures, it can be empowering to be more involved in planning and leading rites of passage. This way, a young person learns the art of creating such rites for themselves and others.

Reflect on the primary focus and movement of the life passage and what type of rite is being called for. The late anthropologist, Arnold van Gennep, identified three subdivisions of rites of passage: rites of separation, transition rites, and rites of incorporation (which articulate an initiate's changed social status and relationships to the family and community). Some rites of passage include all three aspects, while other rites may emphasize one aspect over the others. For significant life passages, consider ways to balance separation, transition, and incorporation rites. For example, while driver training emphasizes the transition aspect of earning a driver's license and independent driving emphasizes separation, a family ceremony to honor this passage might emphasize incorporating the young adult into the family as an independent driver. Whenever a life passage involves a dramatic separation, it's wise to include transition and incorporation rites, so an initiate can experience a sense of support and belonging as they take on their new, more independent status in the family and/or larger community.

Consider what challenges or tests for an initiate are involved in a life passage. Sometimes a challenge or test is inherent within the life passage being experienced. The challenge of a toddler being weaned or a young adult learning to drive may be challenging enough. At other times, a test may be imposed upon a person experiencing a life passage as a tangible obstacle to overcome, creating a "proving ground" for an initiate's growing capabilities. A young adult experiencing a life passage might be tested with one of the adult risks listed on pages 216-227 or by preparing an artistic creation or spoken meditation to share during a rite of passage ceremony. A child's challenge might include taking on a new household chore or learning to ride a bike or swim. Group challenges may be appropriate for particular life passages – such trials as the grail search in the Knighting Ceremony on page 131, or the "Friendship Trials" on page 147. When imposing a challenge, choose one that's age-appropriate and relevant to the passage at hand.

Given the significance, focus, and challenges of a life passage, consider what sort of rite of passage is appropriate. After considering the above three reflections, imagine what sort of rite of passage is called for to celebrate and honor the life passage at hand. Sometimes, the challenge or test involved in a life passage becomes the rite of passage itself. It may need no further articulation, except for the story of overcoming the challenge being told and heard, and the meaning of it lifted from the telling. At other times, an initiate being honored with a special ceremony, family dinner, or community event best articulates the profundity of the life passage and more fully prepares an initiate for meeting the joys and challenges of a life passage with clarity and confidence. If a ceremony is called for, you may want to consider the planning suggestions on pages 326-329.

Planning a Ceremonial Rite

There's no magic formula for planning effective rite of passage ceremonies. As a family plans and experiences rites of passage together, unique styles, patterns, and preferences will emerge. What's most important is to celebrate rite of passage ceremonies that speak to a family's soul and the souls of its individual members. The only way to discover what speaks to you and your family is through experience. As you create and honor rite of passage ceremonies, some will be more profoundly effective than others. However, if held prayerfully, each rite of passage ceremony will have its own gifts to bestow. Trust yourself. Envision, create, celebrate, honor, and reflect. If this is the only formula you use to create meaningful rite of passage ceremonies, it will be enough.

For those who desire a bit more guidance, set aside some quiet time to consider the following suggestions:

Reflect on the significance, focus, and challenges of the rite of passage at hand. Begin planning by considering the reflections and questions on pages 324-325.

Meditate on the images that emerge in your reflections. As you contemplate the significance, meaning, and focus of a life passage, symbolic objects, words, and rituals may emerge during your reflections. Take note of these and imagine how they can be incorporated in the rite of passage being celebrated. What objects, words, images, actions, songs, verses, or sacred writings can you incorporate into the celebration to highlight the meaning of the rite of passage?

Consider who will be invited to participate. Sometimes it's most appropriate and meaningful for a rite of passage ceremony to be celebrated in the intimacy of the immediate family circle. At other times, a larger celebration community may be gathered. Choose participants based on an initiate's relationships of encouragement and support. Ask each participant to prepare for the rite of passage in some way, whether it's writing a blessing or creating a symbolic gift, helping with food preparations, planning to lead a portion of the ceremony, or praying for the initiate. Such preparations will ensoul the event with the interest and love of the participants before the event ever takes place. Consider asking significant elders, godparents, siblings, and friends to take a special part in a ceremony whenever appropriate. Such participation allows those who are intimate with an initiate to reflect on the changes that the rite of passage represents for each of them.

Consider the celebration atmosphere you desire to create. Does the rite of passage call for a raucous, festive atmosphere or a more reverent and prayerful attitude? Some of the most meaningful rites of passage celebrated in my family include fun, spontaneous elements and more reverent, thoughtful interludes. Plan your ceremony with your chosen intentions in mind. Consider how such elements as visual aesthetics and lighting, music, planned activities, setting and time of day, participants involved, and particular ceremonial rites will add to or detract from the atmosphere you're striving to create.

Contemplate the most conducive setting for the ceremony. Through the years, most of the rite of passage ceremonies my family has celebrated have taken place in our home, ensouling our living space with a bounty of sacred blessings and memories of life transitions. If a large group gathers and the ceremony is brief, those who are able can be asked to stand. Of course, there will be times when the size of a celebration community requires a larger space. Your chosen faith community or your child's schooling community may have space available for such gatherings, or consider using an outdoor space. For outdoor settings, think through environmental hazards, such as the mosquitoes that graced Morgan's woman-becoming ceremony. (Of course, even mosquitoes can be considered a rite of passage challenge to overcome – at least, in retrospect.) Also, consider lighting issues for outdoor ceremonies after sunset. If readings are included, you may need torches, candles, penlights, or some other source of illumination.

As you plan the ceremony, vividly imagine its unfolding. Reflect on the elements you desire to include in the ceremony and imagine the movement and flow. When I create rite of passage ceremonies, I imagine four gestures flowing into one another, as follows:

- ◆ **Preparing the Space:** How thoughtfully we prepare the space and ceremonial tools for a celebration can greatly affect the quality and atmosphere of the rite of passage. Decide when and how to beautify the space, gather needed tools and prepare food. Some elements of preparation may be included as part of the rite of passage itself. Distractions can be minimized during the ceremony by planning for the needs of invasive pets and putting a note on the front door to alert people to a ceremony in progress. Immediately before a ceremony, it's helpful to teach unison songs and communicate the flow of the ceremony to participants. Also, remember to ask everyone to turn off their cell phones and pagers.

- **Gathering:** With larger community celebrations, the gesture of gathering includes the way participants are welcomed and encouraged to greet one another as they arrive. Begin the event with elements that promote the atmosphere you're striving to create. This can be accomplished through a community potluck or feast, conversation and interactive games, or simple, collective preparations for the ceremony such as beautifying the space or engaging in an artistic creation to be used in the ceremony. At the beginning of the ceremony itself, gathering can include elements that unify participants and clarify a sense of purpose: imparting words of welcome, singing or speaking a verse together, honoring silent moments of prayerful contemplation, or whatever seems an appropriate beginning for the rite of passage being celebrated.

- **Honoring the Passage:** This is the heart of the ceremony that includes one or more elements that draw forth the meaning and changes of the life passage at hand: spoken reflections, blessings, symbolic acts, storytelling, conversation, guided meditation, prayer, artistic offerings, bestowing symbolic gifts, etc. Arrange the elements in a meaningful flow that build on one another.

- **Sending Forth:** To conclude a ceremony, offer a final blessing as a strong message of support to the one being honored. Before the final blessing, someone may offer words of appreciation to the participants and give each one a simple, tangible reminder of the ceremony – a poem, candle, flower, original artwork, or whatever symbol reflects the theme of the ceremony. Oftentimes, sharing a meal or hors d'oeuvres after a rite of passage ceremony gives an initiate and other participants an opportunity to bask in the joy and meaning of the celebration.

As you plan, vividly imagine the setting and people in attendance. In your mind's eye, see and experience the ceremony taking place. Notice how the ceremony flows and builds. When in doubt, keep things simple and straightforward. The substance of a ceremony is often the presence and blessings of the celebration community gathered.

Create an invitation that assists participants to prepare for the celebration. When appropriate, send or give a written invitation to participants that clarifies the meaning of the event and how those invited are asked to participate. This can be especially helpful for those who aren't familiar with celebrating the rite of passage being honored. Such participants are more likely to engage in the celebration with interest and enthusiasm when they're informed and included in preparations. Those who can't be physically present can be asked to send blessings which can be shared during the celebration, compiled in a blessing album, or placed in a blessing basket or box.

Consider if handouts will enhance or detract from the ceremony. Once the elements of a ceremony are chosen, decide if handouts are needed. Beware giving out verbatim copies of a ceremony, as some participants may be tempted to read along rather than participating. You may want to hand out one small portion of the ceremony such as a group reading, or create an outline of the ceremony for participants with unison songs and verses included to encourage bold participation. When a ceremony includes young children, use a more spontaneous approach. It might be best to use a simple song or verse that the children already know and other participants can easily commit to memory.

Decide who will lead each portion of the ceremony and ask those leading to prepare ahead of time. Guidance for a ceremony can be offered by one individual or shared by various participants. Even when one person leads a ceremony, elders, family members, intimate mentors, or friends of the one being honored can be asked to participate in some special way: imparting a blessing on behalf of the entire group; holding an infant being named, anointed, or blessed; telling a story; symbolically preparing a ceremonial element, such as pouring water into a blessing bowl; or supporting an initiate by helping them prepare for the ceremony.

When planning and preparations for a rite of passage ceremony are complete, relax and let go of your expectations of the outcome. Sometimes a life passage ceremony will evolve in a markedly different way than you imagined it. My family consistently finds that if we don't become overly attached to the outcome, unexpected gifts can arise from a celebration. Sometimes, the most memorable elements are ones we didn't plan or anticipate.

After the ceremony, reflect on the highlights of the celebration. Focus on the elements that worked well and were most meaningful. Lightly take note of aspects of the celebration you'll choose to do differently next time. Engrave the highlights on your memory through sharing stories and reflections about the event with one another in the days and weeks that follow. Meaningful rites of passage can become a vibrant aspect of a family's biography.

Rites of Passage Resources from Birth to 21

Birth and Arrival

Birthing From Within: An Extra-Ordinary Guide to Childbirth Preparation
by Pam England and Rob Horowitz
> An inspired source for parents who desire to experience pregnancy and childbirth as a soulful journey of self-discovery. Includes a plethora of ideas for celebrating pregnancy and childbirth as the life-changing rites of passage they are. (Albuquerque, NM: Partera Press, 1998)

Mother Rising: The Blessingway Journey into Motherhood
by Yana Cortlund, Barb Lucke, and Donna Miller Watelet
> A beautifully designed book with a wellspring of inspiration for creating parent blessings to prepare parents for labor and birth. (Honeoye, NY: Seeing Stone Press, 2004)

Welcoming the Soul of a Child: Creating Rituals and Ceremonies to Honor the Birth of Our Sons and Daughters by Jill E. Hopkins
> An exceptional, enlightening, soulful guide for parents to prepare for the conception, pregnancy and birth of a child. The book is full of helpful rituals and exercises. (NY: Kensington Books, 1999)

Welcoming Ways: Creating Your Baby's Welcome Ceremony with the Wisdom of World Traditions by Andrea Alban Gosline, Illustrated by Lisa Burnett Bossi
> This gem includes nine joyous ceremonies for welcoming a newborn child into the family. (San Rafael, CA: Cedco, 2000; available at www.ambledance.com)

The Wonder of Lullabies by Mary Thienes-Schunemann
> This songbook and CD collection offers beautiful lullabies to inspire times of relaxation and sleep; it will be a joy for little ones and their parents. Available from Naturally You Can Sing Productions (www.naturallyyoucansing.com)

Childhood

You Are Your Child's First Teacher: What Parents Can Do With and For Their Children from Birth to Age Six by Rahima Baldwin
> An invaluable resource for understanding the developmental changes a child goes through from infancy through early childhood. (Berkeley, CA: Celestial Arts, 2000)

Games Children Play: How Games and Sport Help Children Develop
by Kim Brooking-Payne
> An age group specific look at games and sports that foster a sense of fun and holistic development from age three to the teenage years. (Gloucestershire, UK: Hawthorn Press, 1996)

Also see: On the Male Journey – *Raising a Son* and *Raising Boys;* On the Female Journey – *Raising a Daughter*

Coming of Age

Crossroads: The Quest for Contemporary Rites of Passage
Edited by Louise Carus Mahdi, Nancy Geyer Christopher, and Michael Meade
> A rich collection of articles from a variety of sources focusing on issues surrounding the passage into young adulthood. (Peru, IL: Open Court Publishing, 1996)

Also see: On the Male Journey, On the Female Journey, Personal Finances, Soulful Deepening, and Young Adulthood sections

On the Male Journey

Adam's Return: The Five Promises of Male Initiation by Richard Rohr
Richard Rohr has spent decades studying male initiation rites. In this book, Rohr makes relevant five essential lessons consistently communicated through the ages to a male initiate making the journey into manhood. Written from a Christian perspective. (NY: Crossroad Publishing, 2004)

From Boys to Men: All About Adolescence and You by Michael Gurian
A straight-talking book that helps enlighten males on the many emotional, physical, and mental changes they experience during puberty. (NY: Price Stern Sloan, 1999)

Letters to My Son: A Father's Wisdom on Manhood, Life, and Love by Kent Nerburn
A father's wonderfully wise reflections written for his son on such topics as strength, work, money, love, sex, war, faithfulness, loneliness, the spiritual journey, drugs and alcohol, giving, and fatherhood. (San Rafael, CA: New World Library, 1999)

My Body, My Self for Boys by Lynda and Area Madaras
Over 100 pages of fun, fact-filled reading and activities, including games, quizzes, journal exercises and family icebreakers to converse about issues of puberty, changing body image, and sexuality. (NY: Newmarket Press, 2007)

Raising a Son: Parents and the Making of a Healthy Man by Jeanne Elium & Don Elium
An exceptional guide for parents of sons. Covers specific developmental and parenting issues related to the growth cycles: birth to 7, 8-12, 13-17, and 18-29. (Berkeley, CA: Celestial Arts, 2004)

Raising Boys: Why Boys are Different – and How to Help Them Become Happy and Well-Balanced Men by Steve Biddulph
A wise, accessible presentation of the unique parenting needs boys have during what Biddulph calls "the three stages of boyhood:" birth to 6, 6-14, and 14 to adult. (Berkeley, CA: Celestial Arts, 1998)

On the Female Journey

First Moon: Celebration and Support for a Girl's Growing Up Journey by Maureen Theresa Smith
What a keepsake for a girl's coming of age journey! This boxed gift set is designed to support a youth before and during her first year of menstruation. It includes a guidebook, a companion journal, and a flow chart to keep track of a youth's menstrual cycle. (Navato, CA: New World Library, 2005)

My Body, My Self for Girls by Lynda and Area Madaras
Over 100 pages of fun, fact-filled reading and activities, including games, quizzes, journal exercises and family icebreakers to converse about issues of puberty, changing body image, and sexuality. (NY: Newmarket Press, 2007)

New Moon: The Magazine for Girls and Their Dreams (ages 8-14)
A bimonthly ad-free magazine for "every girl who wants her voice heard and her dreams taken seriously." Editors are girls from 8-14; articles, poetry and activities focus on the passage from girl to woman and promoting healthy gender equity (www.newmoon.org)

Raising a Daughter: Parents and the Awakening of a Healthy Woman by Jeanne Elium & Don Elium
An exceptional guide for parents of daughters. Covers specific developmental and parenting issues related to the growth cycles: birth to 7, 8-12, 13-17, and 18-29. (Berkeley: CA: Celestial Arts, 2003)

The Seven Sacred Rites of Menarche: The Spiritual Journey of the Adolescent Girl by Kristi Meisenbach Boylan
Insightful reflections for parents on the emotional and spiritual journey of a girl's adolescence. The author outlines seven rituals or stepping stones she sees as keys to honoring the passage of menarche. (Santa Monica, CA: Santa Monica Press, 2001)

Also see: Young Adulthood – *Understanding Guys: A Guide for Teenage Girls*

Personal Finances

It's tough to find soulful books on teaching young people how to work with money, but here are a few books that will give you some practical wisdom on the subject. . .

Capitate Your Kids; also called *The Sink or Swim Money Program* by John E. Whitcomb
> A practical, step-by-step approach to teaching youth and young adults, seventh through twelfth grades, how to work with money and achieve a high level of autonomy in their financial interactions. (NY: Penguin Books, 2000)

Money Still Doesn't Grow on Trees : *A Parents Guide to Raising Financially Responsible Teenagers and Young Adults* by Neale S. Godfrey with Carolina Edwards & Tad Richards
> Lots of practical, hands-on advice ranging from tipping service workers to credit and cars. Contains quizzes and worksheets that are sure to stir up some energetic conversations. (NY: Fireside, 2006)

Rites of Passage, General

Deeply into the Bone: Re-inventing Rites of Passage by Ronald L. Grimes
> In this scholarly but down-to-earth book, Grimes takes a fresh and creative approach to thinking about traditional rites and re-inventing rites relevant to our lives in the 21st century. (Los Angeles: University of California Press, 2000)

The Rites of Passage by Arnold van Gennep
> A classic from the anthropologist who brought to light the universal functions of "rites of passage" (and coined the term.) Utilizing examples from various cultures, the book reveals rites of passage surrounding birth, puberty, marriage, and death. (Chicago: The University of Chicago Press, 1960)

Soulful Journeys

Buddha in Your Backpack: Everyday Buddhism for Teens by Franz Metcalf (Young Adult)
> One thing many folks don't realize about Buddhist principles is that one can practice them no matter what their religious affiliation. Metcalf presents Buddhism in a straightforward, down-to-earth way that may inspire centeredness and awareness in a young adult at a time of life when young people tend to be overly busy and self-absorbed. (Berkeley, CA: Seastone, 2003)

Chicken Soup for the Teenage Soul Journal by Jack Canfield, Mark Victor Hansen, and Kimberly Kirberger (Youth and Young Adult)
> Includes numerous journaling and reflection exercises to prompt a teenager to consider their inner life, relationships, values, and priorities. (Deerfield Beach, FL: Health Communications, Inc, 1997)

Don't Sweat the Small Stuff for Teens: Simple Ways to Stay Cool in Stressful Times and *Don't Sweat the Small Stuff for Teens Journal* by Richard Carlson (Young Adult)
> Insightful reflections to help teenagers through the difficulties that sometimes accompany homework, dating, peer pressure, etc. Inspires teens to approach life with a greater sense of balance and awareness. The journal includes inspirational passages and relevant journaling exercises on the various topics presented in the book. (NY: Hyperion, 2000/2002)

Dream Symbols by Sara Phillips (Youth and Young Adult)
> Illustrated with exceptional art from the sixth century to the present, this gift book is an aesthetically beautiful, concisely written introduction to common dream symbols and their meaning. It could be given as a gift alongside a dream journal. (Philadelphia: Courage Books, 2002)

Fire in the Heart: A Spiritual Guide for Teens by Deepak Chopra
> A wise and intriguing guide to inspire teenagers to deepen their soulful and spiritual connections, considering such questions as: Do I have a soul? How do wishes come true? What is the supreme force in the universe? How can I change the world? (NY: Simon Pulse, 2004)

The Prophet by Kahlil Gibran (Young Adult)

> A soulful masterpiece offering insight into such life themes as love, marriage, children, work, freedom, pain, self-knowledge, friendship, prayer, and death. Excerpts make inspired readings or recitations for rite of passage ceremonies. (NY: Alfred A. Knopf, 1964)

Young Adulthood

Understanding Guys: A Guide for Teenage Girls by Michael Gurian

> An exceptional little book to prepare young women for the complexities of dating and understanding the differences between males and females in the areas of intimacy, romance, and sexuality. (NY: Price Stern Sloan, 1999)

Also see: Childhood – *Games Children Play*; Coming of Age – *Crossroads: The Quest for Contemporary Rites of Passage;* On the Male Journey – *Letters to My Son: A Father's Wisdom on Manhood, Life and Love;* Personal Finances; Youthhood – *It's Our World, Too!*.

Youthhood

It's Our World, Too! Young People Who Are Making a Difference by Phillip Hoose

> A book that will help empower young people to work for positive change in the areas of human rights, economics, caring for the earth, and creating peace. The book includes fourteen accounts of youths and young adults who have made a difference and practical suggestions for planning, organizing, publicizing, and raising funds for social action projects. (New York: Sunburst, 2002)

Also see: Childhood – *Games Children Play*; On the Male Journey – *My Body, My Self for Boys* and *From Boys to Men*; On the Female Journey – *My Body, My Self for Girls; New Moon*, The Magazine for Girls and Their Dreams; Personal Finances section

Index of Poems, Songs and Ceremonies

Songs

(Alphabetical by title)

Miscellaneous

(Alphabetical by title or topic)

Poems

(Alphabetical by title or first line)

Rite of passage ceremonies

(Alphabetical by title or topic)

About the Author

SHEA DARIAN

is an inspired speaker and workshop leader and has presented keynote talks and workshops throughout the United States. Shea encourages parents, grandparents, and caregivers to transform our often busy, chaotic 21st century lives with a greater sense of balance and peace. She offers practical and inspirational tools to build healthy, joyful family relationships.

In addition to *Living Passages for the Whole Family*, Shea is the author of *Seven Times the Sun: Guiding Your Child through the Rhythms of the Day*, *Sanctuaries of Childhood: Nurturing a Child's Spiritual Life*, and *Grandpa's Garden*, a children's picture book.

Shea received a BA in Speech and Theater from Iowa State University, a Master of Divinity degree from Garrett-Evangelical Seminary, and is working toward certification as a multifaith spiritual director. She has served as a youth minister, minister through the arts, minister of worship, and Waldorf school administrator. Shea is a sacred arts enthusiast, particularly in the area of sacred drama. With her spouse, Andrew, and their grown children, Morgan and Willa, Shea is also an inspired homemaker; she considers her family to be her most sacred earthly sanctuary.

Shea is available for speaking engagements. For contact information, see www.gileadpress.net.

Rebecca Danica Photography, Spokane, WA.